A Tour in Connaught, by the Author of 'sketches in Ireland' [Signing Himself C.O.]

A TOUR IN CONNAUGHT.

Church and Round Tower, Clonmacnoise.

A TOUR

IN

CONNAUGHT:

COMPRISING SKETCHES OF

CLONMACNOISE, JOYCE COUNTRY, AND ACHILL.

BY

THE AUTHOR OF "SKETCHES IN IRELAND."

WITH ILLUSTRATIONS ENGRAVED ON WOOD.

DUBLIN

WILLIAM CURRY, JUN. AND COMPANY,

9, UPPER SACKVILLE-STREET.

1839.

Dublin: Printed by John S. Folds, 5, Bachelor's-walk.

PREFACE.

In offering the following "Sketches in Connaught," the result of a short excursion made in that province during the early part of last summer, I assign one or two excuses for adding to the numerous works of a similar character that have latterly come before the public, and which, to use the words of the greatest of all publishers, have "worn the subject threadbare."

My first plea is, that my volume has not been got up for the purpose of leading or misleading public opinion respecting Irish politics or economics. I aim not at being the precursor of any change, or the promoter of any speculation. The tour I took for my pleasure, and the volume I wrote at my leisure, and during those evenings when I allow myself to relax from the more serious occupations

A 2

of the morning. My own pastime, I offer to the
public, if it so pleases them, as part of theirs; and all
my hope is, that the reader will think better of
Ireland than he will do of the author. The other
reason why I publish is, that I write as a native, who
has made the history, antiquities, traditionary lore,
and social relations of the island, his study, and
therefore may be supposed to be competent to afford
information on subjects not exactly within the convenient reach of an American or Briton. In a word,
I assume that my ARTICLE is what an extern could
not, and, perhaps, if he *could*, *would* not supply.

About ten years ago a volume of mine, purporting
to be " Sketches in the North and South of Ireland,"
was published, and though appearing under many dis-
advantageous circumstances, met with a favourable
reception from the public; and therefore my publishers have not only determined to venture on the
present speculation, but also contemplate a new
edition of the former work.

It is but fair to state, that the three first chapters of
the present volume have already, with some alteration,
appeared in print; the two first under a different
signature and form, in that humble though useful
conveyance of popular knowledge, the Dublin Penny

Journal, to the first volume of which I was a contributor. The third chapter, descriptive of Clonmacnoise, though now considerably changed, has appeared in the Dublin Christian Examiner.

The reader who is about to give these sketches his perusal is hereby warned, that I neither set down distances, nor attempt to describe or even notice every town or place I passed through. These details I leave to be supplied by a valuable road book, lately compiled by Mr. Fraser, and published by William Curry and Co. Sackville-street.

C. O.

Dublin, May 18, 1839.

CONTENTS.

CHAPTER VIII.

CHAPTER XVIII.

CHAPTER XIX.

ILLUSTRATIONS.

A TOUR IN CONNAUGHT.

CHAPTER I.

DUBLIN TO KINNEGAD.

Departure from Dublin—Barrack-street—Phœnix-park—Kilmainham—Old Bull-baiting—Chapelizod—Its name La Belle Isod—Another Etymology—Castleknock—Its Legend—Ballydowd—The plains of Liffey—Ireland a castellated country—Lucan—Rath—Artificial Cave—King John's Bridge—Spa—Steam fatal to Irish Spa—Leixlip—Its Castle—Its position—Its water-fall—Spa—Canal—Aqueduct—Monument of an Irish Job—Carton—A good Landlord—Maynooth—College—Castle—Kilcock—Cappagh Hill—Boyne—Its Character—Clonard—Its ancient celebrity—Kinnegad—Beggar-woman.

VERY pleasant to me was the morning when, escaping out of Dublin, I took my way to the west, through that exceedingly disgusting purlieu of the city, Barrack-street. The road, now made level enough to answer even for a steam locomotive, runs parallel to the river—on the right the Phœnix-park—on the left the lands of Kilmainham—where, in former days, the wild fellows of Dublin came out to bait bulls—as is recorded in that very humorous ballad, entitled "The baiting of Lord Altham's bull." The whole of the fine inches along the river on its north side, and reaching for two miles, were granted by the crown to Sir John Temple, the ancestor of Lord Palmerston, as a remuneration for building a stone wall separating the Phœnix-park from the high road. Fine times these, when estates could be got in the LAND OF JOB so cheaply.

B

To the left is Chapelizod, formerly the residence of the lords deputy—once a place of considerable manufacturing industry, and where the great Duke of Ormonde, immediately after the restoration, set up the linen and cambric manufactures, under the inspection of Colonel Lawrence, who brought a colony of Huguenots from Rochelle, and the Isle of Rhé, and located it here. Old Hanmer, the chronicler, tells a story mighty romantic, relative to the name of this village—it being, according to him, the retreat of La Belle Isod, the frail beloved of a Danish king of Dublin. Here were her bower and her chapel—the devotions of the chapel, (according to the religion of the times,) atoning for the misdeeds of the bower. But this appears but a *rechauffè* of the story of the fair Rosamond, and the more probable origin of the name is as follows—the place of worship here built on the river bank was denominated *Teampoll* or *Seapoll isiol* or *isiold*—in Irish, the low temple or chapel,—to distinguish it from the Teampoll *Naimh Labhrais*, or temple of St. Lawrence, which stood on an eminence near it, called St. Lawrence's brow, and forms the high bluff overhanging that beautiful bend of the river which sweeps round Knockmaroon hill.*

* I cannot leave Chapelizod without directing attention to the cromleach that was last year uncovered in the Phœnix-park, in the vicinity of this village, and which contained, beside half-burned human skeletons, an urn and some curious shell ornaments—these were collected with great care, and presented to the Royal Hibernian Academy, by Lieutenant Larcom, of the Ordnance Survey Department.

Reaching Palmerstown, we rose from the river, and gained the fertile, undulating champaign that extends southward from the Liffey to the Wicklow mountains. To the right the deep-cut course of the river, its steep banks adorned and enriched by the strawberry cultivation, beyond it again the Phœnix-park, and more to the west the two beautiful hills of Castleknock—the one a smoothly circular green knoll, whereon the successive proprietors, as a record of their bad taste, have allowed an unmeaning pigeon-house to remain standing for years; their only excuse, is, I suppose, *that they are accustomed to its ugliness*—the other crowned with its ivy-mantled castle, where the Bruce, some centuries ago, halted his army, when advancing to besiege Dublin, and where *yet* that ancient window remains, of which says Stanihurst, "Though it be neither glazed or latticed, but open, yet let the weather be stormy, and the wind bluster boisterously on every side of the house, and place a candle there, and it will burn as quietly as if no puff of wind blew. This may be tried at this day, whoso shall be willing to put it in practice."

About two miles farther, we arrived at an eminence from whence extend westward and southward the plains of the Liffey, (as in ancient days they were called,) and certainly in no part of the British empire can the eye wander over a richer expanse. To the geologist, it is interesting, as everywhere he finds assurance that before the Liffey had cut down for itself to the sea its present deep and tortuous bed, all before the

view, until it touched the Curragh of Kildare, and
the Hill of Allen, must have been a wide-spread lake;
and when the observer gets down to the deep, dry, circular basin in which the village of Lucan is placed,
he may notice the gradual depositions the subsiding
waters made, and at the same time be led to conclude
that some final force must have operated in the way
of earthquake to form the river's present bed; the force
from beneath, which has been exerted to cause the disturbance of the strata, must have been great, and the
extraordinary disarrangement of the limestone stratifications on the northern bank of the Liffey is worthy
of the attention of the draughtsman or the geologist.

Few of England's favoured vales—few of Scotland's
carses or straths, can show any thing to the farmer's
eye finer or more fertile than the view from the hill
of Ballydowd; to the left is the castle of Ballyowen,
one of those old keeps so frequent all over the island;
and if you look westward, you may see another, and
southward, another; and pass on from this to Galway
or to Cape Clear, and you will see them covering and
commanding, and within signal shot of each other.
They stand as memorials of Ireland's different conquests, and as evidences that when conquered, each subsequent invader considered that what the sword won,
it was needful for the sword to keep.   Ireland is the
land of ruins and memorials—of powers and people
that have successively passed away.   The ruined fortress—the devastated abbey—the lonely *dun*—the
fairy-footed rath—the round tower that sends its

slender shaft on high to assert that the almost imperishable simplicity of its form can survive human record, and even outlast man's tradition—these are what render Ireland a land interesting to the traveller; and not all the magnificence of America—not all its mighty mountains, lakes, or waterfalls, can supply to the passenger such trains of mental association, such stores of romantic thought, as a few miles wandering through Erin.

The castles of Ireland are not only numerous, but of different character. The old massive circular Anglo-Norman—the square and more regularly bastioned stronghold of the Elizabethan era—the more simple and solitary fortalice of the Cromwellian adventurer, who cased himself within his strait four walls like an armadillo or hedgehog, to look out in security on his newly acquired grant, and save his soul alive from the skeins of marauding rapparees.

I scarcely know a more interesting view than that presented to the traveller, when, arrived at the head of the new road, lately made to avoid the old way down the steep hill, he looks down on the valley, or rather river basin, in which Lucan is placed, and sees the village, with its church, its fine single-arched bridge spanning the Liffey, its houses appearing (at least at that distance) neat and prettily mingled with trees, and the fine, rich, full-grown woods that environ it on all sides. To the right, and overhanging a ravine, through which a stream runs and joins the Liffey, is one of the finest RATHS in the vicinity of Dublin, in the centre of which is an artificial cave * or UAIGH, such as is common in the larger and best constructed raths all over the island, but which, as usual, either filled up or rooted up, are rarely to be seen in the perfect state that this at Lucan now presents. Some former tenant of the property in which the rath is situated, (for the present owner has too much taste to fall into such a mistake,) has committed the common error of planting the sides of this stronghold, and so has contrived to hide from the ken of an antiquary what would give him no small pleasure, and now it is passed by as a tastily planted hill, decorated with Scotch and spruce firs—my utter aversion; a rath or dun should never be decorated in this way: the same kind of taste has ornamented a forehead, painted by a Vandycke or a Titian, with a Ramillies wig—a solitary ash or oak tossing its lightning-scathed and storm-vexed branches to the breeze, showing how it has lived long and suffered much—or a fairy thorn bending away patiently from the west—these are what should belong to the rath, these are what the fays and elves would have in the high-places of their resort.

Farther on, about a furlong from the present single-

---

* These caves are thus described in the Icelandic Annals : "Leifr went on piracy towards the west, and infested Ireland with his arms, and there discovered subterranean caves, the entrances of which were dark and dismal ; but on entering he saw the glittering of swords, which the men held in their hands. These men he slew, but brought the swords with much riches away."

arched bridge, is another, the most ancient construction of the kind in Ireland—tradition attributes it to
King John—it certainly is as old as the 14th century—it appears to me, like some others I have seen,
from the smallness and lowness of its arches, to have
been intended to let the floods flow over it in the
winter season.

Lucan, or, as it was anciently called, Lyvecan, was
the patrimony of the Sarsfields—the last owner of that
name was the famous partisan general in the wars of the
Revolution. He forfeited it and followed the fortunes
of his master; and while William took away his
estate, James made him an Earl. The late possessor
of this pretty village and fine property was Colonel
Vesey, than whom a better landlord, a higher-minded
gentleman, or a more devoted Christian, I never
knew. How often have I admired this fine military
old squire walking to church surrounded by a tenantry that he had gathered around him—a tenantry, for whose increasing numbers that church, I may
say, was built—a tenantry amongst whom he might
live fearless of brand or bullet. Half a mile from
Lucan, westward, and between the road and the
river, is the once famous sulphurous spa—it is an
abundant and strongly impregnated spring, and
draws its mineral qualities from that modification of
impure limestone, which has been denominated by
Kirwan and other geologists, calpe, and which, containing an abundance of crystalized sulphuret of iron,
gives out, when the sulphuret is decomposed by water,

the gaseous matter that makes this spring medicinal.
But, alas, for Ireland, steam boats and locomotive
engines now carry away spa-drinkers and pleasure-
pursuers from native wells and pump-rooms to German
brunnens. The hotel here is empty, and lodging-
houses, and all other sort of accommodations unoccu-
pied and going to waste.

Any one arriving at Leixlip must look up and
down with pleasure while moving over its bridge.
To the right, the river winning its noisy, turbulent way over its rocky bed, and losing itself afar
down amidst embosoming woods: to the left, after
plunging over the salmon-leap, whose roar is heard,
though a quarter of a mile off, and forming a junction
with the Rye-water, it takes a bend to the east, and
washes the amphitheatre with which Leixlip is envi-
roned.   Very few Irish fortresses stand in a grander
position than Leixlip Castle, as it embattles the high
and wooded ground that forms the forks of the two
rivers. Of the towers, the round one of course was
built by King John, the opposite square one by the
Geraldines.   This ancient and grandly circumstanced
pile has been in later days the baronial residence of
the White family, and subsequently the residence of
generals and prelates.   Here Primate Stone, more a
politician than a churchman, retired from his contest
with the Ponsonbys and the Boyles, to play at cricket
with General Cunningham: here resided Speaker
Connolly, before he built his splendid mansion at
Castletown: here the *great* commoner, as he was

called, Tom Connolly, was born. Like many such
edifices this castle is haunted—character and keeping
would be altogether lost, if towers of 600 years'
standing, with rich mullioned "windows that exclude
the light, and passages that lead to nothing," with
tapestried chambers that have witnessed pranks of
revelry, and feats of war, of Norman, Cromwellian,
and Williamite possessors—if such a place had not
its legend: and one of Ireland's wildest geniuses, the
eccentric and splendid Maturin, has decorated the
subject with the colourings of his vivid fancy.

Leixlip is memorable in a historic point of view, as
the place where, in the war commencing 1641,
General Preston halted when on his way to form a
junction with the Marquis of Ormonde, to oppose the
Parliamentarians. Acknowledging that his army was
not excommunication proof, he bowed before the fiat
of the Nuncio, and lost the best opportunity that ever
offered of saving his cause and his country from what
has been called "the curse of Cromwell." Rising
out of Leixlip the road leaves the line of the Liffey,
and runs parallel to the small stream of the Rye-
water: over which is thrown, at an immense expense,
the largest aqueduct in Ireland, constructed by the
Royal Canal Company, a speculation got up by an
angry capitalist to rival the Grand Canal Company,
from whose direction he had retired in disgust, and
whose vanity and pique was the cause of this
great absurdity, and of loss and bankruptcy to thousands. It is said that the enormous cost of this aque-

duct was gone to in compliment to the late Duke of
Leinster, who desired that the canal should pass by
his town of Maynooth; it certainly would have been
more advantageous to the commerce of the kingdom
and to the prosperity of the company, had they not de-
flected here to the south, but rather kept northward
through the plains of Meath, made Lough Sheelan instead of Lough Owel their summit level, and met the
Shannon more towards its source, rather than run
their line parallel, as it now does, at only a few miles
distance from the Grand Canal, each starving, and
interfering with the other, and acting like two rival
shopkeepers who, instead of setting up at remote districts of the town, frown balefully at each other from
opposite sides of the same street.

Just beneath the bridge that carries the road over
the canal, is one of the most beautiful and abundant
spring wells in Ireland. If it had been known in old
times it would have been sanctified, as most such are
in Ireland—but it burst out for the *first* time from the
depths of the earth on the excavation of the canal;
and as it was discovered in winter, and its deep-
seated source caused it to appear warmer than other
more superficial springs, so immediately there were
attributed to it virtues of no ordinary degree, and the
crowds that in faith (for the Irish are rich in that
cardinal virtue) resorted to it were enormous. While
the credulity lasted, the harvest of coach and noddy
owners (for jaunting-cars were not yet in fashion)
was immense : strings of carriages, miles long, might

be seen on Sundays issuing from Dublin, containing crowds anxious to apply, internally or externally, its healing waters; and attestations of its curing the blind—restoring the palsied—strengthening the lame, came before the public every day. But alas, the powers of ridicule were brought to bear against it, and *one* wicked wight drew a caricature in which he represented a broken-down noddy as washed by the Leixlip spa water, and all its spokes and shafts, under the mopping of the jarvey, becoming strong and straight. This, certainly, was a pity; and no one in the world was served by dissipating such an innocent and salutary delusion, and after all it is not only a beautiful but an *extraordinary* spring; for, if you believe all the neighbours, not a fish or frog will live in its waters; and though there be a floculent, rusty-coloured, ocherous matter constantly rising to the surface of the well, exactly similar to that which is found in springs strongly impregnated with iron, yet no test, either gallic acid, or prussiate of potash, can detect any iron; but in the centre of this floculent matter is found a *very red* little worm about half an inch long, which all those who have still faith in the salubrity of the well, say, is the sovereignest remedy alive for a sore leg: nay more, let any one who has drank over night from fifteen to twenty tumblers of punch, and whose head is so hot that it makes the water fizz into which it is plunged, let him, I say, but take a quart or two of the water of this spring on the following morning, and he will lose all his whiskey fever, and walk home

as cool as a cucumber. I assure you, gentle reader,
I have seen sundry making the experiment, and I
actually saw them afterwards sober.

And now we arrive at the demesne of Ireland's only
duke—a demesne, according to the exclusive propensities of all those who have this world's wealth, walled
and fenced about with a skreen of trees, through which
the eye of a curious traveller has no chance of pene-
trating. To the left rises an obelisk, built a century ago,
in that remarkable season called in Ireland the hard
frost, by a lady of the Connolly family, in order to
employ the people.   These things are called follies in
Ireland: to give such things such names, only argues
poor taste and sense in those who bestow them; would
that there were many such evidences in the land that the
rich cared for the poor.   Beyond that obelisk, southward, extend the rich wooded grounds, and rises the
finest country mansion in Ireland, Castletown—once
the estate of Dungan, Earl of Limerick—the house was
built by Speaker Connolly, and presents a very
chaste and appropriate *façade* for a rich man's residence.
There, the great commoner, as he was called, Thomas
Connolly, the son of the Speaker, found an income of
30,000*l.* a year too small for the purposes of his expenditure: there were estates encumbered and wasted
in keeping up of huntings and racings—in affording
sport to a whole country, and lavishing of hospitality
on all that would partake of it; so much so, that (as
the legend goes) he once afforded a day's hunting
and a night's entertainment to the devil, who proved

himself the most entertaining companion and the prettiest gentleman of the party.

Now that we are in view of Carton, and the fine estate all round it, brought into its admirable state of improvement by the present nobleman's grandfather, the first Duke of Leinster, I wish I could plant you, reader, for a few minutes, on the top of the tower that crowns a summit in this fine park. Looking east, west, and south, you would observe one of the best managed estates in Ireland. Comfortable slated farm-houses, two stories high, with all their accompanying homesteads; the fences hedge-rowed; the lands well drained and divided, and in the centre of the property a town laid out in the English style—and all this done by one man. Would that all the great proprietors of Ireland had followed the first Duke of Leinster's example, whose desire was to have around him not an idle, sporting, presuming, carousing, set of squireens—but a comfortable, industrious, humble, but at the same time self-respecting yeomanry—a class of men so much wanting, and, alas, still so scarce in Ireland. The first Duke was certainly worthy of all his honours; while living in the splendour becoming one who was lord of 72,000 acres in *this* county we are now passing through, he had the sterling good sense to know how to improve his great possessions in the way best suited to serve his country—he was no rack-renter—he practically applied the old English adage, 'LIVE, AND LET LIVE.' The house at Carton is by no means answerable to the fine demesne. It is what all

houses are where improvements and additions are resorted to, to make up for original deficiency.   It was
not originally intended as the residence of the lords
of Kildare, but erected, I believe, by a General Ogle-
thorpe.   The present Duke has done much—changed
its front, built large additions, and made it as perfect
as good arrangement can; there are a great number
of pictures, and a good collection of books, that once
graced the ducal house in Dublin.   There is a St.
Catherine there, by Domenichino, which, to my mind,
is the first picture in Ireland—but give *me*, after all,
portraits; they furnish the observer with such long
trains of historical recollections.   Here is a noble one
of Gerald, the ninth earl, who so bravely quelled and
brow-beat that haughty prelate, Wolsey.   There, also,
is that extraordinary figure—the Fairy Earl—the
Pilgrim Geraldine.   There, also, before the hall-door
of the eastern front, stands, methinks in rather an
incongruous place, amidst plots of odorous plants and
parterres of dahlias and roses, the ancient cut stone
council-table of the earls of Kildare, when they dwelt
in their stronghold of Maynooth.   It lay buried there
ever since the castle was sacked by the lord deputy in
Henry the Eighth's time, but has lately been dug out.
If I were the Duke of Leinster I would build a great
gothic hall, and place it in the centre: I would hang
the tapestried walls with the armour, and the fretted
roof with the pennons, and would emblazon the deeds
of the bold Geraldines who sat around that table, and
would surround it thus with things in keeping with

its ancient character, and not leave it, as it now stands, a mere support for flower-pots. We entered Maynooth after passing Carton demesne—it looks neat, but *like* all Irish towns, without a stir of business; **unlike** most, as not deformed with mud cabins. It was almost entirely rebuilt by the aforesaid first Duke of Leinster, who desired to make it somewhat like an English market-town; but, alas, it is easier to build houses than to change the spirit and habits of a people. It is now celebrated as containing the great Roman Catholic College, which stands fronting you as you drive down the street. The centre building was erected by a butler of the late Duke of Leinster, who, out of his savings, built it as a private mansion; he little thought of all the Latin, and logic, and dogmatic theology it would subsequently contain. This college is daily enlarging itself; and so it should, if meant to supply the immense and rapidly increasing Roman Catholic population of Ireland with pastors. To me it seems to extend itself without any view towards uniformity, and to be straggling in its hugeness, more like a workhouse than a college. Looking on it as a great factory, where strong machinery is applied to the purpose of bending mind, and assuming that it is more notable for its discipline than its learning, I say, it is deficient in the air, the unction, the scholastic, grey sobriety that characterises Oxford and Cambridge in England, or Padua or Salamanca on the continent. I prefer casting my eye and feasting it on yonder old castle. I remember well, in my younger days, driving under the archwayed tower

that led into the ballium of this Geraldine fortress;
the high road ran under it then. What a grim, gloomy,
prison-like pile is this keep: was it ever inhabited
since the traitor fosterer of Silken Thomas betrayed
it to the lord deputy? Maynooth does not boast alone
of *modern* collegiate notoriety: Gerald, the eighth Earl
of Kildare, the greatest warrior of his race since the
days of his ancestor Maurice—he who was made by
King Henry ruler over all Ireland, because all Ireland
could not rule him—he who excused himself for burning the cathedral of Cashel, by assuring his majesty
that he would not have done so were he not sure that
the archbishop was therein—he who kept all Ireland
under dread of his iron arm—perhaps to make up his
accounts t last, and produce a fair balance-sheet in
the next world, founded a college here, with provost,
vice-provost, and fellows, and endowed it with lands
around the tower of Tahadoe.

Leaving Maynooth, we pass through Kilcock—an
ugly, *triste*, and unimproving place; and still a canal
runs beside it—the great western road through it;
and it is in the midst of one of the most fertile districts either for corn or cattle in Ireland. There is,
however, an excellent corn-market here, perhaps the
best in the vicinity of Dublin.

The hill of Cappagh is now near at hand—what a rich
tract of feeding land. The road, in my younger days,
wended bravely over its summit—and though not
three hundred feet above the level of the sea, it perhaps is the highest point between the bays of Dublin

and Galway.   How unlike most other islands is
Erin—its mountainous districts all around the shores
—its centre only just so elevated as to allow a drainage towards the Shannon, which also, unlike every
other inland river, runs parallel to the greatest
length of the isle.   Cappagh hill forms the high land
that divides the streams falling into the Boyne and
Liffey—from hence is a noble view of almost the
whole of the ancient kingdom of Meath.   Perhaps
not in Europe—except in its mediolanian namesake the
Milanese—is there so much good land mixed with so
little bad, as within its circuit.   No wonder that the
kings of Meath were so often monarchs of Ireland.
No wonder that the hills of Tara, of Usneach, of
Skreen, were so famous.   Here also, was the great
fair of Tailteen, where all the Irish lads and lasses
met to get married, and where, as now at Ballinasloe,
there is a splendid show of fine cattle—so in those
primitive days along the sides of the hill of Tailteen
were ranged pretty girls and brave boys—and then
after the young people had for a sufficient time cast
sheep's eyes at one another, and after the parents had
made proper bargains and arranged family settle-
ments, matches were made; and then games and
sports, and feats of activity began, which were similar, and not perhaps inferior to the Isthmean,
or Olympic games of Greece—human nature is
the same in all times and places—the young must
marry and be given in marriage—and what great difference is there between a mother bringing her

c

daughter to range her with others along the side of a ball-room, and the Milesian mother of olden time leading her blushing girl to Tailteen, to sit modestly on the green clover, and with downcast diamonds every now and then peeping out from beneath her long eye-lashes, to spy whether the *boys* from the opposite side of the line were cocking their bonnets at her. I remember, not long ago, travelling through the county of Down, and witnessing a practice not unlike that of Tailteen. After the cattle, sheep, and pig business of the fair was over—along the sides of the road leading to the fair-green, and on the smooth, grass-covered ditches, all the neighbouring unmarried girls were seated, clothed in their gayest attire; and though nothing in the least indecent or riotous was practised, yet I was assured that here they were assembled to run the chance of getting lovers, and, of course, husbands. Pardon this digression, good reader—it was only resorted to in order to break the dull uniformity of the country from the time you leave Cappagh hill until you get to the Boyne.

We now arrive at the Boyne—and true it is that when you get to that river, it is about as ugly a stream, if stream it can be called that appears to have no current, as need be looked at. You approach it by what reminds you of desolation—a mansion-house, ruined in the rebellion of 1798—a place that recalls all the bitter recollections of that period of " domestic fury and fell civil strife." Yes, look at the potato garden on the side of the road opposite the wasted mansion-house—observe that little mound enced in with gooseberry bushes—there lie, in one large grave, the remains of hundreds who fell in the attack on the dwelling-house of the Tyrrells—God keep such evil days and bloody deeds from ever recurring again! The Boyne flows lazily here amidst sedge and reeds—appearing but the dark drain of an immense morass—the discharge of the waste waters of the Bog of Allen. A strong position in time of war—Lord Wellington knows it well—he has often had his soldier eye upon it, his paternal mansion, Dangan, being not far off to the right, near Trim. How different was the young fun-loving, comical, quizzing, gallanting Captain Arthur Wellesley, when residing in his shooting-lodge between Summerhill and Dangan, from the stern, cautious, careworn Fabius of the Peninsular war; the trifling, provoking, capricious sprig of nobility—half-dreaded, half-doated on by the women, hated by the men—the dry joker, the practical wit, the ne'er do well—despaired of, as good for nothing, by his own family, from the redoubtable warrior of Waterloo—the great prime minister of England— like Julius Cæsar, a rouè converted into a hero.

The Boyne, then, is not here that lovely, picturesque water, which it becomes when it sweeps under the wood-crowned banks of Beau-parc—winds under the limestone bluffs of Slane, washes the castle of the Marquess of Conyngham—or meets the tide

> " At Newbridge town,
> Where was a glorious battle,
> When James and William staked a crown,
> And cannons they did rattle."

But here, though the stream is muddy and ugly, a very pretty new bridge has just been erected.

To the right of the road, after leaving the new bridge, is seen a fine green moat, the sure evidence in Ireland of the ancient importance of the place. These moats have given some trouble to antiquarians in accounting for their use and origin. Evidently artificial—they could not be for defence—could they be for places of sepulture? They appear too large for that purpose; they are generally superior in size to the tumulus or cairn, and besides are always flat at the top. They appear to me to have been constructed for places of assembly, where the chief held consultations with his sept, where the Brehon decided differences among the people. The very name of *moate* attests their origin. Amongst the Saxons, the Wittenagemote was the name given to their popular assemblies. The *mote* was of the same use with them as the *hof* and *ting* were to the Northmen of the Orkneys and the Isle of Man—places of trial and judicial combat, and also before the introduction of Christianity, of sacrifices. Beyond the moat, and farther to the right, on a swelling bank over the Boyne, is the spot where once stood the Abbey and Cathedral of Clonard—*Cluain-iraird*—the field of the western height: but not a vestige now remains but a stone baptismal font, of what was once a bishop's see, and the most famous seat of sacred literature and pious study in Ireland. Here St. Finnian, the most learned of all the successors of St. Patrick, established, in the sixth century, his college, to which three thousand students resorted, not only from all Ireland, but also from Britain, Armorica, and Germany. The venerable Bede describes the English, both of the better and middle ranks, as coming here, not merely for the sake of study, but in the hope of leading a quieter and more contemplative life, (for it would appear that the Irish, in all their feuds, respected learning and the clergy,) and under the direction of holy Finnian, receiving from Irish hospitality instruction, food, lodging, and books, without charge— *céad mille fáilte.* So great was the fame of Finnian, as a commentator on Holy Scripture, that all the holy men of Ireland came to imbibe wisdom from his animated discourses. Hither came the twelve saints whom St. Patrick constituted apostles of Ireland. The venerable Kieran of Saiger, who, with his hair whitened with the snows of an hundred winters, did not disdain to hear Finnian expound to him the sacred book; here also came Kieran of Clonmacnoise, the carpenter's son, who wore himself out in deeds of penance and sanctity, and died in his thirty-third year. The two Columbs, Columbkille and Columb of Tirdaglas, the two Brendans, Brendan of Birr and Brendan of Kerry, Ruadan of Lorra, Molua of Clonfert, and others, as reported by Ussher and Colgan, resorted hither. It would appear that these holy men, while residing at Clonard, did not allow their studies to interfere with their bodily exercises, but that they cultivated the rich and fertile soil

around their abode, and thus by invigorating their
bodies, enlivened their minds, and rendered them
more capable of enduring the mental toil attendant
on the accumulation of much learning. There yet
remains a legend which says that St. Columba, the
son of Crimthan, one night when his lamp failed,
being exceedingly anxious to master some important
passage he had taken in hand, was seen with the
fingers of his right hand tipped with light running
along the leaves of his book, and so, from the efful-
gence which they cast on the pages, he was enabled
to study on while all around him was dark.

Proceeding onwards for a mile or two from Clonard,
the road reaches a long continuous line of gravel hills,
along which it runs for a considerable distance, and
which is, perhaps, one of the oldest lines of road in
Europe. These long lines of gravel hills are all through
Ireland called *aisgirs* or properly *eiscirs:** this one is
that which formed, in ancient times, the grand division of Ireland. I think I could trace this *eiscir* from
Dublin Bay by the green hills of Crumlin, and so
along by the Eskir of Lucan, then south of the Liffey,
near Celbridge, and so across the river near Clane,

---

* These aisgirs are common, I find, in the Scandinavian peninsula. A recent traveller thus notices them: I travelled
great part of the day on one of those singular ridges and mounds
of sand and stones which I met with on the borders of Lapland.
Here it is on a greater scale, running, at least, ten miles. The
road is carried on the top of it. It cannot be an ancient
sea beach, because it slopes equally on both sides.—*Laing's
Travels in Sweden*, p. 209.

onwards by Donadea, until it strikes the line of road
we are now travelling—then trending southward of
the hill of Croghan, until, near Philipstown, another
line of road takes advantage of its elevation, to run
between two bogs; then passing through the barony
of Garrycastle, in the King's County, in a very distinct line, it strikes the Shannon, in the exact centre
of the island, at Clonmacnoise.   This very curious natural *vallum*, just as distinct as the great Roman wall
dividing South Britain from Caledonia, was adopted
as the dividing line between the two parts of Ireland,
and was called *Eiscir Riada*, extending from Dublin
to Galway, the northern portion being called Leath
Con, and the southern, Leath Mogha.   The cause of
this division, as the Irish historian has it, was this:
in the year A.D. 125, Con Ceadcathach (of the hundred battles) was monarch of Ireland, and his reign,
"patrio more" was turbulent; according to the custom of his country, though *monarch* of Ireland, he
found it hard enough to be its *master*.   He fought an
hundred battles, as his name implies, for he was Con
of the hundred *battles*, and not Con of the hundred
bottles, as, by a ridiculous mistake, an Irish work of
character represents him to be.   Yet, surely, even the
Temperance Society would allow that to open an hundred *bottles*, is a more innoxious business than to lead
on to an hundred *battles!*   Con, after being victorious
in ninety battles, over sundry septs, found, at last, a
powerful antagonist in Mogha Nuadat, king of Munster. Mogha, not content with his own share of Ire-

land—fair and fat Munster—must needs try his hand
with Con of the hundred battles, and defeating his
liege lord, compelled him to divide the island, and
this *eiscir* formed the boundary—the northern division being called Leath Con, or Con's half, and the
southern Leath Mogha, or Mogha's half.   But king
Con did not quietly stomach this concession; for, one
morning, he had his rival assassinated in bed, and as
a man-slayer, he was slaughtered himself.   After
wearing his uneasy crown for twenty years, he was
murdered by Tiobraide, son of Roderick King of Ulster,
who, while Con was taking his pleasure, unarmed,
in the hall of Tara, employed fifty ruffians, in the
attire of women, to put him to death.

Kinnegad is, like most towns in east and west Meath,
" a lean place amidst fat lands."   What a sleepy
spot: few up and doing, but the cur dogs and beg-
gars.   The bugle of the passing coach sends its
clangor along the quiet street, it reverberates amongst
the mud walls and dung hills—the lazy cobbler lifts his
head from his last, and scratches, significantly,
beneath his woollen nightcap—the tailor lays down
his goose, scratches also ruminatingly at the organ of
destructiveness, and stares at the passing vehicle—the
tinker's ass brays responsively as the guard blows—
the sow rises from her wallowing in the green puddle
that bubbles and festers before the huxter's door, to
grunt in unison—mendicants and cur dogs rush forth
and surround us, the one barking, the other begging.
Oh, why have we not the pencil of a Wilkie or an

Ostade, a Callot or Della Bella, to picture the grouping of a coach changing horses at an Irish village.
Here I challenge all the mendicant countries in Christendom to match me Ireland in the trade, or costume,
or aptitude for begging—France, Italy, aye, even
Spain itself, must yield the palm. Where, under the
sun, could you find such eloquence of complaint—
such versatility of supplication—such aptitude of
humour—suiting, with felicitous tact, the appeal to
the well guessed character of the applicant? Observe, there is always a leader of the begging band,
who controls the rest, and asserts a manifest superiority in striking the key-note of supplication. Take,
for instance, the queen bee, or rather wasp, of the
Kinnegad swarm that surrounded us: what a tall,
sturdy, sinewy virago—her dark unquiet eye, bespeak-
ing her quick spirit—her powerful form, the danger
of disputing with her—her sallow skin and sharp
features, that the pabulum of her existence was drawn
more from whiskey than from wholesome eatables:
alas, for the body, soul, and spirit of that being whose
existence depends on whiskey and potatoes. Look
at her, with her filthy faltering hand fixed now on the
coach door, in the attitude of threatening requisition,
and almost intentionally frightening a delicate female
within into the reluctant bestowment of sixpence. Again,
see with what a leer of cunning she addresses herself
in flattering guise to an outside passenger, and how
knowingly she *smokes* a youth with a cigar in his
mouth, and while coaxing him out of a penny, which

he flung at her head, she played upon the puffer, offered to lend him her *dudeen*, quizzed him for his parsimony, in attempting to smoke and chew at the same time from the same *tobaccy* twist, and exhibited him off in the truth of his nature, as a Jackanapes. Then she moved off to the rear of the coach, and commenced flattering a farming sort of a young man, large, rude, and ruddy. "Och! then is that yourself, Master Tom—I hope your honour's heifers sold well last market—maybe it's yourself that hasn't the pocketful o'money coming out of Smithfield—and long may your father and your father's son reign, for it's he that's the good warrant to give to the poor—my blessing, and the blessing of poor Judy's children light upon him every day he gets up, for it's he that never passes through Kinnegad without throwing me a silver shilling. Do, Master Tom, and the heaven's be your bed, throw us a half-crown now, and we'll divide dacently. Yes, your honour, I know you'll be afther putting your hand in your pocket. Molly, agra," turning to another beggarwoman, "what a sweet smile Master Tom carries—isn't he as like the dear man his father, as if he was spit out of his mouth—but why shouldn't he be good, seeing as how he's the *rale* ould sort, none of your upstart jackeens." Here a sixpence, thrown at her head, rewarded her pains, and immediately she turned to a respectable looking man, with broad brimmed hat and sad coloured attire, who stood on the other side of the vehicle, preparing to mount. "Do, your riverence, throw

us a tester before you go, and soon and safe may you
return, for the prayer of the fatherless and widow will
be along wid yees,—blessing on his sweet, charitable
face—wouldn't ye see, Honor," addressing herself to
another beggarwoman, with the wink of an eye,
"that there was a heart within him for the poor."
Here Honor interposed—"Judy Mulcahey, and bad
luck to yees, why call the gentleman "his Riverence,"
when you know no more than my sucking child whether he be a *clargy* at all, at all." "Yes, but I do
know, and for why shouldn't I; don't I see his gal-
ligaskins covering so tight and *nate* his comfortable
legs—blessings on his Riverence every day he rises;"
and then, in an under voice, and turning to a beggarman behind her, "Jack, what matters it to the
likes of us, whether he be the right sort or no—what
consarn is it to Judy and the childer, whether he be
priest, parson, or methody preacher, so as I slewder
him out of sixpence. Do, your Riverence, do, and
the poor widow's blessing attend ye, throw something
before yees go amongst us." Thus she carried on
her attacks—praised and joked—prayed and impre-
cated—now a blessing, now a blasphemy—and when
the guard sang out "all's right," and the coach drove
off, she heaped curses, for sheer fun sake, upon all
those whom, for herself and fellows, she failed to put
under contribution—and then for the whiskey shop,
to dissolve, with all rapidity, the proceeds of her
morning's occupation. But "adieu to the village
delights."

"Strange," says a fellow-traveller, as we passed along some beautiful pasturage lands westward of the village, "that a soil seemingly so rich, does not produce cheese: is it the fault of your land, or is it owing to the laziness of your people, that Ireland, even from her richest soils, produces none?" "I beg your pardon, sir," said I, "in my younger days I remember eating cheese made in this vicinity. To be sure, the manufacture of Kinnegad was not equal to that of Berkeley Hundred, and was, in sooth, a tough, thin, leathery sort of thing, very like, when cut into slices, so many razor strops, and I agree with you that it *is* very strange that our confessedly rich pastures cannot supply good cheese, though I have known great pains taken by sundry spirited landed proprietors to produce a good article, and still the attempt proved abortive, though the method of manufacture, the machinery and the makers were brought over from the most approved places in England, as Cheshire, Gloucestershire, Leicestershire; they made cheese to be sure, but it proved not either Cheshire, Gloucester, or Stilton."

"Gentlemen," said a shrewd farming-looking fellow-traveller, "this may not be so strange as many superficial observers might be apt to suppose. The failure, instead of proving a mark of inferiority in our pasture lands, only serves as a proof of their abundant and succulent fertility. The truth is, and on this subject I am informed by a good practical chemist, that our Irish soils laid out for dairy husbandry, supply the cream instead of the curd; or as my friend in learned phrase said, they enrich the cow with more of the *butyraceous* than the *caseous* matter. If unable to produce cheese in sufficient quality or quantity, we can yet supply abundantly our own and foreign markets with butter the best in the world. The bounties of Providence are various, and every country has its peculiar blessing. France has her wine—Italy her oil—England her cheese—Ireland her beef and her butter; and as my farm in Westmeath supplies me with my daily '*mate,* washing, and lodging,' I do not envy the Englishman his bread, cheese, and ale." There was a sensible fellow, and just the sort of intelligent Irish farmer I would like more frequently to meet with.

CHAPTER II.

GAULSTOWN TO ATHLONE.

PASSING by a well wooded and enclosed demesne, with a fine manor-house in the centre, some one remarked that it was Gaulstown, now the property of Lord Kilmaine, but formerly the mansion of the Earls of Belvidere. It is astonishing how previous knowledge causes you, from association, to think well or ill of things and places. Gaulstown, without any grand feature, is as fine as good land, a good house, and large trees can make it, yet, when considered as the prison of a pretty woman, as the lock-up house of a man who was instigated by more than Spanish jealousy, and lived and died under the influence of more than Spanish revenge—even if the sun were shining on it—the thrush amusing its incubating mate with all the harmony of conjugal fidelity, and the ring-dove cooing its querulous love-note from every grove, I could not but consider it as a dismal place. Robert, the first Earl of Belvidere, married in 1736, as his second wife, Mary, the

daughter of Lord Viscount Molesworth; she was
wondrous beautiful, and bore him four children; but
for some cause that excited to dire jealousy his determined spirit, he had his Countess locked up in Gaulstown
house, for nearly twenty years, allowing her only the
attendance of a confidential servant; and this the most
admired woman of her day, lingered away the prime of
her life, neither the world forgetting, nor by the world
forgot—but unknown, and unknowing—guarded with
a vigilance that knew no intermission, until, by her
lord's demise, she was liberated from her thraldom. It
is questionable whether the after-life of this liberated
lady evinced that her long incarceration was instrumental to mental improvement, or even conducive to an
amended life: at all events, during the Earl's life, no
one ventured to call his severe and illegal act into
question, for he was too useful to the government
for it to interfere, and the personal courage of this
clever and handsome Bluebeard was of that exorbi-
tant and reckless character, that no *preux chevalier*
was found hardy enough to attempt the rescue of the
lovely dame from durance vile. In this way they managed matters in Ireland one hundred years ago.

Our next change of horses took place at a village
called Beggar's-bridge—a beggarly place, in sooth, as
its name imports. The cause of its name is not a
little remarkable. In old times, as was the case in
most parts of Ireland, the traveller was obliged to
ford over the small river that crossed the road, and
here stood a beggar, who, as the wayfaring man

slowly picked his passage over the water, from an adjoining bank, asked alms, and invoked all the saints in
heaven to aid and bring to his journey's end, *him*
that lent to God by showing pity on the poor. It
was surely an Irishman who said or sung this stave—

" Of all the trades a-going, a-begging is the best."

Thus our beggarman throve surpassingly, for so ragged,
so wretched, so squalid looked he, that no man could
pass by, (and it was a great thoroughfare,) without
giving him alms, and it so happened that the beggarman died and was buried, and a coffin and winding
sheet were provided for him at the expense of the
neighbours, and his filthy rags, as altogether offensive
and unfit for any use, were cast out on the way-side,
to be trodden under foot, and so resolve themselves
into the element of dirt and dung they had for years
approximated to—but it so happened that as some boys
were playing by the road-side, one of them gave an
unusual toss to the beggar's rags, and out fell a piece
of money, whereupon a more accurate search was
made, and it was found that the ragged inside waist-
coat was quilted with guineas; this money, the young
men who found it, had the honesty to bring to a
neighbouring magistrate, who directed that with it a
bridge should be erected over the stream, on whose
banks stands the little village *inde derivatur*, Beggar's-
bridge.

" What a pity it is that these bogs cannot be turned
to some use," was the remark of one of my fellow
travellers, as we looked southward across some thou-

sands of acres of red bog that stretched towards the Hill of Croghan. " I remember once a near-sighted Englishman, on approaching a gentleman's house in Munster, congratulating the proprietor on the immense quantity of fallow land he was preparing for a crop of wheat; the worthy Briton mistaking the red bog for the red soil he was accustomed to in Worcestershire. "Won't you have patience," said I, "until these wastes are brought under cultivation, according to the process not long ago published as adopted on Chatmoss." "Pooh, pooh—fiddle-dee-dee with your Chatmoss;" said my companion, "convert, forsooth, yonder quagmires on which nothing can stand, and in which nothing can swim; which, are even too wet for a snipe or grouse to feed on—into arable land, producing crops of wheat; sir, I would as soon expect my cook to turn a dish of porridge into roast beef, as to expect that the Bog of Allen should be made arable. No, sir, it is only a great system of combined and national drainage—it is only the slow process of solidification subsequent to this drainage, that can change those at present growing, or, as I may say, living bogs, into recipients for seed corn—into enclosures where the plough and the spade can operate. At the same time," continued he, " I wonder much that a use obvious enough, and very practicable, has not been made of the black, and the more solid* skirts of the red bogs, to manufacture

* These remarks I wish to be considered as written six years ago, and, therefore, before Mr. Williams had made and published his experiments on making his composition of peat and resin answer for steam vessels.

D

charcoal—a fuel so portable, so convenient, so valuable, not only for culinary purposes, but for the different arts and manufactures. Any one who has been
at Paris, and seen the Seine covered with barges laden
with the charcoal that feeds all the culinary fires and
all the furnaces of that city, might wonder why the
citizens of Dublin, and more especially the poor, instead of receiving as they do, cumbrous and expensive
loads of smoky and strong smelling peat or turf, do
not receive their fuel in shape of charcoal. Besides, what a material is here for iron forges. What
is the reason that England, with all her science and
capital, cannot produce iron equal to that of Sweden
or Russia? Why is it that for all strong or safe purposes, artists of every sort must still purchase, even
at double the price, the iron of Scandinavia? Because,
that in the smelting and working of English iron, the
arsenical and sulphureous fumes of the pit coal, still injure the material; and neither in the form of metal, bar
iron, or steel, can iron manufactured with pit coal be
considered perfect. And England, when in former days
she worked with charcoal, and Ireland, too, produced as
good iron as that of Sweden, and it is only necessary
to resort to the old smelting with charcoal, to produce
the good old material. Now what the woods of Sweden
and Russia supply, we may have in abundance in Ireland. I hold it is nearly as easy a process to compress,
dry, and burn peat into charcoal, as to cut down and
cleave timber; and surely, iron ore is very abundant
in our mountains—yes, and at the bottoms of our bogs,

too—and limestone, another necessary, is still more plentiful. What then hinders that we have not iron founderies and forges in Ireland? What but the want of quietness, security, and commercial confidence, by means of which we might and may yet take advantage of the capabilities of the island."

This conversation brought us to the top of a hill which commanded a fine prospect westward and northward. Immediately in front was the pretty hill and dale country of Tyrrell's-pass, which is ornamented with much natural oak wood, and improved by hedge-row planting—presenting in the variety of its surface, and in the number of its gentlemen's residences, a country not unlike some parts of Shropshire. Northward you could see that beautiful oval expanse of water, Lough Ennel, with the narrow Brusna flowing forth and sweeping its tortuous way towards Kilbeggan. This fine lake, full of wooded islands—indented with picturesque promontories, and thickly adorned with gentlemen's seats—presents a rich, soft, *riante* picture, such as Claude or Wilson might paint, or such as Dyer or Shenstone describe. Westward, again, and on a higher level, sparkling like a silver line on the verge of the horizon, might be seen Lough Ouel, in my opinion one of the prettiest of Ireland's lakes. It is of a lowland character, and partakes of the soft *paysage* style of picturesque beauty; no one would presume to compare the gentle naiad of Ouel, with the magnificent deities that preside over Killarney, or Ulleswater, or Katrine—but,

after all, it is a precious *bijou* of a lake, and though
there are no sublime peaks, from whence tumble the
thunder-riven rock and the avalanche—though no
clouds, rolling in mysterious masses, break on the
mountain side, and send down the tumbling cataract—
yet here are the smooth, verdant lawns—the softly
swelling sheep-depastured hills—the wooded banks—
the islands consecrated by all the mournful associa-
tions connected with ruined churches.   I don't know
whether I exactly expressed these identical sentiments
and words to my coach companion, but I certainly
praised, as well I might do, the very beautiful Westmeath waters, along whose banks I have often wan-
dered; moreover, I do not say that it was any of my
fellow passengers who related the following legend
respecting this lake, which, as I have before said, reflected the sinking sun as a distinct but distant
mirror.

"Playful and fantastic was the being who once
dwelt and had power over the sweet valley through
which the waters of Lough Ouel now flow.   The
-times alluded to were those when the Tuatha-Danans
possessed Ireland—when magical power was very prevalent—and a fine town, older still than Armagh or Kil-
mallock, and worthy of its ancient dwellers, covered the
bottom of the valley.   The fisherman, as he in modern days pushes his boat from the shore, and is disappointed in his venture—by the heavens becoming
sunlit, the winds still, and the calm mirror of the
lake assuring him he will cast his line in vain—it is

then when he looks down, for want of something else
to do, into the translucent deep, that he sees stacks
of chimneys, ridge poles, and gables of houses, and
even a round tower—Ireland's most ancient edifice—
and calls to mind the ditty that his nurse has
sung about "the drowning of Old Mullingar." Well
what a purely mischievous person must she have been
that caused this submersion. Yet so it was that a
female caused it. It is very much to be doubted, whether
in any case, save that of our Queen, power should be
entrusted in the hands of women. They are quite too
capricious and they do things too much by the jerk
of impulse. So it was in this instance. The Tuatha-
Danans, who preceded the Milesians in Ireland, were
great magicians. So the historians of our Patron
Saint assure us, there are remains of their feats in the
land even yet, that can only be accounted for in the way
of supernatural power. Could any one but a magician
take a bite out of a mountain in the county of Tipperary, and drop the mouthful at Cashel, where it
now stands as the notorious ROCK—in the same way
with respect to Lough Ouel. Some call her a fairy—
others a witch—any how she had more power than I
would like my wife to possess—and on a fine day she
travels off to the county of Roscommon, to visit a
witch of her acquaintance, who resided on the borders
of a very pretty lough there; and every night in
which witches may disport, she spent her time in
fishing for Gillaroo trout, and when she was in bad
humour, turning a flat stone washed by the waters

of the lake, and as ever and anon the ninth wave passed over it, in cursing her enemies. No doubt she was very proud of her way of life; for, said she, I have here what few possess, that is, hens that have gills, and fish that have gizzards. Now hither the Westmeath wise-woman bent her way; and after certain days entertainment and converse, such as witches alone enjoy, she says—"Cousin, I'll be lonesome when I go back to Leinster, without the sweet sounds of the wave-beating waters of this lough; will you lend it me until Monday; I will just borrow it for the sake of seeing how it will look in my own pretty valley." With all the pleasure in life," says the Connaught woman, mighty accommodating, "but how, deary, will you take it with you or send it back?"

"Och, asy enough—in my pocket-handkerchief— ladies carried no reticules in those days—and so she did, cleverly enough: and full sure it must have been a rare sight to behold it hurrying eastward, high over the hills of Knockcrokery—aqueducting itself over the broad Lough Ree—disdaining to delay on the plains of Kilkenny-west—and then by a slip of one corner of the kerchief, coming down and settling itself, as if it were born and bred there, in the valley of Ouel. No child was ever prouder when paddling in a puddle, than the Westmeath witch was of her borrowed water; and like all wayward and unthrifty ladies, it's little it troubled her that hundreds of acres were drowned to provide my lady with a looking-glass. But what was to be done when pay Mon-

day came? was the lake to be gathered up again in
a shawl, and sent back? By no manner of means.
I have you, my pretty pond, and never again shall
your soft murmuring waves kiss a Connaught shore.
But where's your honesty, Lady Westmeath? Oh,
how ancient is equivocation—how long has the practice prevailed in Ireland, of not paying just debts?
was it from this witch that so many here have found
out, that it was not their interest to pay the principal,
or their principle to pay the interest? Of course the
Connaught woman came in due time, very huffingly,
and demanded her lough. " Did you not," says she,
"promise and vow to return it me on Monday?"
" Yes, to be sure I did," says the crafty witch, " but,
as the Irish have it, it was on the Monday after the
Sunday of Eternity; or, as the English say, it was
on Monday come never in a wheelbarrow."· Bad
treatment this of an honest, confiding, generous
Connaught woman. But it was to no purpose she
stormed and wept; and anger-breathing magician as
she was, she could not blow back the lake, nor could
all her tears create it: what is worse, she had to sit
down contented, in as ugly a turlough, where once
those sweet waters used to flow, as ever Christian
laid eyes on—all covered with limestone flags, as waste
and as sorrowful as a grave-yard. The place is the
Barony of Athlone, I have often passed it—people
dig there for pipeclay; small comfort in those early
days for the loss of her lough, seeing as how tobacco
pipes and smoking to drive away sorrow, were not yet
invented.

The lough itself, it would appear, did not
like to stay on the Leinster side of the Shannon;
and as well became it, forth it sent two streams, one
from its northern, another from its southern end,
both of which trending westward—and called by
the people the gold and silver hands—stretched out
towards Connaught, forming the head waters of the
Inney and the Brusna, and making a very pretty
island of the Baronies of Kilkenny West and Garrycastle. It may be supposed that the Westmeath
witch, with the malice that ever belongs to such a
magical race, did not stomach this hankering after
Connaught, so on a day she says, " my pretty water,
I'll teach you how to long for that land of
bogs and limestone—which Cromwell thought
only a little better than hell—I'll show you, that like
a Roscommon spalpeen, you shan't be ever scheming
to go back to be buried in the land you were born in."
So what does my fairy woman do, but goes and
makes a bargain with the Royal Canal Company, to
sell Lough Ouel to them as a summit level; and she
never rested until she cut off both her golden and
silver hands, and sent the soft, sweet waters, through
the deep-sinkings, locks, and levels, along with canal
boats to Dublin. I do not care whether any one beside myself believes my story; all I know is, that it is
not my own invention; and this I can *assure* you, that
contrary to the natural tendency of these waters to
flow westward, they now, as forming the finest summit level to any canal in Europe, flow eastward, "into
the tea-kettles of the citizens of Dublin."

I would not desire or expect to meet a much prettier village in England than Tyrrell's-pass—wood-crowned hills—dry gravel roads—neat whitewashed cottages—comfortable and well-dressed gentlemen's demesnes—a very pretty new church and steeple—these all meet the eye in and about Tyrrell's-pass; but all these interested me not so much as the old castle that stands a little way westward of the village, and which, placed at the extremity of a line of gravel hills, that rise out of large bogs which skirt it on either side, guards the only passable road leading towards Athlone. This pass—often the scene of bloody contest—has got its name from the ablest partizan soldier that ever Ireland produced, and who lived in the stormy times of Elizabeth, so fertile in every description of great men. This noted soldier was not only remarkable for the courage and devotedness with which he inspired his followers, but also for, in days of unusual treachery, the faithfulness with which he adhered to his cause. True to his employers, attached to his friends, he never despaired of what he thought the cause of his country, which he was the very last to desert. I do not desire it to be understood, that I at all approve of Tyrrell's siding with the King of Spain, against his natural sovereign; but treating historically of him, I cannot but speak of him as a valiant soldier, and a consummate guerilla chief. Of English descent, when Tyrone rose in arms against Elizabeth, he took the command of the light-footed and light-armed Irish Bonnaghts,

and there was not a mountain pass from Malin Head
to Slieve Logher, nor a *togher* across a bog from Philipstown Fort to Galway, that he did not know the intricacies of. When in they year 1597, the new deputy, Lord
Burroughs, formed the plan of his campaign against
Tyrone, O'Donnel, and Maguire, it was arranged that
the Lord Deputy, attended by the Earl of Kildare and
the Lords of the Pale, should march direct upon Ulster,
whilst Sir Croniers Clifford, the president of Connaught, should, with a force of 2,000 men, proceed
into his province, and passing through it, turn in on
Ulster by the head of the Shannon, taking Maguire's
country in flank, and so march on to form a junction
with the Deputy.

Tyrone, one of the wiliest of men, was not
long in ascertaining the details of this plan,
and in taking measures to counteract it; and to that
purpose he despatched Tyrrell, with 500 picked
Bonnaghts, to proceed through the Brenny, into
Leinster, to raise the O'Moores of Leix, Pheagh
M'Hugh O'Byrne, and the O'Tooles, and so with these
united forces oppose and check Sir Croniers Clifford.
Tyrrell, on his way to effect these junctions, was
reposing his men in the woods that lie around Lough
Ennel, when Sir Croniers, whose army lay at Mullingar,
hearing of the Irish partizan being in his vicinity,
despatched young Barnewell, Lord Trimleston's son,
with half his forces, to destroy Tyrrell; who, aware
of his approach, fell back until he gained this pass,
which he made more dangerous by felling trees and

fixing them' on either side of the bogs that flanked
the road, and he directed half his little army, under
Owny M'Rory oge O'Connor, to secrete themselves
in a hollow in the ground, covered with oak copse,
near which the English were to march in order to
gain the pass and assault Tyrrell. Young Barnewell
observing that Tyrrell was making a show of retreating onwards towards Kilbeggan, hastily advanced,
leaving O'Connor in his rear; whereupon the Irish
rose from their ambuscade, sounding their bagpipes—
which was the concerted signal of the English placing
themselves between the two fires—upon which Tyrrell
turned about, and both he and Owny M'Rory fell on.
The English, assailed in front and rear, and unable to
deploy—as enclosed between the two bogs and the
abbatis of felled timber—fought gallantly, as they always did, but were completely defeated and annihilated.
Barnewell was taken prisoner—and not a man escaped
to tell Clifford the disastrous tale, except one who
had plunged up to his· neck in a quagmire, amidst
reeds and sedge. O'Connor, who fought on that
day like a very madman, had his hand so swollen
with fighting and fencing, that it could not be removed from the guard of his sabre until the steel was
'separated with a file. Clifford, with an army diminished to one-half, now finding himself surrounded by
Irish insurgents on every side, was obliged to retreat
on Dublin, and it required the greatest prudence and
skill to effect his retreat in safety. This was not the
only action in which Tyrrell was concerned in this

vicinity. A little to the south, and occupying a similar pass in O'Moore's country, he surprised the most consummate of Elizabeth's generals, the Lord Mountjoy; on which occasion the Deputy was in imminent danger of his life, and had a horse shot under him. Any one who reads the history of that terrible struggle between the English and Irish in those wars, will recognize what an important part Tyrrell took in them—how he was mainly instrumental in assisting O'Donnell to pass into Munster, in spite of all Lord Mountjoy's precaution, who had supposed that he had every practicable road guarded, but which Tyrrell and O'Donnell evaded by passing safely over the hitherto impracticable mountains of Slieve Phelim, and so thence gained the valley of the Shannon, when the English supposed they had enclosed them in the vale of the Suir. Tyrrell led on the vanguard of the Irish forces, at the, to them, disastrous battle of Kinsale. He protected Dunboy as long as it was possible; though often tempted by the English generals, he constantly refused to betray his cause, though thereby he might have saved from an ignominious death, his nearest and dearest friends. Often betrayed, and often thereby defeated, yet too vigilant to be taken—too fertile in resources to be vanquished, he still held out; when even O'Donnell, in despair, retired beyond the seas, and Tyrone bargained successfully for his pardon, and when at last all was over in Munster, because the country was turned into one wide waste—Tyrrell, instead of surrendering, effected, along with his faithful followers, his retreat out of Desmond, and passed in hostile array, from the farthest mountains of Kerry, through the midst of traitorous Irish and watchful English, until he arrived in the fastnesses of the county Cavan—and there history leaves him—for I find no record of his subsequent life or death, after the Lord Mountjoy had the honour to announce to his sovereign, that he had pacified Ireland.

The country from Tyrrell's-pass to Kilbeggan is improved. The hills are generally planted, the low grounds are drained, and gentlemen's seats are to be seen on either side of the road. One in particular caught my attention, as well remembered, having, in my younger days, enjoyed the hospitality of its *then* owner. It has since more than once changed masters; on inquiring who now possessed it, I was informed by one of my fellow-travellers, that its present proprietor was not satisfied with his bargain; and he mentioned, as the common report of the country, how an ingenious trick was played off, in order to induce him to effect the purchase. "The land," said he, "is naturally very light—the upland a dry hungry gravel—the lowland, such as reclaimed bog generally is, wet, rushy, and inclined to return to its original unproductiveness. The gentleman, struck with the beautiful forms of the grounds, and with the tasteful way in which they were planted, appointed a time on which he would come and view the house and land, and previous to that day the owner proceeded to some neighbouring fair, and bought up some forty or fifty of the fattest heifers he could meet—these were, of course, grazing on the land the day the visitor arrived; accordingly, in passing along, he put the question, whether the land could provide good beef and mutton for the table." "My object, sir, is, if I take a country place, to live within myself, to go to market for nothing, to buy as little and sell as much as I can." "Right, sir," says the owner, "that is what I have always done: look yonder, pray, the proof of the pudding may be in the feeding, as well as the eating; do, sir, come over with me and handle a few of these heifers—there is nice beef for you, fit for any market—not better made up cattle from this to Kells." The stratagem was successful—the admiring gentleman, struck with such convincing proofs of good land, soon concluded the bargain. But, alas! since he became possessed of the title-deeds, he has never yet been able to have a good sirloin on his table from his grounds." "Confound the blockhead!" exclaimed a farming man, who was listening to the story, "he must have been some soft Cit to be taken in so—could he not have looked at the blackheads, and fairy flax, and the *traneens?* and they would have told him that he could not expect a fat goose, let alone a fat cow, from such sun-burnt hills." "Sir Henry Piers, in his account of Westmeath," observed I, "written 160 years ago, describes the inferior West-meath farmers as follows:—'The Sculloges, which may be Englished farmers, or boors, are generally very crafty and subtle in all manner of bargaining, full of equivocation and mental reservation, especially in their dealings in fairs and market, where, if lying and cheating be no sin, they make it their work to overreach any one they deal with, and if by slight or fetch, they can hook in the least advantage, they are mighty tenacious thereof.' If the story just told has any foundation, which I trust it has not, this West-meath gentleman played a very sculloge trick.

We now arrived at Kilbeggan, situated on the Upper Brusna river, a small town, though before the Union returning two members to parliament. This was in old times the chief town of M'Geoghegan's country, and there were two religious establishments here, one an Abbey, founded by St. Beccan, a cotemporary of St. Columbkill; and in the year 1200, another religious house, called the Abbey of the River of God— why so called I have not ascertained,—was founded by the D'Alton family under the invocation of the Blessed Virgin; this was supplied with monks from the great Abbey of Mellifont, whose mitred abbot could ride straight forward on lands belonging to his house, from the sea near Drogheda to the Shannon. In Elizabeth's time the Dillon family had the property of the suppressed Abbey; in the following reign, Oliver Lord Lambert was seized of the monastery lands of the Blessed Virgin, and his descendant, Gustavus Lambert, Esq. is now in possession of the property. Passing rapidly through the town, some circumstances connected with it came vividly to my recollection; the

inn of the town *I must* remember as long as I live—
its titled landlady I well recollect—the Lady Cuffe;
never did the fountain of honour play off such a ludi-
crous prank, as when it showered its spray on the
head of an innkeeper; yet so it was, when about seventy
years ago the Viceroy of Ireland dubbed mine host of
Kilbeggan a Knight.   Lord Townshend, the then
lord lieutenant, a man addicted to the most dissolute habits, and who, by the satirical writers of that
day, was represented as one perfectly regardless of
pomp, dignity, or parade—one, who as he walked
the streets, used to scatter his ribbald jests among the
common passengers; whose festivities were often degraded down to disorder, and his recreations to inde-
licacy; he, on occasion of a journey to Connaught,
was, by some accident that occurred to his equipage,
obliged to stop at Kilbeggan for the night, and partake of such accommodation as Mr. Cuffe, the innkeeper, could afford.   In those days good claret was
not an unusual thing to be had even in small country
inns; and it so happened that Mr. Cuffe was able to
send up some fowl and fish well cooked and well
served, and that the claret was in its *bouquet* and fla-
vour adapted to his Excellency's taste; accordingly the
great man unbent himself amongst his boon companions, and so while losing sobriety, he forgot decorum;
and as he on another occasion, introduced his fox-
hounds into the Council Chamber, now as a hair-
brained bacchanalian, he ordered the host to make his
appearance, and when he came into the PRESENCE,

Viceroy, in an affectedly grave speech, returned him
thanks for his excellent cheer, and announced, that
he would not repay the *obligation* in any other manner but in conferring on him the order of knighthood,
and, accordingly, in spite of some of the more sober
of the party, who remonstrated against this act of
whimsical licentiousness, he actually forced mine
host to kneel down, and duly dubbing him in set
phrase and form, said—" Rise up, thou mirror of inn-
keepers, and be from henceforth Sir Thomas Cuffe."
The astonishment of the innkeeper may be well supposed, as he returned to his wife to inform her of her
new honours. The viceregal visitor, as usual, retired
to rest, utterly reckless of what he had done, and rose
in the morning, altogether forgetful, until reminded
of the transaction; at which, when informed, he was
not a little annoyed, but plucking up courage, he said
to his aide-de-camp—" *It* certainly *was* carrying the
joke too far, but curse the fellow, sure he will not
take any advantage of it ? Call him before me, and
I'll persuade him to hush up the matter." Accordingly, the man was introduced—" Mr. Cuffe," says
his excellency, " a circumstance occurred last night,
which I am sure you understood in the proper light;
it was, it is true, carrying THE JOKE too far; I hope,
sir, you feel as becomes you, and that you will say no
more about it, nor let the thing get wind." " Oh!
indeed, my lord, the honour you have conferred on
me, though I am right sensible of its importance, is
still what I, for *one*, would have no objection to fore-

go, under a proper *consideration;* but, please your
excellency, what will my Lady Cuffe say ?" The innkeeper and his wife were Sir and my Lady all their
lives. The man died long before I ever passed through
Kilbeggan, but I perfectly remember my Lady Cuffe.

The remembrance of an ennobled hotel keeper,
however, is not what has fastened the inn so much
on my memory, as a still more *personal* occurrence;
for, be it known, and the part most concerned tingles
while I tell it, I got the greatest kicking ever man
got in Lady Cuffe's yard. The lamentable event
was on this wise:—I, in the summer of 1799, the
year after the rebellion, was travelling from the
county of Westmeath to that of Tipperary, and on
my way rode into my Lady Cuffe's Inn, at Kilbeggan;
there I saw, sauntering about the house, and smoking
as they reclined here and there, a set of outlandish
looking soldiers—gigantic fellows with terrible *mous-
taches* and other accoutrements denoting them to be
foreigners. I was a young, spare, lathy lad at that time,
much under twenty, and like a gaping green-horn, I
must needs proceed to the stables to inspect the horses
and appointments of these much dreaded men, who, I
was told, were Hessians; suppose me then standing in
the stables *" sicut mos est Milesianorum,"* as is the
custom of Irishmen, with my mouth open, admiring
all the stirrups, saddles, and bridles, &c. &c. of the
Germans—moreover, be it recollected, that it was
a token of loyalty in those days to carry a queue or tail
pendant from the back of your neck, and that those

who neglected or lost such an accompaniment were counted disaffected—they were Croppies.   Poor *innocent* Croppy then as I was, there I stood unconscious of coming evil, when I all at once found myself seized on from behind, by the grasp, as it were of a giant—my arms pinioned with one hand, the poll of my neck searched for the deficient tail with the other, and my seat of honour assailed with an immense jack boot, whose toe did horrible execution, such as a battering ram would inflict on a very weak postern, and then a terrible cry was shouted close to my ears, " You be one Croppie rascal, vat te devill bring te yong rebill here ?—take *dat*—and *dat*—and *dat*." So he kicked me in the stable, and he kicked me in the yard, and he kicked me in the street, and he kicked me up the front steps of the inn, and there the cruel monster, who was at least six feet four inches in height, then left me, as a hound would let drop a hare out of his mouth, pounded in body, and wounded in mind. Oh! the toe of that terrible jack boot, never can I forget the infliction—what was I to do ?—take vengeance of course.   Vengeance on whom ?—a common soldier—have the fellow punished—stay in the town until you lodge the complaint before his officer—have him tried, flogged, and what not—oh! but that would take time—I should stop with my Lady Cuffe, that would take money, with which I was not over-burthened, so I thought it better to take patience, call for a chaise, and putting plenty of straw under me, for air-cushions were not then invented, proceed in a

very delicate state to the end of my journey, my only
consolation being, that though a kicked man, the disgrace and pain were not inflicted by a countryman—
by a *rale* O, or a true Mac, but by a brutal Hessian.

Proceeding through Kilbeggan, our next stage was
Horseleap, where a church stands crowning an adjoining height, and where are the remains of a very
ancient fort, anciently called Ardnorcher, but latterly
Horseleap, from an extraordinary leap, said to have
been formerly made by an English knight, over the
raised draw-bridge, when escaping into the fortress
from the pursuit of his Irish foes. This is a curious
specimen of an ancient DUN, of the remotest period,
converted by the military skill of the Norman De Lacy
into a more modern stronghold to quell the conquered
natives. Sir Hugh De Lacy was certainly an eminent
military chieftain, who took advantage of every circumstance and situation to preserve his conquests. In
this way he turned abbeys into castles, and wherever
he found a rath or moat well placed, he repaired and
strengthened it with additional defences of lime and
stone. Thus the ancient DUN or moat of Ardnorcher
seems to have presented itself to De Lacy as a strong
link in the chain of forts and castles, which he drew
along the line of the Pale from the great Bog of Allen
to the borders of Brefney, (now Longford.) There
is a very interesting description of this fortress, and a
drawing and ground plan of it, in the Transactions of
the Royal Irish Academy. According to tradition,
Sir Hugh did not live to finish his plan of Normaniz-

ing this DUN; for while this great man, the favourite of
his sovereign, and one of the most valiant of that
extraordinary race who came over with Strongbow,
was inspecting his rising fortress, and stooping
down to give directions to the workmen, an Irish
labourer, deeply imbued with a sense of his country's wrongs, clove his head with a single blow of
his mattock. Tradition has it, that though one of the
most active, valiant, and sage men of his time, De
Lacy was but small in stature and was called Le Petit;
and from hence the Le Petits of Westmeath derive their
name and origin. Small men have often been found,
not only wise in counsel, but brave leaders in the
field—their energies seem to act with more power,
as more concentrated; and Sir Hugh De Lacy Le
Petit, as well as Napoleon Bonaparte, together with
thousands of other little but great men, have shown
that the mind, the immortal mind, can nerve a little
body to achieve great things. Sir Hugh was an extraordinary horseman—his leap over the draw-bridge
of his fortress is, as I have said, yet recorded, and the
spot shown, and the name of the place and village will
record, as long as time lasts, this feat of a Norman
knight. Alas! for the De Lacys—like the De Courcys
and Tyrrells of that day, they did not respect the prejudices of the people; one of the castles he was building
he dared to found on the site of an ancient abbey.
The Irish were shocked at the profanation, the act
therefore of the assassin was applauded by all, and
even the avenging peasant's deed was counted religi-

ously meritorious, as exciting the anger of St. Columbkill on him who was the usurper of his abbey, and
the spoiler of his churches.   Be it as it will, the De
Lacys were a valiant and noble race.   Hugh, the
founder of Ardnorcher, or Horseleap Castle, left two
sons.· Hugh, the eldest, one of the most politic of
men, contrived to supplant John De Courcy, the
conqueror of Ulster, in the favour of King John, and
eventually succeeded in driving him out of his province, and assuming the government.   The story of
the rivalship of the De Courcys and De Lacys might
be made the subject of a very interesting historical romance.   I have often wondered that Sir Walter Scott,
after introducing the De Lacys into an English story,
did not follow up the subject, by making some use of the
materials which Irish history affords of this noble race;
their strange vicissitudes of fortune—now favorites—
now rebels—defeated to-day by De Courcy—and in a
short space of time supplanting him and driving him
from Ulster—again falling under the displeasure of
their monarch, and obliged to fly for refuge to France,
and there forced to work as gardeners on the grounds
of a Norman Abbot—and again, when unable to conceal their noble bearing, they were detected by the
good ecclesiastic, and by his intercession reconciled
to the king; and restored to their fiefs, we find
the weak and vacillating John writing a letter to
Walter De Lacy, entreating him to forget all ani-
mosities, and assuring him of future favour and pro-
tection.

The next stage is Moate, formerly called the **Moate** of Gren-oge—the Moate of young Grania or Grace. This fine specimen of the labours of the Irish in the erection of these artificial eminences, and which, perhaps, the largest in Ireland is, as I previously said of the rath at Lucan, completely hid by being covered with trees, and looks like nothing more than a hill planted *thickly* (each melancholy fir starving its neighbour) by some *very improving* Quaker. A legend there is concerning a Milesian princess taking on herself the office of a Brehon, and from this moate adjudicating causes, and delivering her oral laws to her people. At present Moate is a neat and pretty place, as all towns in Ireland are that are much inhabited by Quakers. It is really refreshing, after having your senses of sight, smelling, and hearing, outraged in passing through such an assemblage of mud cabins, pig-sties, and dung-hills, as Kilcock and Kinnegad present, to see the cultivated fields, the slated cottages, and the whitewashed dwellings in and about Moate. I have often supposed that Ireland might be advantaged, in a worldly sense, at least, were its people to turn Quakers. What a change my fancy contemplates—a nation of fighters turned into a community of friends; but how cruel would it be thus to cut up the trades of distillers, publicans, pike-makers, and policemen. To be sure this snug, smooth, easy-going people, too, had their hot times as well as others; and the steady, demure, barrel-bodied *Friend*, with his single-breasted surcoat scarcely able to girth in his abdomenic protuberance, or the pale, placid, dove-eyed, and sadly attired sister of the present day, are but cool contrasts to the stern, burning, fervid, bare-boned, proselytizing fanatic of George Fox's time, who roamed the world testifying against parsons, priests, and steeple-houses. When John Parrot, moved by mighty impulse, went to convert the Doge of Venice—and Samuel Fisher rushed to Rome, to testify the truth before roseate cardinals, and instead of kissing the Pope's toe, give it a bite, and tell his holiness he was antichrist—nay more, when the pale Mary Fisher appeared in her simple garb and sweet solemn face before the Turkish Sultan, in the presence of his mighty army at Adrianople, and there spoke what she had on her mind with such simple solemnity and un-veiled modesty, that Mahomet heard her with gravity and attention, and though he might have wished to have such a variety of womankind in his harem, he dismissed her with admiration and respect; so much so, that she passed through hordes of Paynims with-out a guard, and arrived at Constantinople without scoff or hurt—I say, the quiet, sedate, unmeddling Quakers of the present day, are as different from their progenitors, as the frigid from the torrid zone, and occupying now the cool, sequestered character of those who mind their own business, we see them prosperous in themselves, and not interfering with others, except in a *temporal* sense, to do them good. This may be worldly prudence, but its Christian cha-racter I don't understand.

Moate a Gren-oge is surrounded with ruined castles and churches, moates, raths, and memorials of
the wars, the feuds, and the ferocities of former times.
It has had also its day of great Quaker prosperity,
which is, I fear, passing away; for the manufactures
of linen and cotton which these good people encouraged, and which they upheld, perhaps, longer than
any other class of employers, are now undersold and
almost ruined by the overwhelming power of British
machinery. The pretty, grassy, and well cultivated
hills around this town, surrounded as they are by
large bogs, have, as a good military position, been
the scene in the wars of Ireland of many a skirmish
and battle. Here, in the wars of the Revolution, a
severe battle was fought between the forces of King
William under General De Ginkel, and of James under Brigadier Clifford. The Irish attempted to de-
fend the town, which was merely ditched and pallisa-
doed, but were forced to evacuate it and fall back on
Athlone; the horse retreating by the road, the infan-,
try through the bogs and fastnesses with which the
country abounds. Here the rapparees—who, in those
days, were so numerous, and so effective, and who
seemed to be actuated with the same spirit, and to
put in practice the same warfare as the Spanish Gue-
rillas; to the no small astonishment of the English
army, had recourse to a manœuvre with which they
were familiar:—a large party that had skirmished
with the British regiments, and given them no small
annoyance by their bush-firing and desultory attack,

driven by the bayonet, fled to the red bog on the left
of the town, and there, as if by enchantment, hundreds of men in the open day, instantly disappeared:
they were gone as ghosts—and not a single runaway
could be seen as a mark for a bullet, or a butt for a
bayonet or pike. Story, in his interesting account of
these civil wars thus describes this evasion:—" The
rapparees escaped to the bog, and in a moment all
disappeared; which may seem strange to those who
have not seen it, but something of this kind I have
seen myself, and it is *thus* done:—When the rapparees
have no mind to show themselves upon the bogs, they
commonly sink down between two or three tusocks
grown over with long grass, so that you may as soon
find a hare as one of them; and they conceal their
arms *thus*:—they take off the lock, and put it in their
pocket, or hide it in some dry place; they stop the
muzzle close with a cork, and the touch-hole with a
small quill, and then throw the piece itself into a
bog-hole. You see one hundred of them without
arms, who look like the poorest, humblest slaves in
the world, and you may search until you are weary
before you find one of their guns; but yet, when they
have a mind to do mischief, they are all ready at an
hour's warning, for every one knows where to go
and fetch his own arms, though you do not."

The road from Moate to Athlone passes over a
country, as I have before observed, consisting of ranges
of limestone gravel hills, rising from moors and red
bogs; the hills in general range from east to west, and

seem formed by currents of subsiding waters falling towards the great drain of central Ireland—the Shannon. Wherever (as is the case in a great measure between Moate and Athlone,) the hills are planted and the moors drained,. the country is pretty; and more especially about Moate, the patient industry of the Quakers has done much. As you approach the Shannon, the country presents a flat and gloomy aspect; the western horizon exhibits nothing but a monotonous line, unrelieved by mountain or wooded elevation, and the kingdom of Connaught does not smile on you as a land of promise.

As you approach Athlone, high lands to the northwest do not allow you to see the broad expanse of Lough Ree; but on casting my eye in an opposite direction, at the distance of about seven miles—just at the termination of a line of picturesque hills—the round tower of Clonmacnoise rose like the *terminus* of a kingdom, to mark, as it were, the limit of some royal or ecclesiastical frontier—the boundary pillar between O'Melachlin, king of Meath, and O'Connor, king of Connaught.

As you approach the town you do not see much of it, because it is sunk in the hollow through which the Shannon forces its way in order to reach the flats to the south, and nothing in or about the town impresses you with the idea of beauty, industry, or prosperity. It contains distilleries, whiskey-houses, soldiers, and no Quakers. The coach stops at the Westmeath side; neither in the street outside, nor in-

side of the inn where you put up, do you find much that
may administer to your pleasure or comfort; neither is
there any thing in the town, when you walk abroad, to
catch your attention; no antique buildings—no marks
of ancient power or splendour; when you wish to see
the Shannon, you go through a narrow street, or rather lane, towards the bridge, which you find narrow,
and encumbered with mills and houses, besides sundry annoyances moveable and immoveable—but still
if you can with any safety, amidst the rush of pigs,
cats, and Connanghtmen, stand on this important
bridge, and observe the huge volume of the Shannon
rushing rapidly and clearly under its many arches—
look upwards, and you will perceive how the stream
bristles with staked eel-wears—and above them, the
cots of fishermen, and the pleasure yachts of the officers of the garrison; look across the river and you
will see the old castle, commanding the river pass,
once the residence of the Lord President of Connaught, and the well-defended position maintained
for the English in the rebellion of 1641, by the Lord
Ranelagh—and for the Irish, still more resolutely,
by Colonel Gráce, in the war of the Revolution;
who forced General Douglas to raise the siege
in 1690, and in the following year defended it
with a vigour and tenacity which, if supported
as he should have been by the French auxi-
liaries under St. Ruth, must have foiled his adversaries. Perhaps modern warfare does not present
an instance of greater intrepidity and devotedness,

than was exhibited on this occasion; a great interest, indeed, was excited by this siege; the attack, supported by the whole force of Great Britain in Ireland; the defence sustained by the whole combined power of the Irish and French army, led on by a general who had acquired a great name in the wars of the continent. This old bridge on which I now stand, built by Sir Henry Sydney in the reign of Elizabeth, had one arch next the Connaught bank broken down. The powerful artillery of De Ginkel had battered the castle covering the bridge on the western side, into a heap of ruins; every thing sunk before the shot and shell of the well served British artillery. The Irish laboured incessantly to repair the breaches in the walls; the workmen fell as fast as they came to work—but as they were swept away, others took their places, and still men were found ready to labour at a task that brought certain death. But the English general was not yet the nearer to his point; *there* was the hitherto unfordable Shannon, and *there* was the bridge with its broken arch; gun and mortar had done their worst, but Athlone was not gained. It was resolved, then, to force the position by throwing a wooden gallery across the chasm.

The British, under the shelter of the fire of their tremendous artillery, had constructed a breastwork on the bridge at their side of the broken arch. The Irish had one on their part, composed of wattles and earth: but this was set on fire by the continual shower of shot and grenades; and while it was fiercely burning, the English, concealed by the flame and smoke, succeeded in pushing large beams across the chasm; and now it was only necessary to place boards over the beams, and the river was crossed—when an Irish sergeant and ten men in complete armour leaped across the burning breastwork, and proceeded to tear up the beams and planks. The British were astonished at such hardihood, and actually paused in making any opposition—but the next instant a shower of grape shot and grenades swept these brave men away, who, nevertheless, were instantly succeeded by another party, that in spite of the iron hail storm tore up planks, beams, and all, and foiled the enterprise of their foes. Of this second party only two escaped—there is scarcely on record a nobler instance of heroism than this deliberate act of these Irish soldiers, who have died without a name.*

General De Ginkel made another unsuccessful attempt to throw a gallery across the broken arch: when foiled in all his attempts, a circumstance came to his knowledge which saved him from the disgraceful alternative of raising the siege, and which, no doubt, turned the fortune of the whole war. The river, for the first time in the memory of man, was found fordable a little below the bridge—two Danish soldiers, who for some crime had been sentenced to be shot, on pro-

* It is but fair to state, that Story asserts that these men were Scotch, belonging to Maxwell's regiment.

mise of pardon tried the pass, and returned safe.   It
was then given out and believed by both armies that
the siege was to be raised; and when the Irish saw
the English in motion, they lay in perfect security, and
the French camp, a mile beyond, was equally still.   St.
Ruth and his officers had been gambling and dancing
all night in a house, the unroofed walls of which are
still standing, some distance from the town; they had
retired to rest as happily secure as if they had been
in Paris.   On a sudden, at morning's dawn, and with
no other music than the tolling of St. Mary's bell,
sixty chosen men in armour, led on by Captain
Sandys, plunged into the stream below the bridge,*
twenty abreast, and in a very few minutes the opposite bank was gained—the bridge was possessed—and
with cool and steady bravery they set about re-con-
structing the gallery, whereby their comrades could
follow them.   The Irish were taken by surprise, and
had only time to escape out of the town, some without arms, some without clothes, and many were taken
asleep on the ramparts.   The British soldiers did not

* The first bridge I find recorded to be built in Ireland, was
across the Shannon at Athlone, 'by Turlough O'Connor,
king of Connaught.   The Monk of Boyle, who in his annals
states that it was built in 1140, gives us, in a subsequent notice,
grounds to decide on the insecure mode of its construction.
For he states that six years afterwards, said Turlough, according
to the common practice of Irish kinglings, having made an inroad into Meath, in order to carry off cattle, on his return with
his prey—the multitude of beasts, in passing the bridge, broke
the WATTLES with which it was covered, and the bridge was
destroyed by the cattle falling through it into the river.

slaughter the sleeping men, and Mackey, their general, who led them on—a man whose religion was equal to his valour—felt it more necessary to reprove his men for the daring blasphemies which they uttered, as they struggled over the difficulties presented by the ruined masses of the fortress, than to reproach them for want of humanity and courage.

The first express which reached St. Ruth, that the British were passing the river, found him dressing for a shooting excursion. He gave the messenger a deaf ear, and when urged by some one present to take instant measures, he replied that he would give a thousand louis to hear that the English DURST attempt to pass. "Spare your money and mind your business," was the gruff retort of Sarsfield, "for I know that no enterprise is too difficult for British courage to attempt."

In this successful assault Colonel Richard Grace was slain; he who had so gallantly defended the town, and beat off General Douglas. It is with reason supposed that if Grace had not been counteracted by St. Ruth, Athlone would not have been taken as it was; it would appear that he was determined not to survive its loss—he was found amidst heaps of slain. Grace was certainly a noble specimen of a gallant officer and high-minded gentleman—the friend of the great Duke of Ormond, the soul of loyalty and honour; he lived and died faithful to the Stuart cause, and worthy of the ancient line from whence he sprung. He was buried in Athlone with all military honours by his admiring enemies.

There is a curiously sculptured monument on the old bridge, bearing an inscription rather difficult to read, which records that "in the ninth year of the reigne of our most dere soveraign ladie Elizabeth, this bridge was built by the device and order of Sir Henry Sidney, Knt. who finished it in less than one year, bi the good industrie and diligence of Peter Levis, Clk. Chanter of the Cathedral Church of Christ, Dublin, and steward to said Deputy." The inscription goes on to state that "in the same yeare the bridge was finished, the newe worke was begun in the Castel of Dublin, besides many other notable workes in sundrie other places. Also the arch-rebel Shane O'Neil was overthrowne, his head set on the gate of the said Castel; Coyne and livery abolished, and the whole realm brought into such obedience to her majestie as the like tranquilitie hath nowhere been seen." In a compartment of this monument is the figure of Master Levis, attired in his Geneva gown; in his right hand is something which is said to be a pistol, though it is twisted, and more calculated to represent a screw than an instrument of death. On this pistol is the figure of a rat, appearing to bite the thumb which is holding it.

Peter Levis is said to have been an English monk who turned Protestant, and coming over to Ireland was made a dignitary of Christ Church; being a man of great scientific and mechanical knowledge, Sir Henry Sidney sent him to superintend the erection of this important bridge; but being a turncoat, a righte-

F

ous rat, vexed with such tergiversation, followed and haunted him—by day and night, at bed and board— on horseback or in boat, the disgusting vermin pursued him, slept on his pillow, and dipped and dabbled its tail or whisker in all he eat or drank—the church itself could not save him from the persecution. One day in the church of St. Mary's, Athlone, he ventured to preach, and lo, this unclean beast kept peering at him with its bitter, taunting eye, all the time he was holding forth; and when he descended from the pulpit, after having dismissed the congregation, the cursed creature still remained mocking his reverence. This was too much—Master Levis presented a pistol, which he had always about him, to shoot it—the sagacious and unaccountable animal, to avert the shot, leapt up on the pistol, as represented on the monument, and seizing the parson's thumb, inflicted such a wound as to bring on a locked jaw, which terminated in his death.

I will not stake my veracity on the truth of this story; but at all events, this much will I assume, that here we have most satisfactorily explained the origin of the phrase, TO RAT, as applied to changelings; and without wishing to cast MY stigma on Master Levis, who may have been a sincere and honest, as he certainly appears to have been a clever man, I may add, that the conscience-stricken state of those who change their opinions for *worldly* advantages, is well represented as under the haunting molestation of that unclean, selfish, cunning, and voracious reptile, the rat.

CHAPTER III.

VISIT TO CLONMACNOISE.

Departure from Athlone by boat—View of the Town—State and character of the River Shannon—Lonely navigation—Meet a boat—Its freight—First view of Clonmacnoise—St. Kieran—His holy seat—A solitary farm—Field of the Patron—Church-yard—Strange mixture of people therein—Judy the beggar-woman—St. Kieran's tomb—Holy clay—MacCoghlan—Synod of Clonmacnoise—Invasion of Clonmacnoise by the garrison of Athlone—Robbery of bells—St. Kieran's cellar—O'Melaghlin, king of Meath—His fate—Darby Claffy—Fine sculptured cross—Its use—M'Carthy's Church and Round Tower—Origin of these Towers—Beautiful sculpture—Protestant Church—Roman Catholic Sexton—Protestant farmer—Burial-place of the O'Malones—Anthony Malone—Legend of St. Colman—O'Rourke's round tower—Its beauty—Difference between it and other round Towers—Holy Well—Legend—O'Melaghlin Castle—Fairies—Grant of Clonmacnoise to St. Kieran—Treatment of the remains of a M'Loughlan—Description of a Penance-doer from Athlone.

I HAD long wished to visit the Seven Churches at Clonmacnoise; I had been at almost every other place in Ireland, where, by the erection of seven churches, round towers, and other tokens of Cænobitish holiness, the ancient Irish desired to sanctify a peculiar place, and consecrate it to a patron saint. But to Clonmacnoise, the great central place of superstitious resort, the Mecca, as I may say, of Irish hagiolatry, I had not yet gone; for it is much out of the way, it is surrounded by bogs on all sides, except where that extraordinary chain of gravel hills, the Aisgir Reada, leads to it.

Happening, however, to be in the town of Athlone, and having a day at my disposal, I was nothing loath to accept the proposal of my excellent friend, the vicar of St. Mary's, and proceed down the Shannon by boat to visit Clonmacnoise. "It is," (says he,) "the day after the great station held on the 9th of September, the anniversary of the patron saint, Kieran; but you will see enough to surprise you, more than enough to disgust you."

"I am glad (said I) it is not the *great* day, for I have seen such scenes already at Glendalough, and other places, partaking, as is usually the case with all false worshippings, of the orgies of a Bacchanalian licentiousness mixed up with the devotions of a religious rite."

The morning sun was gilding the spire of St. Mary's steeple, when we loosed our little cot and committed ourselves to the Shannon, a broad and rapid stream just here, where the town of Athlone (signifying the ford of the moon*) rises on either bank, and

* So says Vallancey, but the good General was fanciful in his etymologies, perhaps the ford of Luanus, a respected saint in those parts, would be the right derivation.

strongly fortified on the Connaught side—this town has an interesting appearance: and as you glide down the stream, and get away from its narrow streets, and other disagreeable appendages to an Irish town, it has a very fine effect. Just here, says my friend, is the spot where sixty British grenadiers, in 1691, led on by the gallant Captain Sandys, and marching to the sound of my church bell, entered the river, and in the face of a bastion manned with three Irish regiments, passed the water, and so led the way for their fellow-soldiers to win the Irish fortress. Strange it was, that the river never before or since was so low at that season of the year, as to permit even *grenadiers* to wade across.

The Shannon, once you clear the rapids which lie on either side of Athlone, until it enters Lough Derg, is perhaps, the ugliest and least interesting stream of any in the three kingdoms. Surrounded with bogs, it creeps through dismal flats, and swamps; and the narrow tracts of meadow, and small patches of cultivation along its banks only tend like green fringes to a mourning drapery, to mark off, as by contrast, the extreme dreariness of the picture. Oh! how unlike is Father Shannon to Father Severn or Father Thames; here no trade, except that carried on by one steam-barge, no timber, no smiling lawns, no cultivation—the solitary hopelessness of the bog is all around, and nothing interrupts the silence of the waste but the wild pipe of the curlew, as it whistles over the morass, or the shriek of the heron, as it rises

lazily from the sedgy bank, and complains aloud
against our unwonted interruption of its solitary speculations. If ever there was a picture of grim and
hideous repose, it is the flow of the Shannon from
Athlone to Clonmacnoise. We met but one specimen
of way-faring on this great navigable river—as we rowed
down with the slow stream but against the strong
south-westerly wind—a large boat met us half way, it
bore down on us, urged along by a square sail composed for the "nonce" of blankets and quilts, the co-
verings of yesterday's tents, and was freighted with
drunken publicans, "Cauponibus atque malignis,"
belonging to the town of Athlone, who had gone on a
whiskey venture to the patron of Clonmacnoise, and
were now returning drunk with the draining of jars
and kegs of spirits, that they had nearly emptied
for sale on the preceding Sabbath day, which found
horrible and peculiar desecration as falling on the one
dedicated to Kieran.

The experienced man who directed our little boat
warned us not to say any thing to the crew of the boat
that was now nearing us. "Every man of them," says
he, "is drunk; they are all ready for a row; the very
appearance of you as gentlemen is enough to excite
them to quarrel with you, and little would they think
of steering their boat so as to run us down—gentlemen, you cannot but know that the ways of our people are strangely changed, and what some years
ago would be taken in good part, would now be laid
hold on as the pretext for a quarrel." It may be

supposed that we let the abominable barge glide on unnoticed. A tedious row of about ten miles down the most dreary of navigations brought us in sight of Clonmacnoise—as I said before, a line of gravel hills, forming the Aisgir Reada, comes from the east, and cuts the line of the Shannon at right angles, causing the great river to form a reach or bend; and the hills breaking their direct line as they approach the stream, form an amphitheatre, upon the southern curve of which are erected the Seven Churches—the northern terminates in a beautiful green hill, like the inverted hull of a ship, round which the river flows at some distance, leaving an extensive flat of swampy meadow between it and the water; as the wind was strong and steady here up the river, causing the labour of rowing to be almost intolerable, we drew up our little cot into a cove, and ascending the green hill, had at once from its summit a view of the sacred spot before us, and of the extraordinary country all around. The Irish saints of olden time, in imitation of their brethren of the Thebaic desert, chose places wherein to honour God and discipline themselves, which marked the austerities of that superstition, which deceivingly told them that they must not stand up to make use of the liberty wherewith Christ had made them free. What a dreary vale is Glendalough, what a lonely isle is Inniscaltra, what a hideous place is Patrick's purgatory, what a desolate spot is Clonmacnoise—from this hill of Bentullagh, on which we now stood, the numerous churches, the two round towers, the curiously overhanging bastions of O'Melaghlin's castle, `all before us to the south, and rising in relief from the dreary sameness of the surrounding red bogs, presented such a picture of tottering ruins, and encompassing desolation as I am sure few places in Europe could parallel.

We had neither time nor patience to remain long on a remote hill, while the ruins of Clonmacnoise were within ten minutes walk of us, so we proceeded to the first ruin, which lies separate from all the rest, on the northern side of the church-yard—the large field or common on which the patron is held, intervening; little remains of this church but a beautiful arch of the most florid and ornate Gothic workmanship, forming the opening from the body of the church into the chancel; it now totters to its fall—it is even surprising that it does not tumble, and I suspect that it would long ago have fallen a victim to the elements or to the barbarous violence of the people, were it not that it is considered as part of an expiating penance for the pilgrim to creep on his bare knees under this arch while approaching the altar-stone of this chapel, where sundry paters and aves must be repeated as essential to keeping the station; adjoining this is a holy stone on which St. Kieran sat, and the sitting on it now, under the affiance of faith, proves a sovereign cure for of all epileptic people; what a contrast did this ancient arch, so exquisitely carved, tottering in all the grey antiquity of 1000 years, present to a new house erected by a half-pay captain, who has turned

his sword into a ploughshare, and in this dreary place
set himself down on a farming speculation; he
could not be more lonesome on the borders of the
dismal swamp in Virginia—his ugly tub of a house
in all its raw newness had no business at all to
plant itself near that fine old time-touched religious
edifice. I take the man to have a yankee mind who
would bring his geese to gabble and his cocks to
crow near what ages had made lonely and consecrated
to solitariness. Beyond the building, as I said before, is the patron-green, where, on the day before,
even on God's holy Sabbath, thousands had assembled, after doing their stations and performing their
vowed penances, to commence a new course of riot,
debauchery, and blasphemy; to run up a new score,
which St. Kieran was, in the following 9th of September, to wipe out; and so go on the year's sins
and the day's expiation.

The patron was over, and most of the people had
gone to their harvest avocations, and probably so
much the better for us; many a tent was still standing, many were still keeping up the deep carouse that
had continued all through the Sabbath night; and as
we passed along by the unseemly temporary dens that
are called tents, we could hear the impious blasphem-
ing, the maudlin song, the squeaking bagpipe, and
the heavy-footed dance—yes, and now and then we
would meet with some straggler who had spent all
his money, or who had come forth from the feverish
scene to cool his beating temples, and quaff a draught

of the pure waters of the holy well, and *he* would look
on us with a sulky scowl, and so we would move on in
all prudence, lest the fellow would call forth his FAC-
TION and proceed to maltreat us.   Times are greatly
changed in every part of Ireland.   The gentleman
must formerly have given no small provocation before
any of the lower classes, even in their liquor, would
proceed to incivility, but now, under very careful
instruction, much of former deference is disused, and
it is neither safe nor prudent to interfere with them;
we, of course, were studiously cautious in this respect,
and without delay proceeded into the immense church-
yard.

Here is the largest enclosure of tombs and churches
I have any where seen in Ireland—what a mixture of
old and new graves—modern inscriptions recording
the death and virtues of the sons of little men,
the rude forefathers of the surrounding hamlets;
ancient inscriptions in the oldest forms of Irish letters
recording the deeds and the hopes of kings, bishops,
and abbots, buried 1000 years ago, laying about, broken,
neglected, and dishonoured; what would I give could I
have deciphered—I should have been glad, had time
allowed, to be permitted to transcribe them; and what
shall I do with all those ancient towers, and crosses,
and churches, without a guide—I looked around,
there were many people in the sacred enclosure—
some kneeling in the deepest abstraction of devotion at the graves of their departed friends, the
streaming eye, the tremulous hand, the bowed down

body, the whole soul of sorrowful reminiscence and of trust in the goodness of the God of spirits, threw a sacred solemnity about them that few indeed, though counting their act superstitious, would presume to interrupt: he who would venture so to do, must be one, indeed, of little feeling. I saw others straggling through the place—some half intoxicated, sauntering, or stumbling over the grave-stones—others hurrying across the sacred enclosure, as if hastening to partake of the last dregs of debauchery in the tents of the patron-green. One little boy, rather decently clad, seemed wandering about from tombstone to tomb-stone, reading their various legends, and at length I observed him accost a beggar-woman by the familiar name of Judy, and ask where was his mother's grave. " Oh then it's I will tell you, alanna—and more than that would I do for your mammy's son, for didn't I folly along with all the neighbours her berrin when you were not larger than my milk-pitcher, and its little she thought that your daddy would have put so soon a step-mother over her sweet charge; come, jewel, and I will put your two knees down upon the very spot where the bones rest of her who bore you." This woman will do for my business, says I; a beggar is generally an intelligent sort of creature, male or female, if not too old, or quite blind, such have their wits in exercise, they often are the depositories of the traditions of the country, and but too often the con-veyancers of mischief; they endeavour, by being news-carriers and story-tellers, to make themselves acceptable with the people, by reporting not what is true but what is wished for. This woman now before me was such a person, and I soon adopted her, nothing loath, as my guide—and poor soul she did her best. I found that she made it part of her occupation to attend here and direct the people where and how to make their stations, here so many turns round an altar or a church on the bare knees, there so many paters and aves—such a cross you were to embrace to avert the pains of child-birth—yonder stone you must sit on to cure the pain in the back—there is the place you must scrape at to gather the holy clay that is around St. Kieran's remains. After looking about vaguely for a time, this church of St. Kieran's was what caught my particular attention. It was extremely small, more an insignificant oratory than what could be called a church—a tall man could scarcely lie at length in it: a mason would have contracted to build its walls for a week's wages; yet this, my mendicant guide said, was the old church of St. Kieran— the walls had all gone awry from their foundations, they had collapsed together, and presented a picture of desolation without grandeur. Beside it was a sort of cavity or hollow in the ground, as if some persons had lately been rooting to extract a badger or a fox: but here it was that the people, supposing St. Kieran to be deposited, have rooted diligently for any particle of clay that could be found, in order to carry home that holy earth, steep it in water, and drink it ; and happy is the votary who is now able amongst the bones and stones to pick up what has the semblance of soil, in order to commit it to his stomach, as a means of grace, or as a sovereign remedy against diseases of all sorts. Alas! I would ask my dear countrymen, could I obtain their patience but to hear me —is any superstition of Yogees or Fakeers of India more degrading or grovelling than this? Oh! but say the priests, "we do not encourage it, we do not tell you to go to the tomb of St. Kieran, or St. Brendan—to the grave of holy father Tom, or holy father Pat, to scratch up the clay amidst which their bones and flesh have corrupted and festered, in order to infuse it in water, and drink the abhorrent dose." Yes, but gentlemen, ye claim and exercise the power of ARBITRARY excommunication, and ye can and do exert it with fearful effect when your own wishes and interests are concerned, as for instance, when ye desire to put down a school where the word of God is read; say then, why do ye not expose from your altars such as resort to these abominable superstitions —why do ye not curse and ban against holy clay as ye do against Holy Bible—why do ye not exclude from the confession such as make Christianity almost as degrading a service as the garlic and onion worship of the Egyptians!*

* That this clay-scraping round the saint of Clonmacnoise, is not new or unsupported by grave Romish writers, we need only revert to the Hagiologists of Ireland—the historians of her Saints, Colgan, Messingham, and the Bollandists. " St. Columbkill hearing of the death of St. Kieran, made a hymn

From the little oratory of St. Kieran, the woman
led us on to the largest of the ruined churches, which,
after all, is of no great size; but still it is the most remarkable of any, not only for its greater size, but for
the beauty of its western entrance, and the exquisite
and elaborate workmanship of its northern doorway:
this church is said to have been originally erected by
the M'Dermots, princes of the northern parts of Roscommon; a tablet on the wall, near the eastern window, records that it was repaired in 1647, by M'Coghlan, the lord of the adjoining territories.   I remember, in my younger days, when this district of the
King's County was called the M'Coghlan's country,
or for brevity's sake, the Maw's country; and I re-

in his praise, which gave such delight to his successor in the
see of Clonmacnoise, that in rapture he demanded of the
sacred poet how he could or should repay him? " I would
rather have two handfuls of the clay," says Columba, " in which
Kieran was buried, than shiploads of silver and gold."   It may
be supposed that worthy Tigernach did not hesitate in giving
clay rather than silver and gold; and accordingly with his
precious handfuls of earth Columba sailed away for Iona; but
who that knows any thing of the Hebrides has not heard of the
whirlpool of Coryvrekan, for, as it in Irish is spelled, Cari
Bricain, that is, the Charibdis of one Bricain—into this eddy,
in spite of all their craft, and the sacredness of the freight, the
ship of Columba was sucked, and into it they would have been
gorged, had not Columba bethought him of the holy clay of
St. Kieran, when casting in one handful, the water ceased
to whirl, the Caledonian sea became as smooth as glass;
and, arriving safe at Iona the remaining handful was deposited
to be adored by all faithful Albanian Scots.
   Strange, that though I have visited Iona, and saw this
great cemetery of northern kings and chiefs, I heard not a word
of St. Kieran's clay ; but the people are all turned Presbyterians.

member seeing the M'Coghlan, or as he was called the Maw, a fine tall old gentleman of the French school, who lived in the profuse extravagance of Irish hospitality, for which, and for keeping up the old Milesian fighting character, and for other qualities palpable and valued by the people, he was looked on with almost kingly respect. In the midst of the rebellion of 1641, when the Rome influenced Papists had nearly succeeded in driving out the English Protestants, it was then that M'Coghlan repaired this church; perhaps it was within those very walls that the Synod of Popish Bishops met when, preparatory to their removal to Jamestown, they concerted that excommunication which they afterwards hurled against their king's lord lieutenant. Whether the northern doorway into this church existed prior to the repairs of M'Coghlan, or whether executed by his direction, I am not competent to decide; but I am induced to believe that it was constructed in a more auspicious day of taste in Gothic architecture than the seventeenth century; I do indeed consider it the most beautiful specimen of Gothic ornamental architecture in Ireland. It is executed in blue limestone, marble it may be well called, and the elaborate tracery on which the whole fancy and vagary of Gothic licence is lavished, stands forth as sharp, fresh, and clean as if but yesterday it came from under the chisel.

Amongst the other ornaments of this highly finished doorway are figures in alto relievo—one evidently of a bishop giving his blessing, the other of an abbot; the third figure is much mutilated, and that apparently done on purpose. What was the cause of this figure being so much injured?—said I, addressing myself to the woman—"Och then, who *could* do it .but cruel Cromwell's red coats!—a cursed crew that came down in boats from Athlone, and not satisfied with carrying away our beautiful bells that were made of pure silver, and which sung out for mass-gathering amongst those hills, so that there was even grace in living within their sound, the bloody Sassenach hounds came, and not content with the blessed bells, they came up to this church, and after breaking with their pikes that holy image, which they say was the figure of him who was ruler over this place after St. Kieran's death, they then rushed into the church where three priests were at the altar celebrating the mass; those they kilt outright, and after doing other mischief, which myself don't remimber, they set out to return to Athlone; but, my dear, the man who had charge of the bells, in lifting them into his boat, fell into the Shannon, and went to the bottom; the others, as they were going along, fell out about the division of the booty, and so they fought away until they kilt each other outright, and for many a long year, as the people say, that part of the river where the boat drifted after they were all dead, was red in all its waters as if in memory of the bloodshedding." We entered a small arched building south of M'Dermot's church, .which the woman called St. Kieran's cellar; from it arose a curious kind of octangular belfry; where, I suppose, the bells that the English soldiers took away were hung, a proof to me, if any were necessary, that the round towers in this enclosure were neither used nor intended for bell-hanging. "Until lately," said the beggar woman, "Father —— used to make this place his chapel, when, on station days, he used to come to say mass for the people, but now he cele-brate's at farmer ——'s house." "Why does he not come here still?" "Troth and myself can't tell, barring it is, that though he does not say against the patron, he does not think it proper for his riverence to come into the middle, as I may say, of the people when the half of them may be drunk—of late, any how, he has not sung mass here." It was well he did not, for a more filthy, abominable, fetid place I never was in; it seemed as if people on the preceding night had made it their lair, and still, unlike other beasts, they had not been careful to keep unpolluted the place where they slept. "But why call this place St. Kieran's cellar—was he fond of wine?" "To be sure he was at proper times, and small blame to him or any other holy man when his fasts, and prayers, and duties, and stations are all done, and God above is satisfied—if he should take a drop to comfort his poor heart; but, gentlemen, talking of wine, did yees never hear what happened betwixt him and O'Melaghlin, king of Meath, who lived yonder (pointing to the west) in that castle? St. Kieran, (the heavens are his bed,) wanted some wine, whether as a cordial for himself, or to give the sacra-

ment to his clergy; any how, not having any in his
cellar, he sends, and why should'nt he, to king Melaghlin, and he the churl refused—only think of an
Irish king doing the like, bad manners to him, for
being such a negur.   But blessed Kieran was even
with him, for down on his two knees he went, and
prayed that O'Melaghlin might never know the pleasure of a drink again, and my dear sowl so it turned
out, for in the middle of that night he awoke in strong
thirst, and says he to his butler, 'go down to my
cellar and bring me a bowl of wine;' so down the man
went, when the wine was brought to the king and put
to his lips, it fled away entirely out of the cup; he then
called to the dairy-maid, and said, 'go bring me a
noggin of butter-milk;' so away went the maid, but
when she came back with the noggin full, lo, before
it touched his mouth, it went away somewhere, as did
the wine.   'Heigh-ho,' says my king, 'since wine
and milk fail me, sure the Shannon won't—go, fetch
me a pail full of *that*, I was never fond of cowld
water, but you know the saying of 'needs must;' so
they fetched him the water, but when it came before
the king, it also made away with itself, nobody could
tell how: so, gentlemen, to make my story short, the
king died of thirst; and may be no Irish king ever
after refused a saint wine or whiskey, for, sure enough,
refusals of the sort are not nathural."

Proceeding from M'Dermott's church, our attention
was directed to a very fine stone cross, the largest in
the place, formed of one piece, and covered with

carvings in bas relievo and inscriptions, which, had
I the ability, my time would not allow me to decipher.
"Come, my good woman," said I, "tell what may be
the stories told of these figures?" "Why, then, myself
cannot tell you any thing about them, they are all out
ancient; may be Darby Claffy yonder, the ouldest man
about the churches, could tell you somewhat." Now
Darby Claffy was standing idle, leaning not far off,
against the wall of Dowling's church, looking up at
O'Rourke's tower; and a finer studio for a sketcher
than the head, face, and form of the venerable looking-
man could not be seen; eighty winters had dropped
their flakes as light as snow feathers on his head, and
there he stood with his hat off, his fine Guido countenance and expressive face, a living accompaniment
to all the grey venerability that was around. " Come
over here, Darby Claffy, honest man, and tell the
strange gintleman all you know about them crosses and
things—musha, myself forgets—at any rate, I must
run and show Judy Delaney, the simple crathur, where
to find her father's grave—heaven be wid yees, gintle-
men, and don't forget poor Judy." A shilling given
to her seemed a source of unutterable joy; her little
son that was beside her, appearing as if he never saw
so large a coin, snatched it in raptures from his
mammy, and danced about the grave-stones in
triumph. I was pleased to buy human joy so cheap.
The old man did not belie his fine countenance; his
mind was stored with traditionary recollections concerning Clonmacnoise, which, if not according to
recorded facts, were founded on them; and he spoke

with perfect assurance in the truth of what he said,
and of the sanctity of all around. "Can you, my honest
fellow, tell us any thing about the figures carved on
this cross?"   "A little, plase your honour; but *sartain* I'm no scholar: come here now, Mister, do you
see that figure with the keys, that is St. Pether;
and that there beside him is St. Kieran, do you see a
book in his hand?—that is the Gospel of St. Matthew
which Kieran learned so well from holy Finnian, of
Clonard, in the county Meath, where in ould times
there was a great school, somewhat the same as Maynooth now is, whence young Father Finnerty has just
come home, edicated; well, plase your honours,
Kieran was called Kieran of St. Matthew,* because

* That there was some foundation for the old man's legend
about St. Kieran we find in the Bollandists, who relate, when
the saint was studying Scripture under the guidance of St.
Finnian, at Clonard, when he came to the middle of the
Gospel of St. Matthew, where it is said—" Whatsoever ye
would that men should do to you, do you even so to them, for
this is the law and the prophets;"—Kieran cried out on reading
this passage—" Father Finnian, enough for me is the half of
this book which I have read, and now let me go reduce what
I have learned to practice, and do likewise; this one sentence
is enough for me."   Then one in the school cried out—" from
henceforth, Kieran, let this name belong to you, Kieran Leath
Math—Kieran of the half of Matthew."   "No," said the
blessed Finnian, " not Leath Math, but Kieran Leath
N'Erien—Kieran of the half of Ireland; for he shall be bishop
of a diocese whose territories shall include the half of Ireland."
And so it was, for so immense were the endowments of Clonmacnoise, that half Ireland was said to belong to it.   What an
awful ignorance of the Gospel! What an utter forgetfulness
there existed in these story tellers of the work done by Christ
for believers, when a Christian Saint is by them represented to
be contented with a part of a Gospel that had not reached to
the work finished on the cross, which rested merely in the moral
precept of doing as one should be done by.   A follower of
Zoroaster, Confucius, or Mahomet would have said as much.
But more of this by and by.

he knew that Gospel so well; and do now look below
Peter and Kieran, and don't you notice young men
smiling, and one playing the bagpipes?—well, this
represents the young priests that Kieran brought
with him to Clonmacnoise; and as well becomes the
divil, he must needs envy their devotions, and he
used to come by night and play his bagpipes to divart
them there, and draw them off from their vesper
duties—and up they'd get from their knees when the
ould boy, in the shape of a piper, would play a
planxty, and set about (they could'nt for the life help
it) jigging it away; now, St. Pether, in heaven, saw
to be sure, all this,—and so he comes down to tell
Kieran of it; and, moreover, he falls upon Satan in a
thrice; don't you see him there how he has tumbled
the enemy of man?—and, as you see there, is sending
him headlong to hell." There was certainly something like a man playing the pipes cut on the cross,
and a representation of two persons contending, and
one getting the better of the other; but whether old
Claffy was right in his reading I cannot say. This cross
is certainly one of the finest I have seen in Ireland;
I question whether it is even inferior to those immense ones that are at Monaster Boice, in the county
of Louth.

From thence we proceeded, the old man following
us to the church and round tower which stands in the
north-western extremity of the cemetery, and which
is usually called M'Carthy's church and tower. The
round tower, though small, is one of the most perfect

in Ireland: it is conically capped, and the ranges of
stone, forming the cover, are of the most beautiful
and singular arrangement. The tower stands on the
south side of the chancel of the church; and the door-
way of the tower, instead of being elevated ten or
fifteen feet from the ground, is on a level with the
floor of the chancel from which it leads; it is within
a few feet of the altar; moreover, the archway leading
from the nave of the church into the chancel, which
is of the most finished and at the same time chaste
order of Gothic construction, is wrought into the body
of the round tower—part of whose rotundity is sacrificed to give room and form to the display of its light
and elegant span; now these two circumstances con-
vince me that, in the first place, the church and tower
were built at the same time; moreover, that as the
church was placed more remote than other churches,
and nearer invaders coming across the Shannon, the
tower was provided as a look-out station and place of
ready retreat for the priests to retire to with their
sacred vessels and books.

M'Carthy's church, in the north-west corner of the
cemetery, was built by the M'Carthy More of Munster,
the greatest sept in Cork—he who held under his
sway the O'Learys, and the O'Sullivans, and the
O'Donohus, and I don't know how many more Milesian O's and Macs. It is a curious and peculiarly
interesting ruin, because, as I said before, there is here
evident proof that the round tower and church were
built at the same time; for, besides that they both

are formed of the same kind of stone, and are constructed with the same range and character of masonry, there is part of the rotundity of the tower
sacrificed, to give play to the full span of the chancel-
arch, and exhibit one of the most chaste specimens in
the world of what is called the Saxon arch. This
tower is not large or lofty; it measures but seven feet in
diameter within, and is but fifty-five feet high; it has
a conical cap, which is essential, according to antiquarians, to make a round tower perfect; and a free-
mason, suppose he was master of his craft, would say
" well done," to the artist who constructed the beautiful courses of cut stone by which the conical cap was
brought to a point. As I have already said, the door
of the tower is level with the ground; and I think I
could discern the marks of stairs that rose spirally to
the top; unlike all other round towers which, though
there are marks of floors, story over story, in no other
instance present marks of spiral stairs. On the right
side of the altar, connected with the tower, there is,
as usual, a niche in the wall, forming a receptacle for
holy water. It is a prettily carved shallow stone basin,
with a small aperture in the bottom, introduced, no
doubt, to let off, after a term, the water that had been
used, in order to substitute fresh. This receptacle
was now covered, and almost filled with as curious a
melange of articles as ever I saw collected together:—
a bent nail, a shankless button, a bit of unripe apple,
a tobacco stopper, a broken comb, a decayed human
tooth. I might have supposed that such a thievish

animal as a pet magpie, in its indiscriminate larceny, had made this hole its hiding-place, and here was its treasure. "What can be the meaning of this?" said I to my *cicerone*, Mr. Claffy. "Och, plase your honour, this is the greatest place in the varsal world for curing the tooth-ache. Any one that comes here on the pathern day, if a tooth or sound or rotten pained them, so that they could not eat a boiled pratie, always, by course, saying the proper aves and paters, and leaving something as you see behind them, as their offering to the saint, why, as you may say, in no time the pain would pass off, and they might, as a body may say, go crack nuts. But troth, sir, if I must tell the truth, the vartue is very much gone out of this same place ever since a polisman came here, and that not along ago ; for before he came, do you see me, there never was wanting a drop of water here, no, not in the driest of seasons, that a body might take up in their fingers, and put it, hoping in the merits of St. Keeran, to his tooth. But that polisman, may bad luck and fortune ever attend him, drove the point of his walking stick into the hole, and from that day to this never a drop of water came up out of the same, so that it is as dry as any other part of the wall, as your honour now sees."

Removing from this, we proceeded to a higher part of the enclosure, where a slated building appeared, which our attendant informed us was the English church. In any other place it would have been considered a venerable, though a small structure; and there was a chaste and solemn simplicity in the door-

way at its western end that well deserved attention;
but the windows were closed up with jealous care by
wooden shutters, and altogether it looked out of place
in this scene of ruins; and my admiration was, how in
this wild, superstitious spot, where crowds of preju-
diced and ferocious beings assemble, it has been permitted to stand unscathed.   My friend who had accompanied me to Clonmacnoise, and to whom I owe
the pleasure of seeing it, was not only anxious to show
me the interior of the only entire church amidst this
crowd of ruins, but also, as rural dean of the district,
was desirous to take this occasion of inspecting the
interior, so as to make in due time his report to
his diocesan.   Accordingly he despatched a messenger to the house of a man who was reported to have
the care of the church, and to keep the key.   It was
a long time before he returned, during which period
we had leisure to observe the many inscriptions in the
oldest form of the Irish letter scattered about, and
had reason to lament that there is no one here to prevent the destruction of old monuments, or put a stop
to the barbarous breaking, defacing, and utter destruction of inscriptions of kings, chieftains, bishops,
abbots, and learned men: inscriptions that might serve
to verify existing history, or supply the *lacunæ* and
correct the errors in our annals.   The place belongs
to the bishop of Meath; all the lands around are his;
doubtless the parson has a property in the church-
yard.   Surely his lordship has, either directly in
himself, or indirectly by his vicar, a conservative

power over this burial-place of all that was both saint-
like and learned in Ireland; and if these could not,
or would not, exert themselves, why does not the
parish priest? But, as Dr. Doyle has well said,
" Gentlemen, you are very much mistaken if you suppose that the Catholic clergy of Ireland have any
power over the people when their passions or prejudices are in operation." Well, if priest or parson
cannot preserve the monumental and ecclesiastical
antiquities of Ireland from the rapid ruin which they
are undergoing from the hands of a barbarous people,
I wish some society, such as are, I believe, in France
and Germany, would undertake the task. In about
a quarter of an hour our messenger returned, but
without the key of the church. He was accompanied
by a woman, fat, inquisitive, and rather impertinent,
who desired to know, in the first instance, who we
were; and who, after endeavouring by many evasions
to put us off from the desire of seeing the inside, at
length told us that we could not get in, for the man
who was in charge of it was unwell and would give the
key to no one out of his own hand. "Go back, my good
woman," said my friend, "to your husband or master,
whichever he is, and tell him that I charge him
at his peril to let me see the interior of the church."
Accordingly, the woman went and brought back, as
soon as might be, a stout, short, broad-backed, broad-
faced man, half-farmer, half-publican in his appearance, who, with the maudlin countenance, codled eye,
and brutified expression of face and form that denoted

one who had been tippling for two whole days, asked
us stammeringly and yet sturdily, what business we
had to take him away from his customers, " when
the woman (as he called his wife) had already tould
yes that by no manner of means would we let busy-
bodies and lurking strangers into the church."
" Yes," answered my friend very civilly, " you, my
good man, are quite right in keeping out strangers,
but I am *not* one. I come here once a year to inspect the church, pursuant to my duties, and if you
have charge of the key, you are bound to give *me* ad-
mittance." " And how am I to know that you have
any claim or right to get into the decent man's church
in his absence. I was taken in once by a man with
as smooth a face as any of yees, and when I let him
into the church to satisfy, as he said, his curiosity,
what did he do, but set about defacing an ould tomb-
stone of the Malones. Yes, in troth, a man calling
himself Counsellor M—— did this upon me, in order
that he might carry a lawsuit his own way ; and
ever since I have been in dread concerning strangers
getting in there." " Pray, my friend," said I, " are
you the clerk or sexton, that you are so vigilant."
" No, Mr. Nobody-knows-who, from Athlone ; I am
not clerk or sexton. I wouldn't take all the land the
Shannon flows by, and have any thing to do with this
English place, barring it was to keep the key for the
minister, who, in his way, is a decent man enough,
and a good neighbour. Sextin, forsooth! I'd have
the likes of yes to know, that all of my ould name

stick to the ould religion." "No offence, Mr. M——, but are you aware, that by your refusal to admit the clergyman, who has a *right* to enter, you subject yourself to be brought before the bishop's court." No Roman Catholic likes the name of a bishop's court, and I perceived that the threat had its effect on him, when a respectable gentleman-farmer sort of a man, with a Petersham great coat, covered with broad wooden buttons, and wielding a huge whip in his hand, came up, and having listened for a time to the altercation, interposed and said, "Oh, Mr. M——, you need not dread that these persons will do any injury to the church. I know that this gentleman," pointing to the vicar of St. Mary's, "is the person he represents himself to be, and I'll be answerable that all is right." This had its effect on the Clonmacnoise publican, and he proceeded, growlingly enough towards the church door. While approaching it, I was bold enough to ask the new-comer in the Petersham whether he had arrived to perform a station: and if I had offended the publican by asking was he the Protestant clerk, I still more provoked my present companion, by asking was he a Papist devotee. "No, sir; I wonder you'd ask the like of me such a question. I'd have you to know that I'm as good a Protestant as yourself. I abhor all that is going on here, as much as any man can do, and I have more reason, for I suffer more." "Excuse, sir, my impertinence," said I soothingly; "I meant no offence. I altogether beg your pardon, but allow me to ask how it is you are a sufferer." "In this way, sir: I have a considerable tract of land in this vicinity, and, as perhaps you may have remarked in every other part of Ireland, the more superstitious the people are, the more also are they lawless and ferocious. It is fully exemplified here. My farm latterly has become totally unprofitable—it lies waste, because I ejected the old tenants who would pay me no rent whatsoever. The people will neither allow me to cultivate it myself, nor any other person to take it. If I run cattle on it, they are in danger of being houghed; if I build a house on it, it is likely to be burned; if I make fences on it, they are sure to be thrown down, and I came here to-day, not, as you supposed, to go the rounds of the churches, and keep a station, but to go the rounds of my farm, and see what state it is left in after yesterday's doings." By this time the Protestant church was opened by the Roman Catholic keeper, Mr. M——. It was in pretty fair repair within; very small, and without any ancient ornaments or tombs. It was in former times called Dowling's church. For the last two centuries it has been the burying-place of the Malone family. Here lies buried the once famous Anthony Malone, who filled the highest law stations in Ireland, in the early part of the reign of George the Third, and who, (as an elegant writer described him,) " to a benign and dignified aspect, an address both conciliatory and authoritative, joined the clearest head that ever conceived, and the sweetest tongue that ever uttered the suggestions of wisdom, and who executed the

highest law offices with such ability as stands unpa-
ralleled in the records of justice." This may be
overstrained praise, but it is not conceived in the bad
taste of an epitaph upon another Malone, whose marble does not blush while telling that he had *every*
virtue under heaven. While some one of the party
read aloud this panegyric, the gentleman-farmer, with
a significant and sad look, exclaimed, " I deny the
truth of that eulogium, seeing as how he did not
exactly possess one important virtue—namely, that of
paying his just debts; for the worthy gentleman died
in *my* debt, to the tune of 1200*l.*" " Perhaps, sir,"
says I, "debt-paying is not an Irish virtue." "May
be not," says he, "especially within the bounds of
Clonmacnoise."

While standing in this little Protestant place of
worship, surrounded as it is with all the grey memorials of ancient superstition, I cannot well imagine any
stronger contrast than that of a few Church of England
Christians performing their quiet devotions, amidst this
scene of superstitious dissipation and riot. It was, I say,
a day not of superstition and debauchery, but of riot;
for the Protestant gentleman who had accompanied
us in viewing the church, asked old Claffy, " Well,
Darby, how did you get on yesterday?" "Oh,
very well, *plase* your honour; all was regular until
after the priest came down to say mass, things went
mighty cordially, indeed, until his reverence was gone,
but then the boys turned out, and there was as purty
a fight as ever myself saw at the Seven Churches.

Many this day are sore enough with broken heads
and shins. They say it will go hard with Jem Dunne,
who got his scull laid open with a cloholpeen." On
returning from the Protestant church, we repassed
the fine cross opposite the west end of M'Dermot's
church; a number of persons were attempting to span
the shaft with their arms—few succeeded. It required a tall and thin man so to do. Such being my
case I succeeded; and my guide in praising me for
my success, assured me that I merited for my wife
that no evil should happen her in her next accouch-
ment. This ought to satisfy me, as, no doubt, it
would every affectionate husband. "Do you know
any thing, Mr. Claffy, about the erection of these two
crosses?" "But a little, sir, and it is this:—There
was one of our ould saints, called Colman, that once
took a great fancy to gadding away from his church,
and his excuse was that he must needs go and kiss
the foot of his Holiness the Pope, and nothing would
satisfy him but off he would go; so a brother saint, of
the name of Berachy, came to him, and very dacently
and wisely gave it as his advice, that it would be
much better for his own sowl, and that of others, to stay
at home and keep minding his devotions and offices—
but to brother Berachy he gave no heed. Well, says his
friend, come off to St. Kieran, and maybe he will say
what will satisfy you. So off they came here to
Clonmacnoise, and to be sure our saint did his best,
but if he was arguing with the wilful man until the
cows came home it would avail not, for go he would,

to bless his own two eyes with the sight of the holy
father of the Christhen world. Well, as wilful will
do it, to be sure St. Berachy and St. Kieran gave him
their blessing; and St. Kieran, moreover, lifting up
his hand, made the sign of the cross over his head;
whereupon, my dear sowl—for wonderful is God's
power in the hands of his saints—St. Colman saw all
Rome, and his holiness the Pope sitting in his easy
chair, as plain as I, Darby Claffy, see O'Rourke's
tower that is there fornint me. This, by course, satisfied my curious gentleman, and he gave up his
gadding; and more than that, in memory of all the
time and money that was saved him, he set up these
two crosses; the little one in memory of the miracle,
the larger in honour of St. Peter, St. Patrick, and St.
Kieran." Mr. Claffy's allusion to O'Rourke's tower
directed my particular attention to it—particular, I
say, for it is the great prominent eye-attracting object
of the whole scene; without any exception it is the
most beautiful round tower in existence; it stands on
an elevation at the western side of the churchyard,
and in a line with the principal buildings; the ground
sinks from it abruptly towards the Shannon; and just
under it, to the north, is the holy well. Nothing
can equal the beautiful effect of this simple pillar-
tower, cutting, as it does, on the horizon, and relieved
by the sombre back-ground of the bog on the other
side of the Shannon, that spreads for miles, cold, flat,
and desolate; and then the tower itself is so beautifully time-tinted, I think I never saw any thing

erected by human hands so painted by fortuitous vegetation. I might conceit that time, proud of his
secret, so well kept by these Irish towers, had called
on nature to deck out this master-piece in its kind,
with all its lichens and mosses, producing every colour that could or ought to harmonize, in order to present what art could not imitate, and what the painter
would despair of picturing, or the narrator of describing. Other round towers that I have seen, and few
have seen more of them than I have, are excellent
specimens of masonry; some of them more, some less,
exhibit indubitable proofs that in early times the
line, plummet, and hammer, were used with considerable handicraft in Ireland; but here, instead of the
asler or the stone-chisel work of other towers, a marble
pillar has been erected almost as smooth as Pompey's in
Egypt, or, if a more familiar comparison will better suit,
almost as smooth as the chimney-piece in your drawing room. It is composed of that immense secondary
limestone formation that covers, with little interruption, the central plains of Ireland—which in many
places assumes the compactness, the ringing sound,
and the capability of polish, which constitute what in
commerce is called marble. The stone of the tower
is of an ash grey colour, full of madreporic concre-
tions; and as a proof how much more permanent such
a marble is, when polished, than granite or any other
material, these stones, though exposed to the elements
for a thousand years at least, are as untouched by the
tooth of time, as if they came yesterday from under the

H

polisher's hands; for, I repeat it, that every stone in
the courses of this building must have been polished,
and fitted as you would set up your chimney-piece;
and there it stands, not encumbered with a rude
bush of enveloping ivy, or with the rough garnish-
ment of wall-flowers, sedums, and maidenhairs—no,
but with the softest harmonizing tints of lichens and
close-creeping mosses. The doorway into the tower
(as is usual in all perfect specimens, and where there
are not occasions which require it to be otherwise, as
is the case with M'Carthy's tower in this cemetery,
and with that on the rock of Cashel) is fourteen or
fifteen feet from the ground; it is of beautiful and yet
simple construction. I could not get into this tower
to ascertain the interior arrangement of its lofts. In
almost every other tower the interstices between the
ranges of stone are sufficient to put in your toe at
least, and with the help of others, you can get up;
but here, instead of a resting-place for your toe, you
could scarcely find a place for the introduction of
your toe nail. Commend me to O'Rourke, prince
of Brefney, for his spirit, taste, and devotedness, in
the erection of this tower.* Did he die before his ad-

* " And the same O'Ruairk, of his devotion towards the
church, undertook to repair these churches, and to keep them
in reparation during his life, upon his own charges, and to make
a causeway or togher from the place called Cruan na feadh to
Pibhac Conaire, and from Pibhac to the Lough; and the said
Fergal should perform it, together with all other promises he
had made to Cluin, and the repairing of that number of chapels
or cells, and the making of that causeway or togher; and hath
for a monument built a small steep castle, or steeple, commonly
called in Irish, Clairtheagh (quere Cloghtheagh,) in Cluin, as

mirable work was finished?—did the wars which
have, from the beginning of time, wasted and neu-
tralized nature's blessings in this island, extend their
ravages to his fair domains?—was he *forced* to stop
before he brought to a finish his beautiful work?
But so it is; the tower that rises, as one fair polished
shaft, to about 55 feet, then presents a quite different
aspect; some "'prentice hand" has added about ten
feet of additional structure, which, though perhaps as
well built as most other round towers, presents such
a contrast to the remainder,* that it seems strange

a memorial of his own part of that cemetery; and the said
Fergal hath made all these cells, before specified, in mortmaine,
for him and his heirs to claim; and thus was the sepulture of
the O'Ruairk's bought." Mr. Crofton Croker, from whose
work on the South of Ireland, I make this extract, says, that he
took it from a MS. in the British Museum, which appears to
have belonged to Sir James Ware; and he applies this donation
and erection of Fergal O'Ruairk to Cloyne. But I think there
is every reason to refer it rather to Clonmacnoise. At Clonmacnoise the largest round tower is called, to this day, O'Rourke's
tower. The cemetery of the Rourkes, princes of Brefny, is at
Clonmacnoise, a much more probable place of sepulture for a
prince, whose territories were not far distant, than at Cloyne,
one hundred miles off. Besides, I have an old map in my possession, of lands in the vicinity of Clonmacnoise, in which a
togher, or causeway, leading to the churches, across a great
red bog, is laid down as the Pilgrim's Pass. For further particulars respecting the above passage, see Appendix.

* The imperfect construction of the upper part of this tower
may be accounted for in this way. The first and most perfect
part may have been erected by means of an exterior scaffolding,
and when arrived at a certain height, it became inconvenient, or
impossible, to scaffold higher, and, accordingly, the masons had
to finish from the inside, over-hand, as it is, I believe, called,
just in the way that the tall factory chimneys are now constructed.

how any one could have the hardihood to make such
an unseemly finish to so exquisite a work. Centuries,
one might suppose, must have intervened before this
additional work, with its eight windows, was added;
and it only confirms me in my opinion, that these
towers were erected as places of retreat and watch-
towers. For both purposes, O'Rourke's is admirably
circumstanced; even at the elevation originally given,
it was high enough to take cognizance of the coming
enemy, let him come from what point he might; it
commanded the ancient causeway that was laid down,
at a considerable expense, across the great bog on the
Connaught side of the Shannon; it looked up and
down the river, and commanded the tortuous and
sweeping reaches of the stream, as it unfolded itself
like an uncoiling serpent along the surrounding bogs
and marshes ; it commanded the line of the Aisgir
Riada—could hold communication with the holy
places of Clonfert, and from the top of its pillared
height, send its beacon light towards the sacred isles and
anchorite retreats in Lough Ree; then it was large
and roomy enough to contain all the officiating priests
of Clonmacnoise, with their pixes, vestments, and
books; and though the Pagan Dane or the wild Mun-
sterman might rush on in rapid inroad, yet the solitary
watcher on the tower was ready to give warning, and
collect within the protecting pillar all holy men and
things, until "the tyranny was overpast."

Underneath this tower, and in the low ground to the
north, at the bottom of the limestone rock on which

the tower is built, is the holy well, round which it is
necessary to go as part of the station. A few women
were still about this pool, whose clear, bubbling, and er-
ratic waters had scarcely cast off the muddiness and
abuse which those who trampled in it and around it yesterday had inflicted on it. For the present it only
answered the purpose of affording a cooling medium
into which the tent revellers might cast the fiery
whiskey with which they were brutalizing themselves.
A well of clear water is at all times, and in all places,
a scene of interest—beautiful in itself, beautiful by
association—the bubbling issue of its pellucid
waters—the irridescent play of the pebbles and minute shells, as they rise and fall in the clear depths
from whence it rises; these make a spring lovely in
every clime, from Iceland to Borneo. Leaders of a
people's religious hopes have turned to their own advantage this natural feeling; and the Pagan priest,
the Mahometan Santon, the Hindoo Brahmin, the
Budhist, the Parsee, as well as the Romish saint,
have identified themselves with the refreshment of
clear flowing waters, and left their names there. And
yet in Ireland, after all, these wells are but ugly
things; no watchful guardianship is observed to keep
the fountain clear; the mud caused by the people's
tramping is allowed to accumulate; the rank weed is
permitted to choke up the fountain's flow, and create
a swamp all around; and the hideous garniture of old
rags hanging on some neighbouring bush gives a sort
of beggarly accompaniment to the place, and you turn

with disgust from a spot that superstition has deformed
rather than consecrated—where the deformity of superstition, and not the beauty of holiness is personified.—
Such was the well of Clonmacnoise.   It is the only
spring of good water in the neighbourhood; the Shannon water is unwholesome and unpalatable; and while
taking a draught from this fine spring, as it welled forth
clear as crystal from the limestone rock, I pondered on
the vast varieties of people that for twelve centuries
have made use of its stream.   Kieran, who first settled
here, little thought of the many superstitions that
have been enacted, as it were, under the sanction of
his name.   He, instructed by the holy Finnian of
Clonard, the mighty master of the Scriptures in the
sixth century, perhaps like his successor, St. Eangus,
in the eighth century, cried aloud to his followers,
"Aspice Christum"—"Look unto Jesus;" and
though he fell, as one of his earliest errors, into Ce-
nobitish superstition, yet it is most likely, with all
faithful tenacity; he held to the Head, and would have
been grieved to the heart had he but foreseen how,
taking advantage of the practices that he had weakly
given birth to, others had beguiled the people " by a
voluntary humility, and a worshipping of angels—
intruding into those things which they had not seen—
vainly puffed up by their fleshy minds."

    " Pray, Mr. Claffy, can you give me any informa-
tion as to how or when this well was made holy ?"
" Ah, then, don't your honour know better than I
can tell yees.   I am but an unlarned man, and how

could the likes of me give you right and square knowledge about them holy things? How could I know
any thing but by remimbrance of what those that have
gone before me had to *say ?* This holy well was not
blessed either by St. Patrick or St. Keiran, but by a
poor afflicted man, that sacred Patrick took pity
on, because he was covered with sores from top to
toe, and who, though humble in body, was beautiful
in soul. The man who gave the word of life to Ireland, wherever he journeyed, took him always about
with him. But soon, dacent man as he was, he began to find that the sight and smell of his sores were
too much for Christhens; and so he searches him out
for a secret place; and, sure enough, if he had his pick
and choice of all Ireland, he could not get a more
lonesome one than this. Here, then, he lay down,
and made his bed in the hollow of an ould oak tree.
And it came to pass, that he had not lain there
long until he saw a comely-looking young man pass
by, with a black bag thrown over his shoulders,
' Where are you going, my dearest lad?' said the leper,
' I'm coming from Rome,' answered he, ' and I'm on
my way to Croagh Patrick, to find the convarter of
all Ireland, and it's I that am bringing what the holy
St. Patrick will value more than a silver mine—a present of precious relics from the Pope.' ' Stop a bit,'
says the leper, ' my purty young man, and for the
love of our sweet Saviour, just go down to that hollow
place under the hill, and pluck me a bundle of rushes,
upon which I may rest my poor bones.' ' With all

the veins in my heart, I will,' said the young pilgrim.
So down he went, and, my dear life, the moment he
made a pull at the rushes, up they come, and with
them the finest flow of spring water, clear as the very
air, and on it flowed over the meadow. You may be
sure my man was not long until he ran back with the
rushes, and tould the poor leper about the new-found
spring. 'The very thing I want—blessed be he that
sent it,' says he; 'I'm about to die, and it is for you
young man, when my soul has given itself into the
hands of angels, to wash my poor remains in that
wonderful spring.' Immediately on saying this, he
gave up the ghost; and though it was any thing but
a pleasant job, the poor youth brought the body on
his back down to the spring; and, oh, the wonder!—
the moment the messenger of Patrick applied the
water to the corpse, it, that was all foul with sores,
became as clean, and clear, and sweet as the bosom
of a sucking child. This was enough to tell the son
of piety that the poor afflicted beggar was a friend of
God, and that his sowl was in the company of saints.
So, my dear, he straightway buried him in the high
ground just above the well. This was the first body
that was ever buried in Clonmacnoise. But, will
you, howsomdever, listen to me a little longer, for
my story is not yet all tould. The pilgrim, after all
his dutiful labour and charity, with regard to the evil-
touched man, began now to bethink him of the bag
of relics, and, wonder of wonders! what should be
seen but the ould oak tree sucking into the hollow,

where the poor leper lay, the holy bag; and, though
he ran with all his might, yet the tree had closed,
and the bark had covered it so, that you might as well
draw the marrow out of a man's bones without breaking the limb, as take the relics out of the tree without
cutting it down. Then it was all to no purpose that
the honest man went to the next carpenter's shop for
the loan of an axe—in vain, when he got it, did he
hack away; I might as well attempt to cut yon limestone rock with my tabaccy knife. Well, as it was
better for him, away he went to St. Patrick, an' he up
and tould his story, and, in his anger, all as one as
accused the poor leper as being an agent of the wicked
one, for being the occasion of his losing his relics.
'No, by no manner of means,' says holy Patrick;
'those relics were not intended for ME; they are re-
served for one that is to come after me, the holy St.
Kieran, who will come to that very place—stand beside that very tree, which will open its bark, and from
its sanctified hollow let fall into the hands of happy
Kieran these blessed relics."

"Well, Mr. Claffy, you have really told this story
most fully. Can you tell us, further, what these relics were?" "Why then, musha, myself cannot tell,
seeing as how long ago, they were carried away by
the Danes; but, as the saying is handed down,
there was a lock of the blessed Virgin's hair;
there was a skirt of the little coteen our blessed Re-
deemer wore, when he disputed with the docthors;

and a feather which St. Mary Magdalene carried in her bonnet when she was a wicked woman."

Having now seen the most remarkable things in the churchyard, we proceeded south-westward towards those picturesque ruins which are called the castle, and which writers concerning Clonmacnoise call the bishop's residence, but which, according to the people's tradition, was the palace of O'Melaghlin, king of Meath. It stands out, in singular loneliness, on the last spur of the southern limb of the amphitheatre of gravel hills that formed the Aisgir Riada. The slow-flowing Shannon forms a bend round it. If I wanted to call forth a draughtsman to exhibit with his creative pencil a building that time had ruined in the most grotesque and singular manner, I could not expect he would venture on such a vagary as this. It stands on a moat, where art has added to natural elevation of the ground, and is surrounded with a dry but deep fosse. I have just said that time had ruined it—that could not be; some mine, some explosive shock, must have rent the massive works, and thrown them into the various positions and shapes they now exhibit; some parts lie in masses, larger than human habitations in the fosse; others lie rolled in immense heaps in the ballium, or court-yard; an immense curtain-wall, at least ten feet thick, undermined, lies at an angle of forty-five degrees, reclining upon about half a foot of its thickness, and presents at a distance one of the most singular and picturesque hanging ruins I ever looked on. It is surprising, how coarse are the materials of this building—what a large proportion the mortar bears to the stones, which consist of rounded pebble-stones taken from the adjoining hills; and it would appear to me, such is the predominating proportion of mortar to stones, that the building was erected by forming a sort of case-work of boards or hurdles, within which these stones were thrown at random; and that then a grouting mortar was poured in, which was left to settle and solidify; and then the exterior casework was removed. I cannot in any other way account for the extraordinary proportion of mortar in this building. I am quite sure, that, if any mason at present were to attempt to rear up a wall, twenty or thirty feet high, of rounded stones, cemented with so large a quantity of lime and sand, the whole concern would tumble at once about his ears. But the works of Clonmacnoise castle are now any thing but crumbling—no breccia, no pudding-stone can be harder than the composition; time has made the mass so compact, that I am sure it would be just as easy to break the limestone pebbles of which the walls are composed, as to separate the mortar. The view from the staircase is very fine; the tortuous Shannon sweeps calmly underneath; southward are the high grounds about Shannon bridge; and more to the west, the wooded elevation on which the ancient episcopal church of Clonfert stands, where St. Brendon erected his seven altars, and which, amidst surrounding bogs, like Clonmacnoise, seems to challenge equality of desert seclusion.

Mr. Darby Claffy, whose age approached to eighty, was nothing loth to follow me up the broken and tortuous staircase, which I had ascended to view the surrounding country. What a fine vegetable is the potato that can give to extreme old age such an elasticity of step, such a lightness of limb, which many of the beef-eating, turbot-gorging, calipash-swilling citizens of London or Bristol, of half his years, could not imitate! Potatoes are fine food for man, woman, or child, provided there is little *hard* work required. Darby, I believe, was all his life a herd, and had little to do with spade, shovel, or pickaxe. "These are pretty green hills, my good friend, here all around," I observed to my companion; "all quiet and lonesome, except on station days—a likely spot, as one may suppose, for a meeting of the *good* people." "Och, then, it is yourself may well say that. The stars on the sky that covers us, or the merry dancers around the plough-star, are not so plenty of a frosty night as the good people are on these hills and lonely meadows in the middle of the moonlight." "Well, now, Claffy, do tell me, did you ever see them?" "See them! ah, then it's I that did, and hear them too." "On what occasion?" "Why, then, your honour, if you *must* know, 'twas about ten years ago, when there was great want and sickness hereabouts, and the praitie crop failed, and the corn was not much better; and as there was a great price for wheat at Athlone, I was employed by one farmer Dooly, to watch his wheat that he had laid down on the river-brink, ready to send up the river in

boats, at the break of day to the market. The night
was bright almost as day, for the moon was nearly at
full, and all was silent as the dead in yonder graves,
except now and then the plash of the otter might be
heard in the river, or the owl would hoot as it fluttered
round church and tower. So I bethought me that I
might as well go and do a DHURUS for a friend far away
in England, and say for him a few paters, and go on
my two knees round the holy well; when what should I
hear 'whiz, whiz!' over my head. Master, did you ever
hear the whirr and the whiz that a flock of wild ducks
makes of a snowy winter's evening, as they come to
settle down upon the river?—just, then, such a noise
did I hear, and troth myself thought it might be a
flock of frightened peewits or widgeon; but I looked
up, and what should my two eyes behold, but a fine
child carried through the air, and, oh! mother of
mercy, how it did cry! I thought as how it said, 'O
Darby, save me!' But what could I do? Away it
and those who bore it went, and on I saw them go
over the callow meadow as straight as a sparrow-hawk,
until I saw them strike upon Bentullagh hill, which
opened as easy as the chapel door, to let them enter,
and then I saw no more, and there, for aught I know,
they may remain until this day. Well, to be sure,
my mind was full of this, and after my charge of the
corn was over, away I went misgivingly home, when,
what should I hear, but the whole village in a pullaloo!
little Paddy, my wife's sister's grand-child, was fairy
struck, and nothing was in the place of the finest child

that ever took breast-milk, but a little crutheen of a thing, as crooked and as crawling as a dhowlduff.* But this is not all. The cross of Christ cover us from harm! don't I recollect, as well as yesterday, when farmer Mulloy's daughter was carried off, and a dead child put in the cradle, and after its being buried, it came, in a night dream, on the father's mind, that all was not nathral; so out he goes to the grave, and he digs away, and opens it, and, as sure as I stand here, to tell it, there was nothing in the coffin but a wisp of straw."

"Is there any thing here that is worth seeing, besides these old walls?" "O yes, sir," says Claffy; "may be, it would be as well to show you the returning stone." "What is that?" said I. "Why, it is a stone that the holy St. Kieran stood on, when he parted with his friend St. Shannon; and it is our opinion, that no one who, in the right faith, implores St. Kieran's blessing, and says the regular rounds of paters and aves, if he leaves this place, but will return in safety to it again."

We soon arrived at this spot, which was a mere hollow in the rock, such as a man's heel might make in any clayey substance. Of course it was the identical mark of the saint's heel. "I wonder, Mr. Darby Claffy," says the Protestant farmer whom I have before alluded to, "did your nephew, who is now in

* A dowlduff is a black insect about an inch long, which all the lower classes consider the representative of Satan, and as such, kill it whenever they can.

jail for the murder of Mr. ——, take his turn round
on the stone before he got into the trouble in which
he now is: report says it will go hard with him at the
assizes—may be he won't come back, except with his
heels foremost." Old Darby looked at the man who
made this observation with a sinister cast of his eyes,
which denoted that though aged, all the savage passions that belong to unchristianized human nature
were still dwelling in his bosom. The day was now
beginning to turn—the sun was westering, and the
impatience of my friends began to evince, by many
outward acts, that their curiosity was slaked, though
mine was still unabated. Our way back lay through
the burial-ground, and Darby Claffy, as not having
received his shilling, was still in attendance. "Can
you tell me any thing, Darby, about the beginning of
these buildings, and about the consecration of the
place." "By course, I can, sir," said he; "I recollect, at any rate, what all the people before me have
said about it:—Kieran, the carpenter's son, came
directed by God's finger, to this place, which was then
called Drum Tipraid, or, as one would say in English,
the brow of the hill that is in the centre of the land.
It was a green sheep-walk in those days, and belonged
to Dermot O'Melaghlin, king of Meath. 'Give me,
says the saint to the king, 'a spot of ground where I
may build a house in honour of God, and enclose a
place where the dead may receive Christhen berrin.'
'I cannot afford to give my best land for that purpose,'
said the churlish king. 'Go,' said he, 'to some moun-

tain, or some good-for-nothing place amongst the
rocks of Connaught, and make the best you can of it;
but, as for me,' says the proud king, 'never, until this
staff in my hand fastens in the ground, and growing
there, throws out root and leaves, will I give away
the purtiest sheep-park in Ireland. O! blessed
day; no sooner said than done. The staff that he
had used as a walking-stick for many a long year,
suddenly fastened itself in the ground; branches began to sprout; green leaves began to appear, and before the saint had time to say credo, it had grown
into a big tree that covered with its shade many a
perch of ground. 'Father Kieran, says the king, 'I
see it's God's will that you should have this field:
take it, with my blessing, and all I ask is, that when
I die you may put me in a place that your reverence
will *particularly* bless, where I and all my seed, breed,
and generation may be buried.' ' I thank you, king,'
says St. Kieran, ' and though you refused me at first,
I now grant for yourself, and all that die belonging
to the Catholic church, who are buried here, that
none, though they may go—as surely you and all will
go—to purgathory, shall ever be plunged into the deeps
of hell.' " How many bodies have been buried here
since, sure of the privilege that Kieran granted to
King O'Melaghlin, heaven only knows. It was now
time for us to hasten away to our boat, so making
old Darby happy with his well-earned shilling, we
wished him good bye. Poor old man! with what
tenacity his memory adhered to these legendary lies.

With what perfect assurance his naturally comprehen-
sive mind retained a belief in ghosts, fairies, and
lying miracles; and yet there are thousands in this
island, christianized thirteen centuries ago, that are
just as deluded and as ignorant as he.   " I dare say,"
says one of my companions, (as we were retracing our
steps across the burying-ground, and in our way passed
by M'Dermot's church,) " this Darby Claffy, knowing well you were a Protestant, did not tell you how
the people annually visit the grave of the first
M'Coghlan buried here, who turned Protestant."
Here he related a practice of the people on every station day, which I must not commit to paper, but
which singularly characterised not only the brutality,
but the deep malignant hatred that has been engen-
dered in their minds against Protestantism.   " I
wonder much," says I, "that with those feelings,
thus annually revived by such a revolting practice,
they have not long ago rushed on, maddened by their
superstition, and hot with the fiery orgies of the patron
debauch, to pull down the Protestant church that
stands in the centre of all this bigotry." " Wait
awhile," was his reply; "let us see what a year may
bring forth, coming events cast their shadows before
them; other churches, as well as yonder humble
building, may yet find that it is little the existing laws
can protect them in the great hour when fanaticism
runs rampant through the land." We still, as returning
through the cemetery, observed many persons performing rounds and offering up prayers.   One woman

I

who had risen from such an exercise, called out after
a gentleman of our party, who had come with us from
Athlone, and had, as a medical practitioner sent down
from Dublin during the prevalence of cholera, with
singular success, ability, and humanity, fulfilled his
arduous functions there.   The female penance-doer,
addressed herself to the doctor, and wished that God
might bless him.   "Alas!" said he, "is it such characters as this that come .to Clonmacnoise.   This
wretched woman—the vilest of her sex, in a garrison town—for the sake of getting the clothes
that are usually given out to those leaving our hospital, actually feigned herself in cholera.   I was
obliged to turn her out; and now I see her performing a religious duty, such as it is.   I hope she has
noted down in her long score the scene at the cholera
hospital."   "Oh! indeed, sir," says another companion, "it is surprising how they get on here with
their rounds and duties.   I remember, not long ago,
being here in company with two gentlemen, who came
down from Dublin to make drawings of these ruins.
Both were occupied with their pencils, sketching the
old nunnery arch that we are now drawing near to:
they were intent on their work, and so was a middle-
aged woman, who, on her bare knees, was creeping
along under the arch; and on she urged her painful
way over the sharp stones, while she counted with
intense carefulness her beads, fearful that one pater,
ave, or credo should be omitted.   Just at this time
one of the sketchers took some instrument out of his

pocket, which the woman's two children, that were
playing near at hand, took for some murderous wea-
pon, and immediately they both set up a shout and
ran towards their mammy; whereupon the woman
broke off from her devotion, and in an instant poured
forth such a volley of curses on the children, and imprecations on those who occasioned them to interrupt
her, that I was as much shocked at her blasphemy
as surprised at the versatility of her inclination, that
could dispose her to pray and curse almost in the
same breath."

Passing the old exquisite arch that, in the beginning of this description, I had represented as
near to the half-pay officer's new house, my attention was directed to a rounded ridge of moderate elevation, which, I was informed, was the covered secret
way which led from the building—a nunnery built by
Devorgilla, daughter of Murrough O'Melaghlin, king
of Meath—to the churches. I had no time to explore this curious passage. Tradition records many
such between monasteries and nunneries in Ireland,
I suppose they were intended for *useful* and *sanctified*
purposes. It may not be too uncharitable to suppose
that they were sometimes applied to the furtherance of
pious frauds, or to what was worse. The hagiologists
of Ireland describe how St. Ita, one of the early female
saints, was desirous to receive the eucharist from the
holy hands of the monks of Clonmacnoise; and that,
pursuant to her desire, she did receive it without any
one seeing her going to the place or returning from it.

Might not the beatified dame have made use of this covered passage, and, unseen by vulgar eyes, have been at the eucharistical altar?

It is now time for me to close this too long chapter. I am fully aware that the few hours I spent at Clonmacnoise were not sufficient to give me an adequate picture or intelligence of the place. I should feel the deeper regret at the cursoriness of my inspection, were I not sure that in the forthcoming work of Mr. Petrie, all that I have overlooked will be supplied. In fact, I only, in this case, look upon myself as the brief indicator of what will be amply supplied by a more practised hand. Like an insignificant bird in the American forest, my only use may be, by my garrulous noise, to call the attention of the traveller to where the honey-tree is to be found.

CHAPTER IV.

On leaving Athlone you proceed westward, through
a district very ugly by nature, and instead of being
improved, deformed by its inhabitants. Chains of limestone gravel hills, rising out of red flow bogs, stretch
away, their ranges being nearly at right angles with
the Shannon, and it would appear that at the subsi-
dence of the waters under which this country was
once submerged, the decreasing torrents, in seeking
the great central drain of the island, left these enormous deposits of sand, gravel, and rolled stones.
These gravel hills, covered with a shallow but kind
and warm soil, support a superabundant population;
a population, no doubt, encouraged to increase, more
especially here, by the great facilities of obtaining fuel,
the only comfort of the poor—this increase seems to
have met no discouragement from the prudence or
fears of the proprietors of the soil, and the consequence is, that, as you proceed to Ballinasloe, you
pass through an almost continuous village, and are

forced to observe a wretchedly clad people inhabiting
wretched houses, and carrying on a wretched and
destructive tillage within minute enclosures, fenced
by dry stone walls of the rudest construction possible;
indeed the soil seems miserably exhausted, and you
see very deficient crops of potatoes and corn, and at
once can explain the cause in the almost entire absence
of cattle to make manure, and therefore burning of the
already too light soil is resorted to as the only means
of stimulating the ground to produce a crop—and
such a crop, the white lumper—the tired earth unable
to bring to perfection even a *red* potato—the people
thus reduced to subsist on the very weakest and least
nutritious variety of the lowest kind of food—moreover, (and indeed this must surprise an Englishman
not a little, considering the great abundance of people
and the actual idleness of the larger portion both of
young and old,) the crops are not kept clear from
weeds—weeds that children might pull up and collect
for manure, are allowed to grow and run to seed, and
as they do so, not only deform the face of the country,
but actually help to exhaust the soil.   It was to me,
as I passed along, a matter of great wonder how the
landlords could allow their properties to be so subdi-
vided and maltreated—how allow a tenantry to increase and multiply beyond the means of subsistence,
beyond the power of drawing much more than mere
existence from the land they cultivate—and if such
be the results already, what must be the more alarm-
ing ones hereafter—and what is to become of such a

people when one of those very frequent failures of the potato crop takes place; and how will a Poor Law then operate—how affect the relative states of land-owner and occupier. Such considerations engrossed my mind as my jaunting-car swept along, and I could not help observing to my fellow-traveller—"Well, of all parts of Ireland I have seen, I know no portion that upon the face of it exhibits more symptoms of the perhaps *now* inert existence of the Rockite disease—as sure as effect follows cause, so must this plague spread amongst such an ignorant, half-fed, and abounding people, who cannot possibly be worse off, except under a famine of the potatoes; and who must ever remain under the apprehension of their only means of subsistence failing, and thus their great poverty ending in absolute destitution. My friend, who was well acquainted with the state of the country, and had peculiar opportunities of knowing the habits and feelings of the people, told me (in corroboration of what I had apprehended) the following circumstance.

A family once highly respectable, and possessed of considerable property in this district, in consequence of that inconsiderate extravagance, so much the characteristic of Connaught gentry, were reduced to very embarrassed circumstances, and so in order to meet the numerous charges on the estate—jointures, annuities, interest on younger children's portions, and on money borrowed, it was resolved to turn the fine old sheep walks, of which the estate principally consisted, into tillage, and make settings to tenants who flocked in, covenanting to pay high rents, and who, while the soil remained fresh, and markets for corn good, actually paid the rents they had engaged for. But by and by these tenants are allowed to underlet to other PROMISERS of higher rent, and from the small farmer springs up the cottier as sure as bad husbandry produces weeds; and then the war ceases, and prices fall, and Mr. Peel's bill for the resumption of cash payments comes into operation, and creditors insist on the payment of the debt in gold, which was lent in paper—and now arrives the time when there takes place a lamentable difference between the promise and the payment of rent; and in the mean time join-tures *must* be paid, and the creditor *must* have his pound of flesh—and then ensue foreclosures of mort-gages, custodiams, and law-court receivers. Attorneys alighted on the vexed estate and fastened their claws on it, and fattened as flesh-flies do on a festering sore. In this state of things the owner, who was a young man, did what was wise and honest—he broke up his establishment, he let the fire out on his paternal hearth, and went to live poorly but secretly on the Continent, leaving the nursing of the estate to a younger brother—perhaps he would have done better had he sold it; but those only who are reduced to the dire necessity of selling their ancestral inheritance can tell how bitter it is to take such a deep plunge downwards, and what way will not be tried before this last leap is taken?—besides, perhaps, he could not sell—it is not easy in general to make out a clear and marketable title to Irish estates—but be this as it may, the owner had confidence in the firmness, the integrity, and discretion of his younger brother, and he left him as his agent, and *he* honestly and with diligence set about to force the tenants that were solvent to pay the rents they had undertaken for, and those who were not solvent, and incapable from idleness, ignorance, and bad habits, of meeting their engagements, he endeavoured to force off the property, giving them every aid that the limited means at his disposal would permit, to remove to some other location—he gave them their potatoes and furniture, and if they desired it the materials of their cabins. It does not appear that he did any thing unjust or oppressive, either to those he allowed to remain, or those he evicted. But still he became exceedingly unpopular— even those who *could* pay, combined to refuse payment, either from fear of their neighbours, or from the expectation that they could evade it altogether, in consequence of the landlord's embarrassments, and in the midst of hostile legal proceedings. In all parts of Ireland attorneys are to be found who stimulate tenants to such evasions, and who live upon the differences between landlord and tenant. Such became now the state of this deranged property—some were forced off the estate—others under ejectment, by advice of their lawyers, were taking legal steps to retain their holdings, without paying rent at all.

Alas for the poor young man who undertook such

an agency. The dire spirit of Rockism rose in its
wrath against him, and he *must* die.

In this vicinity, as in many others similarly circumstanced in the south and west, a character is to be
found—a fellow from his youth up given to dissolute
practices; with considerable natural ability, with great
vigour and activity of body; a violent temper* that
never has been quelled, and strong passions that have
always been indulged; such a person is given to no regular labour—he will work, it is true, more than any
other at certain times, and under strong excitement—
he will be found digging out a poor widow's potato field,
or his reverence the priest's—and that more especially
when whiskey and a dance are to be at the end of the
job; but if inconstant at labour he is a regular
attendant at fair, market, patron, wake, or hurling-
match—if there ensue a row, *and* HIS presence almost
insures such a result, he is at the head of it, the
ready promoter of all kinds of RUXIONS—his skull,
shins, and arms, are covered with scars of cudgel
wounds received therein: you may be sure he does
not go near the confessional—he dare not go down

---

* I consider the lower classes in Ireland to be particularly
negligent in curbing the tempers of their children. The little
ones of the cabin are, year after year, accustomed to be over
fondled or over punished, and all according to the instigation of
the present passion—and victims as they are of an affection that
palliates serious faults, and of a wrath that punishes without
reason—no wonder we see so many instances of passionate
excess—no wonder that the savage hand is so often lifted up to
strike and commit homicide.

and "whisper at a priest's knee"—and he never mar-
ries, but neverthelessis the neglectful parent of a multitude of children. In this way he is the cuckoo of the
parish—his birds are found in many nests;—at
times well, and at others shabbily dressed, he has
always the air of a rake, and the leer of a profligate—
he is sometimes sober and good-humoured, and good-
natured, and would go through fire and water to serve
one of his own faction—he is oftener drunk, and that
for days together, and then he is a ferocious dangerous
brute; it is not exactly known *how* he lives, and no
one can exactly tell his "whereabouts;" but he is
known to be a good shot—killing wild duck by night,
forms part of his ways and means, and though so
often light-hearted and joyous in his deportment, it
is known that he cares no more to shed human blood
than he would to stick a pig.

The aggrieved party on the estate in question, consisting of fourteen, having resolved to take the agent's
life, cast their eyes on a man of this character, and they
hired him as one whose heart was firm and aim sure,
to fire the shot; but still fearful of their bravo, they
determined that one of them should accompany him,
and that individual was fixed on by lot. Accordingly
the two waylaid their victim at a spot they knew he
must pass, on his return from dining with a neighbouring gentleman. The scheme succeeded—the
bullet was true to its mark—Mr. ——— was shot
through the heart, and the murderer and his companion walked leisurely away—known as they were

to thousands, not a man gave information—the event,
of course, for a time made a great noise—rewards
were offered—the police were on the alert—and then
all blew over. The bravo for a time kept out of the way.
This was not extraordinary in one who had no settled
home; but by and by the money he was supplied
with was spent, and he returned to give his employers
very broad hints that he *must* have more. The Rock-
ites now took counsel together—they saw the danger
they were in from being in such a reckless ruffian's
power, and they resolved on their remedy. He was
called to their meeting—he got more of their money
—he was then informed that they wanted another
cast of his hand in order to put out of the way another
obnoxious gentleman who lived on the other side of
the Shannon, and they engaged him, nothing loath,
to come along with them to do the deed. On a dark
blustry night they accordingly embarked in a cot on
this dreary river, that here steals through bogs and
morasses its deep and silent course, and while in the
middle of the stream, the bravo was suddenly caught
hold of, and before he had time to collect himself for
resistance, was tossed overboard, and as he rose
after the plunge and attempted to catch the boat, a
heavy oar's blow, aimed with vigour and certainty at
his head, sent him again to the bottom, and as it was
hoped, never more to rise. But in this they were
mistaken, for by and by he was seen swimming
steadily and lustily towards shore, and then it was that
one of the party, resting the ruffian's own gun on the

gunwale of the cot, fired with sure aim, and sent the
bullet through his brain. The fellows waited till they
saw that he would *now* rise no more—they then went
home—kept their own secret, and all was safe. But
some time after in the usual process of decomposition
the body rose to the surface, and was found amongst
the reeds. A coroner's inquest was summoned, a
doctor, *pro forma*, called in, and after a cursory inspection, the usual verdict of "found drowned" was
about to pass; but while the coroner was writing out
the proceeding, one of the jury passing a small
switch through the profuse curls of the dead man's
head, found his switch enter, and as through a hole,
pass out at the other side—this, of course, led to a
more exact examination, and the man was found to
have died of a gun-shot wound inflicted by some person unknown. Still a year or more passed on, until,
in the dusk of a winter's evening, as the chief constable of the district was sitting by his fire, a message
was brought to him stating, that one in his hall wished
to speak with him. He accordingly had him introduced, when in a way not at all common with the
Irish, and in apparently the deepest agony of remorse,
he told the guilty story from beginning to end. He
said that though he had confessed all to the
priest, and gone through many penances, yet he
could not find ease for his conscience—that life was
a burthen—that he desired to die, even suppose it
was by the hangman's hand. He named to the constable all the individuals concerned—said that a

large portion of them were at that very moment on their way to the gaol of Galway, to visit others of the confederates who were confined for some other crime. By means of this information the constable succeeded in arresting almost every one of them. I do not know what became of the repentant murderer, for *he* was the one upon whom the lot fell to go along with the bravo to shoot the agent. I must conclude this, I fear, too long narrative by stating, that the chief constable, a most trust worthy and efficient officer, declared that in all his experience of Irish criminality, this informer showed the only evidence of genuine and uncontrollable remorse. And reader, after all, I do not regret having told this story—because I think it goes a great way to explain much of the predial evils of Ireland. I think it goes to show that Ireland's over population, with a barbarous reckless vindictive multitude, is, in a great measure, owing to the improvidence and pecuniary distresses of the landlords. Are not the present race blamed for the faults of many generations ? This would qualify the censure— that there has not been that watchful and protective guardianship on the part of their fathers—that *they* have been as improvident in the selection of their tenants as they have been profuse in their hospitalities, and heedless in the choice of their guests. The truth is, that the present generation is suffering for the sins of their progenitors—the fathers have sown the wind, and the children must reap the whirlwind.

There are a few gentlemen's places between Athlone

and Ballinasloe, but they are not large or beautiful.
One or two seemed to belong to that race now rapidly
wearing out in Ireland—the middlemen, who, let
people say what they will, were in their time useful,
and without whom, bad as Ireland is, it would be much
worse than it is. They expended capital which either
the owners of the soil could not or would not expend.
They became the stock-farmers of the country, and
introduced the fine breed of long-woolled sheep, that
now is the ornament of our western pasture lands.
The fact is, with regard to the middlemen, we are
too apt to argue against the use from the abuse: the
respectable, careful, well-educated middlemen in process of time rose above their condition; they became to
all intents the resident landlords; they formed a sort
of intermediate proprietary between the owners of the
large and unwieldy grants from the crown, and the
people incapacitated by the penal laws; they increased
and improved their holdings—they generally farmed
their own lands—they restricted their under-tenants
from subletting;—they discouraged rack-rent tillage,
and are now the principal stock-farmers who supply
Ballinasloe fair with the sheep and black cattle that
are so much in demand. It is only the hunting,
racing, duelling, punch-drinking, carousing, *squireen*
middleman, that has been, and is, a nuisance in the
land; who takes ground on speculation, to sublet it—
who gambles on land as he does on the cards—who
plays, as I may say, spoil acres as he does spoil five,
—who, because he is a spendthrift, must be a tyrant,

and as he knows nothing of economy, cares not a fig for the political economy of his country;—such middlemen, and they are, alas, still too numerous, having long leases, and who still cling to the determination of extracting all they can out of the soil, no matter in what way, are the curse of the country. I passed by a demesne, and such a demesne !!! it was owned I may suppose by one of these transition gentry—an *improvement*, as I would guess, of about 30 years' standing, begun in the war time, when thedem and for Irish corn increased wonderfully the incomes of middlemen, and booted many who heretofore wore brogues; and so here was built a thin tall canister of a house, with its multitude of little windows, and its great gaunt gables—and then its plantations—little clumps of unsightly firs, dotted here and there over the light limestone pasture, where they grow so thick, so spare, and so unsightly. If tired of the world you might choose such a grove to hang yourself in, could you but find a branch to fasten your rope to. Then the belt all round the low-walled demesne—you could see the sky and the distant bogs through it, and now the wall being here and there thrown down, you might observe pigs rooting, and mangy sheep rubbing against the stunted timber and leaving their loose wool on every ragged sloe bush, and there was a gateway and lodge—but the gate of it was gone; a sprawling root of bog timber supplied its place; the lodge was nearly roofless—the avenue grass-grown and thistle-grown. We were near enough the mansion to see that rags

and old hats served for stuffing to the broken panes;
that the offices were partly ruinous; and that here
and there straw supplied the vacancy where slates
once had been. Here was a true specimen of a broken
down middleman's hall; I believe a race-course was
not very far off.

Ballinasloe is a good town, wonderfully improved
since I saw it first, twelve years ago;, it stands upon
the Suck, which is very like its elder brother
the Shannon, the same slow dark-flowing stream,*
gliding like a black snake through callows, moors,
and red bogs; wasn't it very poetical in a Roscommon bard to call the punch-drinking squires dwelling
on the banks of this sedgy stream—the sons of
Suck!!! There is a canal navigation to Ballinasloe,
and as it terminates here, so it is of advantage to the
place. I believe in every instance a canal in Ireland
has been found to be of little good to any place except where it terminates. Ballinasloe is certainly the
most improved town I have seen in the province; it
bespeaks the attention of an intelligent and assiduous
proprietor—it belongs to Lord Clancarty, the head of
the Trench family, who are, I may say, a race, and
that a númerous one, of improvers. I never passed

---

* Perhaps the first canal in the British Isles was made by a
king of Connaught. The Monk of Boyle, in his Annals, states
that " In the year 1139 Turlough O'Connor digged a canal
from the river Suck that came to Tuam, Dyskert, and Turlough hugh, that it made two great loughs, and came to the
river of Eidne and Lough Ri, and the gathering of Connaught
was doing that act."

K

through any part of Ireland where I found one of the name located, that I did not see their demesnes well ordered, their farming well managed, and a benevolent and prudent attention paid to the education, the comforts, and, as far as they were allowed, the religious instruction of the lower classes. I shall say nothing concerning the great fairs that are held in this town: I never was present at one, I hear that they are rather on the increase, and believe the sheep fair is the largest in the British dominions—from 80 to 90,000 were offered for sale last year. Westward of the town is the fine demesne of Lord Clancarty, well wooded, well kept, and well enclosed. Judicious planting, rather a rare practice in Ireland, seems here carried on to perfection;* and this is all I can say of Garbally, for I had neither the desire nor the opportunity of seeing more. I did not come to Connaught to see fine houses or fine demesnes—I would rather see a well cultivated poor man's farm, a neat

---

* What an amazing loss has occurred to Ireland by injudicious planting—planting in improper places in an improper or imperfect manner, and bad kinds of timber; what an absurd attachment to that ugly and worthless tree the Scotch fir, while the oak, the ash, the wych-elm, so suitable to our soil and climate, are comparatively neglected;—and then the planting in thin belts and round little clumps—and the rage after the larch, which, though undoubtedly a good timber tree and very handsome in its proper place, is in most respects unsuitable to our climate, whose westerly blast it is quite unable to stand against, I dont know any outward sign that marks off the gentleman and the man of taste so much as his planting. Wherever a tailor or a grocer buys an estate he immediately sets to stick down Scotch firs and larches as thick as cabbage plants, and then leaves them to struggle with each other and starve like children in a foundling hospital.

cottage garden, and clean and well ordered tillage—I would rather see a red bog reclaimed, or an old ivy-mantled abbey protected from the avaricious hands of the spoiler, or the wanton waste of the savage. Or what is best of all, I would rather see a landlord, living constantly in the midst of his tenantry, and exhibiting in the peace, comfort, and order of all around him, that his prudence, principle and fortitude had got the better of all difficulties; and who, setting himself the example of obedience to the laws, and a love for the Gospel, had found many imitators in those within the happy circle of his Christian influence.

By the way, I met a bog improvement outside the demesne of Garbally; it no doubt belonged to Lord Clancarty, and though only in *progress* towards perfect reclamation, it was producing a crop of rape. It seemed drained and levelled, and promised a fair crop of seed-rape; but I have as yet seen no red bog of *any extent* turned into good meadow, with a firm sole of grass on it; but I shall for the present pass by this subject, designing to revert to it again, merely making this observation, that it is one thing to commence a bog improvement, and another to bring it to a permanent and profitable termination.

CHAPTER V.

AUGHRIM.

Aughrim—Formation of country—Hill of Kilcomedan—St. Ruth the French General—His ability shown in the fine defensive position he chose—Hesitation of De Ginkle as to the expediency of attack—Council of war—Result—St. Ruth's speech—Father Stafford's speech and bearing—Attack—Repulse of British—Contest in the morass and the hedges of Kilcomedan—Confidence of St. Ruth—Onset of Talmash—Consequences—St. Ruth's fall—Panic of Irish—Utter defeat and slaughter—Fatal results of want of confidence and cooperation between the French and Irish Commanders—State of country after battle—Anecdote of a dog—Irish prophecy—Fatal and unexpected fulfilment—Aughrim not only famous for fighting but for Fairies—A herd's happiness marred by the GOOD PEOPLE.

ABOUT three miles south-west of Ballinasloe rise the high grounds of which the hill of Aughrim stands most prominent. It may be supposed that I would not pass near the memorable battle-field without walking over it, which I accordingly did. Even were it not the scene of one of the most important events in European history, it is a beautiful eminence to look from—a fine farm of grass land, and near it is rather a pretty village. The hill which St. Ruth, the general commanding the united French and Irish forces, chose as the ground where he would make the last great struggle for the house of Stuart, is called Kilcomedan. The Frenchman, surprised as he was at Athlone, and brought to shame and confusion in the midst of his boasting, determined to show here that he knew how to choose a good defensive battle-field—and certainly (speaking, as I confess I do, as a mere civilian) I may say, that, not in Ireland, could a better position be selected. I have been at Waterloo—at Culloden—at Oldbridge—those great fields where the fate of religions, empires, and dynasties were decided, and none of them can at all be compared to Kilcomedan. The hill rises, a fine green eminence, to the height of about four hundred feet. The ascent is so gradual, that both cavalry and artillery can easily manœuvre. Along the north-eastern side, upon which the Irish army was drawn up, there were parallel rows of lofty whitethorn hedges, which partly remain to this very day. On either flank were red bogs—in front a morass, only passable, and that with great difficulty, in two places. The only approach for cavalry or artillery was by a narrow causeway that passed under the castle of Aughrim, a stronghold of the O'Kellys, and along which but two or three could ride abreast. It was no wonder, then, that St. Ruth, with his usual complacency, felt satisfied that his position could not be forced—it was no wonder that De Ginkle, the British commander, summoned a council of war to discuss whether it were possible to beat the enemy from this position. The fog, that covered the whole country during the early part of the day, and the irresolution of the British officers, did not allow the attack, which was now resolved on, to begin till about two o'clock; and St. Ruth, observing that the assault *was to be* made, addressed a speech to his army, in which he took great merit to himself for the wars he had waged, ·and the desolations he had been so successful in perpetrating on Protestants in France and Germany. He stated, that now or never was it for the Irish to stand by their religion and country, and he closed his harangue, as follows :— "Stand to it, therefore, my dears, and be assured that King James will love and reward you—Louis the Great will protect you—all good Catholics will applaud you—I, myself, will lead you to victory—the church will pray for you—posterity will bless you— angels will caress you—God will make you all saints, and His holy mother will lay you in her bosom."* This speech, of course, could be heard but partially by the officers and men; but a priest, of great eminence, Dr. Stafford, crucifix in hand, went along the lines, and with astonishing eloquence brought all the inducements of time and eternity to bear upon the feelings of the soldiery. There can be no doubt but this man was sincere, and his devotions had a wonderful effect; he stood to his work the whole day, from the beginning to the end of the fight—there he was, passing from line to line, animating the men, and when all was over, amidst the thickest heaps of slain he was found, cut down while exhorting the Irish to fight for God and their country. The Irish were superior to the British in numbers, especially in cavalry, but much inferior in artillery—they mustered about twenty-five thousand men. As I said, the battle began about two o'clock; the English attempted to turn the Irish right, near the house and high

* Story.

ground of Urrachree, but they were repulsed, with so much loss, that about four o'clock a council of war was again held, to consult whether it would not be better to draw off the troops, at least for that night; but, by General Mackey's advice, (one of the best men and bravest officers in William's service,) it was determined to persevere, and to send forward the centre to pass the marsh in front. That which was then a morass, requiring caution, even in those who knew it well, to pass over without sinking up to the middle, or being swallowed up altogether, is now a fine tract of meadow and pasture ground. Across the firmest, most practicable parts, the English now ventured to make their way, protected by their well served artillery, *which* fired over their heads, and played upon the Irish who lay along the hedges that just commenced where the hill rose from the morass. The English having passed the marsh found themselves in face of the enemy, who had lined all the hedges, and had also made open and convenient places through which cavalry and artillery might manœuvre. Here the Irish fought most heroically, and the push of pike and bayonet through the hedges, reminds us of the same kind of desperate struggle that took place at La Haye Saint on the field of Waterloo. The Irish regiments even drove back their opponents, who, told by their commanders that they must force the Irish from the hedges, or fall back on the morass and be swallowed up, fought like tigers; yet, they *were* driven back, and were, while swamping in the bog, either

killed or taken prisoners.   Beaten thus, on their left
and centre, the evening was closing, and the Irish
had *all the advantage*.   St. Ruth was heard to say,
now I shall beat back the English to the walls of
Dublin.   Nothing could retrieve the battle but a
charge of the English cavalry from the left, to try
and take the Irish in flank, and this charge must be
made along a narrow causeway under the guns of the
castle of Aughrim.   They did attempt it, led on by
Talmash, a man of ready enterprise, and of the most
undaunted courage, and, like most valorous attempts,
it succeeded.   But, while in the act, while struggling
with their great difficulty—while scrambling over the
torn up causeway, and plunging on, St. Ruth was
heard to cry:—" What are these fellows about?"
"Why, they are about to turn your left," was the
reply.   "Then they are brave fellows," said the
Frenchman, "but every man of them will be cut to
pieces."   It was not so—they passed on like a hurricane—they took the Irish centre in flank, and were
doing horrible execution, when St. Ruth, seeing that,
against all military calculation, the English horse had
forced the pass and were doing valiantly, rode down
the hill with a view of directing a battery that was
raised to flank the pass, to play on the successful enemy.
When in full career he was shot by a cannon-ball.   The
place where he fell is marked by a small whitethorn
bush; an aid-de-camp threw his cloak over him, but
not before it was known to the Irish cavalry who
swept by, and subsequently it ran along all the Irish

line, that their commander was no more. The Irish
are subject (more especially in their own country) to
sudden panics. On this occasion, though they had,
decidedly, the best of the day, though they had
fought with a courage and discipline such as in their
own island they had never shown before—though
they had fresh troops in abundance, yet all seemed
paralyzed—the battery ceased to fire—the Irish horse
halted, and delayed to charge. Talmash, who at once
saw that something was gone wrong with the enemy,
took instant advantage of the delay, he called on the
English, both horse and foot, to advance—the columns
that were unbroken, at the edge of the bog, moved
forward—those that had been dispersed returned to
their ranks, and the whole centre charged up the hill.
In the mean time, no one stood forward to command
the Irish—not one direction was given—those who
commanded the cavalry rode off the field in despair
and indignation—the foot, seeing themselves aban-
doned by the horse, fled and dispersed over the bogs,
and all was cutting down, and remorseless slaughter,
until night put an end to the pursuit. Sarsfield, who
had the character of an active officer, and had proved
himself able to act wisely in an extremity, should have
taken the command on the fall of St. Ruth. It does not
appear, however, he did; it is, therefore, doubted by
some, whether he was in the battle ; at all events there
was evidently a want of confidence and counsel between
the French commander and the Irish officers; the
presumptuous and ill-conceived contempt for the Irish

which possessed the boastful Gaul was exceedingly
offensive, and, it would appear, that he did not com-
municate his plans to any one; the result was as we
have seen. Providence, in the midst of almost certain success, confounded the allied arms; and the
death of St. Ruth sealed the destiny of the house of
Stuart. The Irish left one-third of their army on
the field. The dead lay, day after day, exposed—
there were none to bury them—the country people
had all fled—and the carrion-birds came and ban-
quetted, and wild dogs, in packs, frequented the field,
and became so fierce, feeding on man's flesh, that no
one might pass by that way: and amidst this scene
of pestilence and horror there was one dog, a wolf-
hound belonging to an Irish colonel that fell, and lay
upon the hill-side: on this body the attached creature
remained day and night, with the rest of the prowl-
ing animals, dogs, foxes, wolves—he fed upon the
corpses that lay around, but he would *not allow* any
thing, either bird of the air, or beast of the field, to
touch his master; and when the bodies were all reduced to skeletons, when he was obliged to go far away,
and prowl by night through the neighbouring villages,
yet he came back presently to the place where his
master's bones lay festering in the slow process of
corruption, there to keep watch and ward. A soldier
quartered in Aughrim, six months afterwards passing
by chance that way, saw the dog seated by the skeleton, and drawing near out of curiosity, the animal,
fearing he came to disturb his master flew at him,

and the man surprised at the suddenness of the assault, levelled his musket and shot him dead.

I shall conclude my sketch of this important battle, by noticing a prophecy which was prevalent among the Irish respecting it. A year before it took place a Protestant gentleman living near Aughrim met a number of that nomadic race that existed in Ireland during the sixteenth and seventeenth centuries, called Ulster Creaghts, who roamed the country, desolated as it was by the wars of Elizabeth, Charles, and William, from north to south, and drove their herds before them, pasturing on the devastated lands wherever they chose. Meeting this gentleman just near the castle of Aughrim, they demanded of him what castle that was, and upon his telling them its name, they pointed to the hill of Kilcomedan, that rose to the south of the castle, and declared that before long a great battle would be fought *there* between the English and Irish, and that the English would find their coats too heavy in climbing up the eminence. This prophecy was two-handled, and was interpreted by the Irish, to mean their foes casting off their coats while running away from them. Colonel Gordon O'Neill, who lay wounded on the hill, and was (before he was trampled to death) taken prisoner and brought off the field, when he saw the British casting off their coats, in order that they might more lustily pursue and overtake the Irish before they got to the bogs, called to mind with no small grief the prediction of the Ulster Creaghts.

The green hill of Aughrim is not alone memorable
for the conflict that confirmed the dominion of England over Ireland, but like every other fine green eminence, it is the domain of the fairies. One rich in
reminiscences of the "good people" told me the following " FACT."

Just on that side of the hill where the battle raged
and St. Ruth fell, there dwelt a poor man, whose business it was to herd cattle. He was married to a
neighbour's daughter, fair, mild, and good; and they
had three fine children, and the mother was just
brought to bed of a fourth, and was doing " as *well
as could be expected*," and the midwife had settled
her snug for the night, and went home, expecting
to find her and the baby well in the morning; but
when morning came, to the husband's utter grief, and
all the neighbours' great dismay, instead of the living
wife, was found a corpse, livid and loathsome, with
grim features, totally unlike those of the gentle and
pretty creature who was laid to sleep over night.
From such a change all knowledgeable people came to
the conclusion, that it was the work of the " good
people;" and this lump of loathsome flesh was left as
a substitute for the woman who was carried away. Of
course, the corpse was buried as soon as possible, and
the little sister of the infant took to rearing it with a
spoon. In this way, the family continued for some
time; the poor husband remained desolate, and when
he looked on his poor motherless children, he turned
his head away, and dropped a silent tear for his own

and their bereavement. But it so happened, as he was sitting up one night minding a sick cow, and had just laid down in his clothes in bed, not desiring to sleep *soundly all out*, and the children were all enjoying the steady repose of health and innocence, the fire raked out, and the round moon ascending high in heaven, sending its slanting light in at the little cabin window, the man saw the door open, as if stealthily, and a woman enter, whom he at once recognised as his wife. Supposing at first it was her ghost, he lay still and said nothing; but he saw her go to the fire, pull out a coal, light a rush, go to the press, take out some boiled potatoes, lay them on the coals, and then go to the churn, take up some milk, and make her supper heartily. When, moreover, he saw her go to the cradle, take the infant in her arms, and give it suck, then he was sure the woman was alive, and he bounced up and took her in his arms, and in his surprised joy cried, oh! whence come you, my own dear Mary? and then she told him how she had been carried away by the fairies—that she was used as the nurse of their king's daughter—that she was allowed to step home for an hour at midnight—and she moreover said that she might be *yet* released, and restored to him, for that she had *as yet eaten none of their food*, but she came home every night, and eat the boiled potatoes that were left, and that her fond heart was yet with her own dear man and the children. " Well, but, MARY ASTHORE, how are you to be released from their power?—or how could a poor lone man like me, hold

you back from these wise and dangerous people." "I
will tell you," replied she, " we will be removing on
Saturday night next from the rath, where we now
are, and we will pass through the old gateway that
leads down to the castle, and you will first hear as it
were a sigh, as if the wind was passing through the
big ash trees, and then a rushing of (as it were)
dried leaves in a whirlwind; and then's your time,
Darby dear; and have with you a vessel, in which is
mixed the blood of a black hen and salt, and all-flower
water; and when you see the dust curling on the road,
and the whirl of the dry leaves, as it were, passing by,
then dash what is in the pitcher on the spot, and it
will fall on me, and I will be left behind." Having
said this, the wife departed, as needs she must, and
the husband prepared himself for the disenchantment;
and having concocted his mixture, he, on the night
specified was at the spot, and prepared to do so as
desired; but, when the moment came—when he heard
the midnight silence broken by the sough of the
coming whirlwind—when the rush, as of a multitude
came hurtling along, his teeth chattered, his sight
failed, his knees knocked, down fell the pitcher out of
his hand—it seemed as if some knowing Fay gave it
a kick with his heel as he passed by. At any rate the
man failed of his purpose—the dusty whirl came and
went, and was *not* sprinkled, and poor Darby, in the
midst of his trepidation, thought he heard a departing
moan, and a voice that said, " Mary is gone from you
and the childer for ever." In about two years after,

Darby was found under the side of a ditch, paralyzed, and without the use of his left arm, eye, and leg, and his speech utterly gone. "I saw the man," (says my informant,) in the year 1835, he wrote me this account, for he could not speak, and maintained, (which he will do to his dying day,) that he was thus struck for not releasing his wife from the fairies."

CHAPTER VI.

KILCONNELL.

Kilconnell Abbey, its position—Picturesque appearance—Place of Sepulture—Tomb of Trimlestone—Cause of his interment here—Who built
Kilconnell—Character of Connell—His merits—His demerits—St. Patrick's
anger not ill placed—St. Connell's fault not uncommon in latter days—St.
Connell's dispute with his sister—With his friend—Saints wrathful at
times—Strife of tongues—Effects of holy cursing—Holy Priests—Father
Christy and the Fairies—Christy and Grace—It loses him his supper—His
disenchantment and return to sober seriousness—Father Christy at a
Funeral—The dispersion of his whip.

FROM Aughrim I proceeded to Kilconnell*—I was
desirous to see the ruined abbey there, which is as
usual placed in the middle of very fertile land, close
to a fine spring of water, and is as picturesque a ruin
as can be, where there are neither hills, rocks, lake,
nor river, and but a few distant trees to improve the
scenery—perhaps its ivy-mantled tower and time-
tinted roofless gables, with all their salient angles,
producing the happiest effects of light and shadow,
were better in keeping with the waste and desolation
that presided over the place, destitute as it was of any
modern improvement or decoration whatsoever. The
wretched houses of the adjoining village did not at
any rate take away from the dreariness of the scene.
I walked through a rich meadow, entered the enclosure, and the first thing that met my view was an
immense stack of human bones. As I mean to speak

---

* When I visited Kilconnell, the glebe-house was not
built, and there was not, as there is now, a resident and pains-
taking minister. My visit took place twelve years ago, I
include it now in this present tour, because if I had not visited
it before, I should have done so on the more recent occasion.

in another place of the state of Irish abbeys, I shall
say nothing further here, because my memory is not
fresh, and I took no notes of what I saw of Kilconnell. I shall only observe that I scrambled over
nasty graves, and sauntered through tottering and
wasting away enclosures that once were nave, transept,
choir, cloister, dormitory, and chapter-house—and
observed that what the original devastators had spared,
the heedless and tasteless people had altogether demolished and removed to make uncouth ornaments
for the graves of the vulgar people that lay all around;
my feelings were vexed and melancholy, and this
mood was not altered by observing a tablet placed on
the wall of a side chapel, on which was the following
inscription:—

HERE LYETH THE BODY OF MATHYAS BARNWALL THE
12 LORD BARRON OF TRIMLESTOWNE WHOE BEING
TRANSPLANTED INTO CONAGHT WITH OTHRS BY OR-
DERS OF THE VSVRPER CROMWELL DYED AT MOINIVAE
THE 17 OF SEPTEMBER 1667 FOR WHOME THIS MO-
NVMENT WAS MADE BY HIS SONNE ROBERT BARNE-
WALL THE 13 LORD OF TRIMLESTOWNE, HERE LYETH
ALSOE HIS VNCKLE RICHARD BARNEWALL, IAMES BARNE-
WALL WHO DYED ATT CREGAN THE 2 OF OCTOBER
1672 AND IAMES BARNEWALL OF AGHRIM· GOD HAVE
MERCY ON THEIR SOVLES.

Poor Barnewall, how much you must have felt the
exile from your rich property within the English pale,
from the smiling and exuberant plains of Meath to

L

ugly and stony Connaught—yes, and to one of the ugliest parts of the trans-Shannonite province—boggy, melancholy Monivea.

That order of Cromwell's was certainly a "horrible decree," it was "*væ victis*" with a vengeance. It is a sad thing to emigrate at any time; for the *last* evening to sit round the paternal hearth—hear for the last time the closing of the door of home—home sanctified and made precious by the births, marriages, and deaths of all we have loved—and from the last eminence whence it is visible—cast a look, and then another, and *it* must be the *last*, on the scenes of our playful youth—the very pleasant places where our young ideas expanded, and our young affections budded and blossomed—yes, to go away deliberately, without any force but the constrainings of prudence, to where profit or ambition may call us, *that* is sad enough—but there is this *great, fond* alleviation— thank God we *may* come back and find a welcome! But when pushed away by the stern decree of a tyrant—a resistless tyrant; when the exile is taken hold of as you would an obnoxious plant, and torn up by all its roots ; when thus the delicate fibres are snapped, by which were assimilated all that consti- tuted life's pleasures, and the outcasts are sent forth on their EXODUS, and they lift up their wringing hands and say,

"Nos patriam fugimus, et dulcia linquimus arva,"

and they are gone to sigh out life in a barren and dreary, and unwelcoming land. Oh! this is indeed a transplantation—untimely, unnatural, hopeless like that of a large tree—see it *there* in its new position, with its top withering, its branches decaying and snapping off with every wind; its stem loose and bending from the blast that vexes it with all its storms—no wonder that poor Lord Trimleston soon ceased to sigh for the pleasant land of his birthright, and sought refuge where the weary are' at rest.

. KILCONNELL.—The church or cell of Connell (Connell, a cotemporary, as legendaries, or, if you will, *historians*, say, of St. Patrick,) was one of the multitude of sees, existing in Ireland at that time, for it is reported that there were upwards of three hundred and fifty, and that the means of support of a bishop consisted of the milk of one or two cows. Now as the credible history of Colgan goes, Connell was mighty good in the way that Irish saints are reported to have sanctified their characters; yet he fell under the displeasure of St. Patrick, and of his own saintly sister, and his conduct brought down a double curse on the place he had chosen, and that curse remains to this day.

Connell, I repeat, was a good man, as goodness was appreciated in that day, for each epoch has its peculiar goodness, and, no doubt, the goodness of St. Connell was very different from that of his namesake, and, for aught I know, blood-relation, the *big* O'Connell of the present time. Now his goodness . was in this sort, into the cold, cold spring-well he would go down and kneel every morning, and minding the water as little as a frog, would say all his paters and aves, and repeat every verse of the one hundred and fifty psalms—nay more, he used to starve, flagellate, and macerate his poor body, and undergo acts of mortification, enough to turn his carcase into a mummy in the same way (as we may suppose) the men of Kent turn pig's meat into brawn. But he had better have been less ascetic, and more circumspect, and minded his Bible more than his Breviary—for while he did what he need *not* have done—he left undone what he *should* have done—he laid hands suddenly, and without due examination on certain men, and ordained them bishops, and confided the crozier to those totally unfit for the office—and his imprudence coming to the ears of Primate St. Patrick, he not only rated him well for it, but he punished the place he was so partial to, and decreed that to the end of time Kilconnell should continue a poor place. I wish more of St. Patrick's vigilance, and less of St. Connell's negligence, had descended to the primates and prelates of the Irish Church—and this I *must* observe, that if the sees of bishops where their lordships lay hands suddenly on presbyters and prelates were to dwindle down to ruin like Kilconnell we should have many poor sees, where we now find rich, in the length of the land, from the Causeway to Cape Clear—from * Derry to

* In making these observations, the tourist anxiously desires to have it understood, that he means no allusion to persons now living.

Aghadoe. St. Connell's sister's curse was more intemperate and certainly (as Colgan says) less deserved. She took a fancy to erect a nunnery near the cell of her brother, and he, the religious churl, in his extreme-asceticism and self-suspicion, did not think well of woman-kind being so near him; and she in anger cursed the place with poverty, which, alas, I fear, the present vicar feels, for I am led to suspect that Saint Atracta, for that was the name of the abbess, who was attracted by the " *amœnitates loci*" of Kilconnell, was the primal prophetess who foretold of parliamentary interference with, and plunder of, church property: especially when the true blue and staunch Protestant squires, composing the legion-club in College-green, first took away from poor vicars the tithe of agistment, and so the pro-Protestant Whigs of the eighteenth century taught the pro-Popery Whigs of the nineteenth to *appropriate* church property and starve the parsons.

So far written story goes concerning Kilconnell and its saints—tradition, as it was communicated by one whose mind seemed to delight in these matters, informed me as follows :—

At the time that Connell was about building the steeple of his abbey, another saint, one Kerrill, was intending to do the same at a place called Clonkeen, about seven miles to the west, and it so happened that Connell had his materials ready *first*, and he came to the other and said—" Brother Kerrill, let me now have your masons to help mine, and when you are ready I will in return send you mine back along with your own, and so there will be no time lost to either of us." "Agreed," says Kerrill. So Connell soon ran up his steeple, and was proud, as he well might, of his edification—but by and by, when Kerrill was ready, he sent to Connell for *all* the masons—but he, it is supposed, conceiving that when pious intentions are to be fulfilled, it is no harm to break a promise, said, that indeed he was busy in building a chapel for the Virgin, and he could not send *his* people until that *good work* was finished. So Kerrill, in great wrath, came over to Kilconnell, and then the two saints set to rating one another most roundly; and not content with this public strife of tongues, they retired to a lonesome field, called Ballyglass, about a mile off, where there were lofty echoing rocks, and each kneeling down, with his face to a high stone, they set to, most methodically, to curse each other, and wish evil against whatever they respectively held dearest in the world—among other anathemas Connell hurled this at Kerrill—" May Clonkeen Abbey never see a Monday morning come to noon, without a corpse coming to be buried." "Thank you for that," says Kerrill, and now have you done your worst?" "Yes," says Connell. "Well now," replies Kerrill, "see how I come over you and your pitiful curse—for my prayer is, and I am sure it will be granted, that the corpse that is to come shall be that of a * blackbird"—and

---

* A darigg or starling, according to some handers down of the story.

so it is, for every Monday morning since that day's
cursing-match, a blackbird is found dead in Clonkeen
Abbey. And now it came to Kerrill's turn to curse,
and his was a most catholic and general curse,
attending not only on the place of his dislike, but, as
I deem, extending all over the land of Ire—his curse
was—" May Kilconnell never see a fair-day without
a fight—and may there be as many black eyes and
bloody noses there and then, as there are cock black-
birds, with red bills, in Clonkeen." Poor Connell was altogether powerless to avert this curse; fate was too stern
for him, and so it is—every fair day that comes, fighting
follows as sure as a luck-penny concludes a bargain;
and so when the cattle are driven out of the green,
and whiskey has done its duty, then comes the clash of
cloholpeens, and the joy of battle sparkles in each
reddening eye—" *Bello gaudentes, prælio ridentes.*"
On they rush, the Kilconnellites to batter the Long-
fordites—and the ruxion rages. Reader, if ever you
go to Kilconnell be sure to examine the heap of skulls
you will see there; and pray *observe* the wonderful
thickness of those brain bowls. Nothing but constant
cudgelling could have caused this characteristic cras-
situde, and so St. Kerrill's prophecy is fulfilled to
the letter—and why should not the inhabitants of
this barony continue as long as fire burns, or water
flows, to fight at Kilconnell, to keep up the credit of
St. Kerrill?

Now worthy reader do you doubt the truth of this
tradition—rest satisfied that the *facts* are unques-

tionable, for there are visible proofs of its being well founded. I told you before that the conflicting saints retired to fight out their wordy duel, to a field surrounded by precipitous rocks, and grassy hillocks; you were told that each saint, in order that his curse might reverberate and roll more imposingly upwards, turned his face, as he execrated, to the tall rock, and there and then holy rage was so great, and as they muttered their terrible rhymes, and

" Sternly shook their raven hair,"

blood spouted from their nostrils, and as the sanguine stream struck the rock, it forced an entrance as would an auger—and there, even in the hard limestone, the red holes are to be seen to this day, and you may put your fingers in, if you will, where the hot and burning blood once penetrated. The fairies, who were ever and always fond of this grassy and sunny field, surrounded, as it is, with little knolls, looking like green china cups turned upside down on a tea-tray, were not over pleased at their pleasant dancing-green being tormented with all this cursing; they, therefore, (as they say,) have no fondness for what are called 'holy priests, and excommunicators, and exorcisors, and *that* not only for the reason that they are the well-known successors and representatives of such saints as Connell and Kerrill, and that they still love cursing with bell, book, and candle: but also, as said holy priests are apt, by night, to see double, therefore, as having much to do with SPIRITS, they also sometimes spy the fairies, and follow will-o'-the-wisps into bog-holes and ditches, while other, less gifted people keep never minding them. Now, there was in this neighbourhood a holy priest. "My grandmother (says my informant) often drank the water steeped in the blessed clay in which he was buried, but no matter for that." And the fairies had a grudge against Father Christy, and watched to take him at an advantage; so one night, it was close up Hollantide, if it was not the very eve of All Saints' itself, any how, Father Christy was coming home to Kilconnell, from the hospitable house of one of his *gentlemen* parishioners. I think the place is, or was called Hillswood, and the moon, the deceiving moon, was up, and she threw her shadows and shinings in such a way, that it would be hard for any man, especially when coming from a place overflowing with hospitality, to pick his way quite straight; but at any rate the priest thought he had the path, and on he went, expecting every moment to see the abbey tower—when, mighty strange!!! his reverence found himself at the door of a great house, and standing at the hall-door, clad in green and gold lace, was a servant who bid him welcome, took his horse, with a low bow, and pointed to the open hall-door, and requested him to enter, which he did, nothing loath, for all round seemed as kind as it was lightsome and gay. At the entrance of a splendidly lit up chamber, he met a lovely lady with a goblet of wine in her hand, as clear and sparkling and enchanting as her own dark rolling eye, and she led him into

where tables were laid out, and gallant gentlemen, and
gorgeous dames sat intermingled, and, as the priest entered, one and all rose and cried, " You're welcome,
Father Christy;" and they were all equally so kind
and so encouraging. " Here's a seat by *me*," says one;
" No," says another; " come beside ME, and have
your back to the fire this cold night, dear, sweet
Father Christy." But all this kind and invitatory
bustle was set at rest by the little splendid man dressed
in green cut velvet, with a golden hunting-cap on his
head, who sat at the head of the table, and who summoned him, with an air of superiority, to take a chair
at *his* right hand, as the post of honour. And now,
the work of the festive hour was being begun—each
seemed about to address him, or herself, to the food
they liked best; when up stood the Amphitryon of
the feast, and with that satisfied air which denotes
that the speaker is about to address a willing audience, he said, " Gentlemen and ladies, before we set
to, I propose that we drink the health of our guest,
Father Christy, AND LONG MAY HE REIGN AMONGST
US." To which all, with one accord, assented, and
were in the act of filling bumpers, and crying hip,
hip, three-times-three, when the priest, on being
offered the wine, as it went round, with all due gravity, and as became his calling, said, " Most noble,
my unknown entertainer, and you, ye gay gentlemen
and gracious ladies, I do, from my heart, respond to
your hospitalities, and shall most willingly partake of
your cheer, and especially your wine, for as you all

may know it is more pleasant to set to drinking again
than to eating; but this I must say, that it has ever been
my own practice, and I do my endeavour, as becomes
my cloth, to teach it to others, never to sit down to
table without saying grace," and, with that, his reverence, with his usual slight and agility, *cut* the sign
of the cross on his breast, and said off his Latin with
such holy rapidity, that none, but a practised eye and
ear, could see or hear the reverend office; but, wondrous were its effects:—like a flash of lightning, or
the shifting of the FATA MORGANA in the straits of
Messina, or on the coast of the Giant's Causeway, all
vanished: light, people, goblets, and good cheer—and
lo, the priest rubbed his eyes and felt very much as if
he had been just a sleeping, at the stump of an ash tree
near the village, and nothing was very wrong about
him, save that the knee of his thickset small-clothes
was burst, and the rein of his good and quiet mare
broken, which was altogether of no consequence,
as the gentle beast was grazing but a few yards off.
The priest used, in after times, when wrought up to
good humour at a station, to tell this adventure
amongst the fairies.

"I remember (says my informant) on one of those
occasions, my grandmother asked his reverence what
would have been the consequence had he drank off
that bumper without saying grace. 'Why,' says the
holy man, ' I never would have got away from them,
they would have as hard a *hoult* of *me*, and I would be
as *far in them* as any of the other people they have
taken.'

"My grandmother, God be good to her, was a great favourite with this priest, and good reason there was for it, for she was of the *thrue* three orders, the scapular, the cord, and the sacred heart, he, therefore, told her of many other doings he had with the "good people;" amongst the rest, how one day he met on the road, of a fine summer's evening, (by-the-by it was always after dinner he saw the "GENTRY,") a hearse, followed by a long line of gentlemen's carriages, and then horsemen with scarfs, country people in thousands, and the *keening* going on as if it was quite Christian, and his reverence turned back, as it is always decent to do so, and he followed them a considerable way along the road, but never a word could be got from any one, nor would they say whose burying it was, and where they were going, but by-and-by they came to an old building, and he saw every mother's soul of them, with coffin, carriages, hearses, and all, go into a hole in the wall, not bigger than what leads to a wasp's nest, and so, says the priest, "My nice little people I'll be after following yes as far as I can," and with that he thrust the butt end of his whip into the hole after them, but when he took it out, the lead with which it was loaded was all melted, and he could not carry it any more, it smelt so strong of brimstone."

CHAPTER VII.

AHASCRAGH.

AHASCRAGH is rather a neat village, it rises from a
small sluggish river over which there is a bridge. You
may be always sure in travelling through Ireland
wherever you find a place beginning with A or Ath,
that there is a river which either is by nature fordable or has been made so by art. The practice of the
ancient Irish was to make streams fordable by casting
small stones into the stream so as to make a sort of
under-water causeway.* This practice was no doubt
the cause of the great number of loughs, morasses,
and bogs which prevailed through the island. The

---

* This and the similar practice of making passes of hurdles
across the morasses and sluggish streams, which were called
toghers, tended to enlarge the morasses or bogs, and flood the
upper levels by the back water created.

Irish in this instance acted like the beaver o f North
America, they did the same mischief without showing
the same constructive intelligence.

There is a neat church and parsonage-house adjoining this village; both one and the other show that the
resident minister is an improving man—in every sense
of the word—I hope and believe he is. That man's
bigotry must have eradicated his common sense
who would say that this place, or indeed any other,
would be better without the parson—the parson's
wife—his house or his church. In the absence of
the landed proprietors, who as lords or commoners
must, or *think they must*, for the greater part of the
year be in London, I ask would the as yet ill-
educated middlemen, or the bachelor priest, surrounded, beset, and biassed as he generally is by his
low, narrow-minded relations—would they make up
for the parson and the contents of the parsonage,—
the educated, moral, independent, pious inhabitants of
that clean, modest, well-regulated dwelling. No; great
indeed must the animosity be, which, while deprecat-
ing, as it will venture to do, all absenteeism, would
drive away the three thousand of the most intelligent,
moral, and useful country gentlemen that Ireland now
possesses. To exemplify what I say, the parson of
Ahascragh has instituted in his small town a lending
fund, which is established on such good principles
that though it circulates three thousand pounds annually amongst the lower classes, and has been the means
of giving comfort and competence to hundreds, yet

is not decreasing its capital. On the contrary, its accumulation is certain, though moderate, and there are very few instances indeed where the people who take advantage of the loan, do not strictly discharge their engagements.

There is a holy well at Ahascragh which I did not see: near it are fir trees of great virtue, and around which the devotees, in pursuance of penances imposed either by priests or friars, or by their own wilful vows, circumambulate, or rather circumgenuate, creeping on bare knees, five, fifteen, twenty times, and so on, saying multitudes of paters and aves; and where, as I am told, they bow down to a picture of the Virgin, suspended by the priest for the occasion. In this holy well St. Cuan, the patron saint of Ahascragh, used to descend and stand up to his middle, until he repeated the 150 Psalms of the Psalter. Like his near neighbour, St. Connell, he was a WATERPROOF saint. This was, I believe, the same saint who sailed across Lough Corrib, along with eight of his disciples, on one of the flat limestones that are so abundant along its shores; and the same also who, when his mother admired his beautiful black eyes, lest the flattery should make him vain, gouged both one and the other out with his forefinger, which, as he cast away from him, two ravens came and carried off; but which (while he was, as no doubt he should be, in great pain and darkness,) were snatched from the ravens' bills and restored back unto him by angels. The legendary who tells this savoury story asserts, that when holy Cuan thus got back his eyes, he could sing as the Psalmist did in the 109th Psalm, "Open thou mine eyes and I shall behold the wondrous things out of thy law." The fame of this miracle of course went abroad, and thousands of saints flocked from all parts to see him. Of these he formed a sodality, which assembling one day in order to unite their suffrage for suffering souls in purgatory, a bell was seen flying and ringing over their heads, at which, while all were wondering and asking what this could mean, St. Cuan said, "Brethren, that is St. Fursey: the good man is so busy that he cannot come himself, but in order to show that he will join our fraternity, he has sent his bell." And upon the brethren further inquiring where he was, and what he was doing, Cuan said, "Brother Fursey has left Ireland and gone to France; and at Peronne he is now abbot, and he cannot come, because he has made a covenant with his friend St. Magnence, which is rather inconvenient, for in the strict ardour of their fellowship, they have *swopped diseases!!!*

"Fursey had a dysentery which, by prayer, has been transferred to Magnence; and Magnence, full of sores which constantly bred loathsome worms, has sent his sores, insects and all, to Fursey. This is indeed a wonderful communion of the saints, and you cannot wonder that Fursey in this predicament should send an excuse to us." It is scarcely possible to suppose that HE who would invent such absurdities as these are, *he* who would collect them and with all solemnity of purpose, as Colgan has done, in his "Acta sanctorum Hiberniæ," embody them in his folios, intend any thing else than to bring all miracles into discredit by such disgusting caricatures; and also they must have been the most beastly or the most unbelievingly satirical of mankind: as Primate Ussher has well said, they must have had a front of brass and a heart of lead.

In the neighbourhood of Ahascragh there are two fine demesnes, one Castlegar, the mansion of Sir Ross Mahon; the other, Clonbrock, the seat of the lord of that ilk (as the Scotch say). They are both very different indeed from the middlemen's demesnes I have lately described. As far as great extent, full grown timber, and roomy but not handsome houses, kept in excellent order will go, they are fine establishments. Both owners were from home, as indeed I may now say *for once* was, every owner of a fine demesne, except one, that I passed during my whole tour. I observed that the soil was poor and hungry in their demesnes. Though it was the latter end of May, the surface was covered with a thick vesture of moss. I had, before I visited this quarter, imagined that the central plains of Galway were of a finer quality of land than what I now found them. The finest oak-wood I have seen in Connaught is at Clonbrock; the timber seems to stand in its natural *habitat*, and is full grown. Part of it was being cut down, and I observed that, contrary to the Irish practice, the bark was stripped off before the tree was felled; this, I believe, is the

M

practice in the royal forests in England, and improves the quality of the timber. I saw here pheasants running along the skirts of the wood. This rare species of game being abundant here showed that his lordship was careful of manorial rights. I confess I would rather have seen a fine peasantry than a pheasantry; and I am not sure that I saw any thing like the former. In the immediate vicinity of the great house, I saw some pretty porter's lodges, &c. &c., but outside of the demesne (on land, which, no doubt was still his lordship's property) I did not observe any great improvement in the dress, the houses, or the tillage of the people. No doubt there is a slow process of improvement going on here, as in every other part of Connaught, and a change is coming over the language, and dress, and the habits of the people. Respecting this very district and property of Lord Clonbrock's, I remember being told a circumstance which occurred half a century ago, and was witnessed by a relation of mine then on a visit at Clonbrock. The then lord was getting home his year's fuel, and as was the custom, the tenantry, according to their villages, took it in turn, day after day, to draw home, with men and horses, the lord's turf; and during the process, each set of villagers got their dinners in the servant's hall; but when it came to one set, which were located far off in an island, surrounded by red bogs, and when they were called to come in to the house to dinner, nothing could persuade them to do so—in Irish, their only language, they declared that they dared not do so, lest the big building should fall upon their heads while under it. Such barbarian ignorance, if ever it was shown, could not *now* at least be exhibited. Lord Clonbrock is, I am told, a great improver of red bogs, and I regretted much that my time and engagements did not allow me to go and inspect what he has done—but when I asked was the improvement finished, is the red bog become good pasture, meadow, or tillage land, I was told that it was not so yet,* and it was more than hinted that his lordship was growing tired of his speculation.

On leaving Ahascragh and its vicinity, I was in doubt whether I would proceed to Tuam by Moylough and Mount Bellew, or take a road more to the south, and see Knockmoy Abbey. I could not see both, and, therefore, though I should have much liked to have seen the vale of Moylough, and the improvements of Mount Bellew, I decided on Knockmoy. But though not taking the first mentioned road, let me say something about it. There is some uncommonly fine pasture land about Moylough, and near it is a lake called Lough Lasarae, or the illuminated lake. This was celebrated as a place of religious rite, even in the time of paganism; and its waters are said every seventy years to possess this luminous quality in excess, and then the people bring their children and cattle to be washed in its phosphoric waters, and they are considered to have no chance of dying that year.

* Indeed, this NOT YET, is the end of almost all inquiries respecting the reclaiming of RED bogs in any part of Ireland.

Mount Bellew, I understand, is a pretty village, and there is a fine house and demesne belonging to Mr. Bellew, a Roman Catholic proprietor. There also is a monastery, and the whole place and arrangements connected with it have a Romish air. I understand that the house contains a very fine library, particularly rich in manuscripts and rare works relative to Ireland. The predecessor of the present owner was an elegant gentleman of the old school; a finished scholar, and though highly devoted to his own religion, could be hospitable and useful to Protestants, and that more especially if he found a person attached to Ireland, and desirous to acquire knowledge concerning its ancient history.

I said I took the road that led towards Knockmoy. This central part of Galway is by no means interesting;—you either pass through lands miserably cut up and portioned out into small tenures, where the people pursue their miserable tillage of potatoes and oats, or you pass through sheep pastures, treeless and dreary, divided by the transparent stone walls that you can shoot a snipe through, and which look so loose and frail, that you would think they could not stand an hour,—yet there they *do* stand,—the wind seems to think it not worth its while to cast them down, seeing that it gets a free passage through, and the cattle spare them in their own defence, lest, if they touch, they should fall on and crush them. I suppose there is some knack, which Connaught men alone possess, in the construction of these fences, which the

setting and rising sun can shine through; occasionally in this district you come to plains entirely
covered with flat masses of limestone—they look
like huge grave-yards—nothing can surpass their
dreariness, and yet they form good pastures for sheep,
for as it is impossible for the plough or even the
spade to be there employed, there grows up an extremely succulent herbage between the rocks, which
fattens sheep admirably. But independently of the natural ugliness of the country we were passing over,
there was a smoke floating over the whole surface,
arising from the burning of the soil for potatoes. The
season happened to be peculiarly favourable for this
operation, and the people were taking advantage
of it; all before us and behind us smoked like a
brick-kiln, and the smell (to me) peculiarly offensive,
was almost as annoying as that of the bogged-flax,
which salutes you towards the end of autumn as you
travel through the province of Ulster. Observing
this universal burning of the soil that was going on,
for in this inland district the poor have little else to
depend on as manure for potatoes, I asked what
would become of the population in very wet seasons.
The answer I got was, that "God was good." It
must arise from this precarious preparation for the
growth of potatoes, that scarcity is so much more
prevalent in Connaught, than in any other portion of
Ireland. It is supposable that this system of burning
the soil must deteriorate it—the ashes of the roots of
vegetables and the burnt clay can *only* stimulate. I

cannot understand how they can supply food for plants, and hence I believe it is that the people in these districts must now put up with an inferior kind of root, *the white*—the stronger and more nutritious *red* potatoes cannot now be raised. What is to become of such a population as this ?—with the lands in their own holding run down and deteriorated, so that it can only supply the poorest and weakest kind of food, will they not, unless something is done speedily, possess themselves, one way or other, of the fine fresh pasture lands now in the hands of the graziers? Hunger will break through stone walls. I deem that a Connaught wall will yet prove no obstacle before the rush of a starving multitude,—or will the new poor law find a remedy? I trow not, for why should it?

I have before observed that I took a western and rather circuitous road to Tuam, in order to visit the abbey of Knockmoy. Some twelve years ago, when much less interested in antiquarian matters than I now suppose myself to be, I had visited this interesting ruin,—and what I then saw, urged me now to make a longer and more interesting observation. The abbey is situated in a fine country, and as you approach it, you pass the well wooded and fertile demesne of Abert, where I saw, and I am sure I don't know *why* I saw *there*, deer stalking through the full grown wood, without any wall to keep them in, or any one to molest them—they seemed to range quite at their ease. I approached the abbey along a road that ran parallel to a river, on the other side of which

are the ruins, and which road divided a rising hill to
the left from the rich meadows that lay along the stream.
It was necessary to go up this road and pass westwards
of the abbey in order to arrive at the village, and the
bridge over which you must pass; and in going along
I was on the look out for some one who would come
and show me the place, and give me all the traditionary and local information he possessed.   In this instance I showed neither my usual tact, nor had my
usual success; I should have chosen some boy of
twelve or thirteen years of age, or some old woman,
the boy's fresh memory and youthful unsuspectingness
would have helped me to all the traditionary lore he
had heard during the winter's night; or the old
woman, from her garrulity, *when properly managed*,
would have poured forth all her store.   But here I
lit upon one who was singularly tall, and though not
fat—for whoever saw a potato feeder fat ?—he was
comparatively full. I, though not little, was as a pigmy
beside him; but, in sooth, he was but a lumpish animal after all—he let out afterwards that he dieted on
Connaught lumpers.   But this is nothing to the purpose, I have seen men as lumpish and doltish, fed on
bacon and beef, and allow (though I should not) that
James the First was a shrewd observer of men, when
he remarked, that as the upper stories of lofty houses
are badly furnished, so were the heads of *tall* men;
but it could not be helped, and I had as my leader
Mr. O'Connell, if it so pleases you—big Mr. O'Connell !!! With this companion, who was both ignorant

and suspicious we proceeded; and in walking along from
the old bridge to the abbey, our way was through as
fine a piece of pasture as ever my foot pressed; the
limestone rock rose here and there through herbage of
intense verdure, and you were forced to observe that
these Cistercian monks knew where to build their
rookeries and feather the nests well and warm; or
rather, on second thoughts, were they not improvers,
and might not their long and assiduous care have made
what was once a barren and waste wilderness, smile and
blossom like the rose; yes, 'tis true, they were improvers, but selfish esoteric improvers, who left the
people poor, pugnacious, and barbarous, while they
kept the wisdom, the knowledge, and the gastronomy
to themselves.

Immediately before the western entrance to the
church, I observed an excavation as if recently made.
I asked MY *great O'Connell* what that meant. He
said it was sunk some time before in search of money.
I asked were the persons successful. He said he believed they were; and assigned this as his reason, that
the following morning some gold pieces were found
lying about, and he made me acquainted with the
fact, that those who dream of hidden money, and find
it in consecrated ground, never consider that they will
have luck with the money, or grace in their lives, if
they do not leave some of the treasure near the spot
on which it has been found. Please to remember
this, good reader, in case you should at any future
time become a gold-finder. I think there is a *moral*
in this superstition worth observance.

The nave of Knockmoy is not long—it has no pretence to either beauty or grandeur. The whole place is woefully dilapidated, and shamefully deformed by the people. The choir, however, is interesting,—here is the tomb of the founder, Cathol Crovederg O'Connor; and here are the curious fresco paintings. I know of nothing like them in Ireland, except at Quin Abbey, in the county of Clare; and as we shall speak of *them* hereafter, it is as well to make no further allusion to them now.

Cathol Crovederg,* or of the red hand, founded this abbey in the year 1189. Cathol, as a brave and clear-sighted Irish prince, had seen that it was the disunion amongst his countrymen that enabled a handful of foreigners to overrun the island. He, therefore, though fully aware of the military prowess of the Norman leaders, raised a strong, and, as he thought, a lasting confederacy against them, and to this he was the more encouraged by the dissensions between the two leaders, De Courcy and De Lacy. Crovederg having made his preparations, had soon an opportunity of keeping his right hand red, for Almeric St. Lawrence, the brother-in-law of De Courcy, and perhaps the stoutest and bravest man, next to De Courcy, of his day, had, with singular temerity, and no doubt trusting to the armour in which his party were cased, ventured to penetrate into the heart of Connaught with only 30 horse and 200 men at arms; Crovederg

* For the cause of Cathol's red hand, see the Appendix.

came up with this handful at the place where this abbey now stands, and surrounded them with his multitudes. St. Lawrence saw his danger, and assured that there was no chance at all for the foot, he proposed to leave them to sell their lives as dearly as they could, while he, with his thirty horse, effected his retreat; but against this the footmen remonstrated, and St. Lawrence, though he knew there was no escape, consented to fight and die with his fellow-soldiers; so accordingly sending off two of the horsemen to a neighbouring hill to witness how bravely they fought and died, and then proceed to report their fate to De Courcy, St. Lawrence ordered the rest of the horses to be killed, and then this little devoted band awaited the shock of the Irish. The historian says, they fought all day—they killed ten thousand of their enemies, and there actually fell and died more under the fatigue of the fight, than under the blows of their enemies—be this as it may, not a man escaped but the two scouts.

It may be said that Crovederg had no great reason to be proud of his victory; but it seems he was so, and as when his Connaught men were hacking away at those sassenachs, who were as hard to kill as cats in armour, he vowed he would build an abbey. Accordingly he, under the invocation of the Virgin, founded this—handed it over to the Cistercians, and called it Abbey Knock Mogha, or the abbey of the hill of slaughter. There is nothing at all remarkable, at least as far as I could observe, in the tombs or inscriptions, which are in fact so moss grown, that unless I

had the chisel and time and patience of old mortality,
I could not decipher them; of this I satisfied myself,
that there is no inscription in the Irish character.

On the left side of the choir, as you front the altar,
are the fresco drawings that have got considerable notoriety—over the tomb of Cathol is represented, in
what I conceive to be a spirited manner, the taking
down of our Saviour from the cross. The outline of
the drawing is firm and free; and though the colours
are almost gone, and all is rapidly obliterating from
damp, and what is worse than time's neglect, wanton
abuse—yet, you may still see the features of the
Saviour, shewing the muscular tension as of one
who had died in great pain. Nearer to the altar,
and on a large compartment of the wall, are two de-
signs. The upper represents six figures, clothed in
rich and flowing robes—the one in the middle is said
to be Roderick O'Connor, monarch of Ireland. He
holds a shamrock in his hand, as the emblem of his
sovereignty over the soil of Ireland. On either side
are the princes, his vassals—one holds a hawk on his
thumb, the other a sword. The costume of their
figures is well represented, and as far as deficiency in
perspective will allow, they are executed with spirit.
Below this is a man sitting with what appears to be
a roll of paper in his hand. To his right is a young
man fixed to a tree, and transfixed with arrows; and
two archers are in the act of shooting more at him.
For a mere outline it appeared to me exceedingly spirited; and it reminds you of the frescos which recent

travellers have delineated, as copied from drawings in
the temples and catacombs of Egypt.   It is said that
this youth, pierced with arrows, represents Mac Murrough, son of the king of Leinster, who betrayed Ireland to the English, and that Roderick O'Connor con-
demned the youth to this fate, in revenge for his
father's treason.   The whole of these representations
are interesting and singular, and are well worth inspection; and the sooner they are visited the better,
for they are daily obliterating.   I have seen them
twice—twelve years ago, and lately.   There have been
great and evident obliterations during that time—the
plaster on which the drawings are made is evidently
decomposing, and even suppose boys did not, which
I believe they do, play ball against such a smooth,
and therefore *to them* tempting surface—a few years
more of time's work will efface all.   It is curious to
observe the way in which this plaster decays; it
seems to have been put on without a mixture of
hair, and applied of as loose a texture as possible—
in order to prevent cracking; therefore, it is decomposing in volutes and circles.   In the cathedral on
the rock of Cashel, the ancient plaster is decomposing in the same manner.   It has been said that this
fresco painting is not as old as the foundation of the
abbey, but is the work of artists employed by the
Roman Catholic clergy, who, in the early part of the
seventeenth century, and the more lenient reign of
James the First, were allowed to repair and re-occupy
the abbeys in Connaught.   I do not think *this* to be

the case. I agree with Mr. Dutton, the author of the
Statistical Survey of Galway, and Mr. Petrie, who
consider that they are of the early Norman period,
and were, if any thing, only repaired and retouched by
the priests of the seventeenth century, who, if they
painted any thing, would have represented some saintly
legend, or some scene which magnified their church.
The youth slain by arrows is like in its spirit, design,
and costume, what is represented on the Bayeux ta-
pestry, and other works of early Norman art.   In the
southern transept, which formerly contained two oratories, or lateral chapels, are now two vaults—one of
the French family, another of (if I mistake not) the
Blakes—both are open—the vault of the Frenches
has the property of drying up the bodies of those that
are placed within it—similar to the quality that the
vaults of St. Michan's in Dublin possess.   When first
I visited Knockmoy, about twelve years ago, I arrived
there in the evening, between seven and eight o'clock.
Proceeding along the road that runs parallel with the
river, on the other side of which the abbey is situated,
and nearly opposite it, I encountered a handsome
carriage, in which was a lady dressed out, to all appearance, for an evening party; doubtless, she was
proceeding to the hospitable house of some of the
neighbouring gentry, and had not been sparing of the
decorations of the toilet, in order to set off the advantages of her fine face and person—either her complexion was high, or " Betty " had given her "cheek
a little red."   The "tout ensemble" of this fine

woman, in all the full blow of beauty, gaiety, and pomp,
had still possession of my imagination, when I entered
the abbey.   The little boy that accompanied me
brought me, by way of a short-cut into the building,
over some broken walls, and a space that once was the
cloister, and the first part I entered of the edifice was
the oratory, in which is the vault of the French family,
and in one corner of this little chapel, sheltering themselves from the sun that was streaming in from the
west, was a group of boys enjoying noisily a game of
marbles—in the other corner, and over the tomb, was
a little figure reclining against the wall; it was of a
brownish yellow hue, it was partly furnished with skin
and dried flesh—its skull and face was covered with the
same material, that gave a horrid tension to what were
once fine features, features still so delicate as to tell
they were female.   The feet were gone from the ancle
joints—she stood upon her stumps—all under the ribs
had fallen in, and the horrid cavity was but partially
covered with torn filaments of what seemed smoky
parchment; the same mummied integuments enveloped
the limbs, and kept the joints together. The whole presented what you might suppose was a dried baboon
that had been hung over a fire until it was exsiccated
and prepared to be hung up with a preserved croco-
dile and a flying fish in the museum of some virtuoso,
or the penetralia of some mountebank astrologer of
past times.   I asked my conductor who and what this
was ?   "Oh ! plase your honour, this is Lady Evelina French, the grandmother, or great grandmother,

faix myself an't sure, of that lady who passed you by a while ago in the coach." My imagination fastened on the great contrast, and I thought of that fine plump rosy lady I had seen, coming in due time to this vault, and all her costly robes are laid aside, and her rosy cheek dries in, and her plumpness corrugates and exsiccates, until it becomes in the slow process of that horrible vault, such another shrunken, horrid, and mummied specimen of mortality, as that before me— as that poor abused Lady Evelina, who was once the beauty and the pride, and the ennobled daughter of an ancient and honourable family.

" How long, my boy," said I, " is Lady Evelina here?" "Oh sir, she is here hundreds of years." He pointed out to me an inscription over the vault, and it stated that she was entombed in the year 1686. On asking were there any more bodies in this state, I was shown where the side of the vault was opened, and there I saw bodies, reposing in broken coffins, with their flesh dried up, and somewhat of the colour and texture of saddle leather, and, while stooping and prying in, in order to take advantage of the last rays of the setting sun, something in the dark distance darted before me; you may be sure I drew back. Can, (said I to myself,) can these dried Frenches come to life again? I needed not to have conceived the silly thought—the merriment of the boys could not comport with ghosts. " What noise is that I hear, my little fellow, in the vault ?" " Oh! it's only a rabbit, your honour; the place is all out alive with them."

On my late visit to Knockmoy, things respecting this burial-place were much altered. I found boys no longer playing marbles in the oratory; they were only playing ball in the ruined refectory. Lady Evelina was taken from the corner where she had been heretofore planted as a most disgusting object of mockery and profane jest; her remains now repose in an open coffin, and are much more decomposed. The bodies are also coffined, and covered in; and as there have been no late funerals of the French family, I had no opportunity of ascertaining whether this vault still retains its drying and preservative efficacy.

In Knockmoy, you may observe the usual destruction I complain of going on; all the ornamental parts torn out of their places, whenever they could be reached at by the people—to make head-stones, and uncouth decorations for their ugly graves. This monastic establishment was once of great consideration, and had large possessions. Hugh O'Reilly, the abbott, in Henry the Eighth's time, gave up the pope, and got the property restored to him, on conditions of furnishing the king, when he or his deputy came a warring into Connaught, with sixty horse, a battle of gallowglasses, and sixty kerns—pretty strong following for a *cidevant* priest.

CHAPTER VIII.

TUAM——ROSS-REILLY.

HAVING satisfied my curiosity at Knockmoy, I returned to the village, to try and get some dinner, before proceeding to Tuam; and I may as well mention,
for a warning to other travellers who may venture
when hungry, to call for food in an unfrequent-
ed village, that I was flatly refused at two
houses, where our guide informed us we could be
supplied; at the first house we called at they said
they had nothing to give us; at the second we
were refused, because we did not, in the first
instance, call *there*, but afterwards when we saw a pot
boiling over on the fire, out of which steamed a savoury smell that caused hunger to twinge cruelly, and
when we used all the eloquence we possessed to turn
"mine hostess" from her cruelty, she condescended
to give us a share of the food she was preparing for
some sheep-shearers, and this consisted of the saltest
and toughest parts of a pig, namely, his feet, and

N

these with the hair not altogether scalded off, and bristling sharp on our tongue and palate, and only garnished, with lumper potatoes, very like lumps of bad soap, and a very small portion of whiskey to keep down the feet from tramping up out of our stomachs, formed our repast, and for this she had the conscience, and may the priest, when she goes to confession, put her to a hard penance for her extortion— I say she had the conscience to charge us seven shillings.

We proceeded across a very ancient bridge, to take advantage of a short cut over a bog, to Tuam. The bridge was one of those low-arched unbattlemented passes that were thrown across our rivers in the seventeenth century, when it was intended that in flood times the water should flow *over* as well as under the arches, which were only designed to be used in summer time, and when people *ought* to travel. We soon saw Tuam, for the tower of its new Romish cathedral called our attention as it rose above the mist that settled on the smoking country.

Tuam—no one can expect that much will be said of it; with a Connaught town it is not out of character. Of course, MY imaginative prejudices made me consider it had a Romish look—that indolent, unbusiness-like, "ne'er do weel" look—which belongs to most towns all over the world where priests enjoy much power; but as it was a fine evening, and too early to go to bed, off I started to see the great sight of the place, the Roman Catholic cathedral, and, certainly, while

approaching it, where it stands a little to the north-
east of the main-street, I felt astonished at such a
building being erected within these few years in the
poorest country, and by the poorest people, perhaps,
in Europe.   Ever since I had entered Connaught, my
eye, I may say, (except in a few instances, when
observing the demesnes of absentee Protestant proprietors) settled on nothing but poverty; and yet, here
stands a building that must have cost thousands upon
thousands.   I cannot suppose it possible that such a
poor town and poor vicinage as Tuam could do all
this? No; I suspect that all Romish Connaught, nay,
all Romish Ireland was taxed to effect this wonder.
In Tuam was built the first stone building, not a
church, by O'Connor, king of Connaught, and it was
called "Castrum mirificum," the wonderful castle.
Archbishop M'Hale is determined to have his " Basi-
lica mirifica" also, 'and exhibit what wonders purgatory can effect. The whole established church, with
all its tithes and church lands, with all the machinery
of its ecclesiastical boards, nay more, with all the
private and public influence of its valuable clergy,
could not raise such a splendid edifice as this.   No;
Purgatory thou art a most profitable dogma, and well
may we apply the Italian adage with respect to you,
and say, " Si non e vero e ben trovato."

This reminds me of an incident told me by a Me-
thodist preacher. While on his circuit through the
northern part of this province, and riding, as most of
these worthy men do, rather a sorry horse, with

his travelling appurtenances, " methodistico more," strapped behind him—he was overtaken, as he slowly jogged along, by a moon-faced, able-bodied person, the ample calves of whose black stockinged legs protruded from top boots which hung, with all their straps, in wrinkles about his ancles. This goodly man, whose shoulders taxed the black broad cloth which covered them to its full measure, was riding on a huge mare, whose feeding and whose breeding, and that part of her which the northern jockeys call the " Farewell," bespoke the abundance with which the owner was thrice blessed. One person scarcely ever in Ireland passes another on the road without some friendly accost, and, of all men, the parish priest, *except where he meets the parson*, is the most kindly in his* accostings—he does it patronizingly, for he is powerful—he does it benevolently, for he really is a kind-hearted, good-humoured, accommodating being, full of good words, good common sense, and intent on

---

* I have sometimes had occasion (and will, I fear, have to do so still) to speak disparagingly of Roman Catholic priests, and while doing so, it is with much regret, and more certainly with the desire of exhibiting the SYSTEM under which they are trained, disciplined, and constrained, than with any view to represent them as individually evil. I believe the Irish Roman Catholic clergy to be, in general, not only clever, but kind, generous, hospitable, and charitable. I believe that a large portion of them regret that they are forced to stand aloof and show an alienation from the clergy of the Established Church. I know that many, against the grain of their hearts, feel it incumbent on them to pass the parson without wishing him God speed. I know of one whom it would be a pleasure to me to name, if I did not fear that by doing so I might injure him—who has done acts of kindness, by stealth, to the parson of his parish, which were as delicate in their performance as they were beneficent in their intention, and who almost with tears in his eyes,

kind actions. So the two soon got into conversation, and "talk of various kinds beguiled the road;" but in the midst of their chat, the poor rosinante of the preacher made a stumble, and down he came on his knees, casting the rider over his head; luckily, not being much hurt, and finding his horse's knees not much worse than they were before. Reader, did you ever see a man get up after he fell over the neck of his *own* stumbling horse, who did not cast his first glance at the nag's knees. He remounted, and immediately the priest began to remonstrate with him, in a soothing way, for riding such a bad horse. "Why, sir," says the preacher, "perhaps I cannot help it—is it not a fair excuse to say, 'my poverty and not my will consents.'" "Why, who are you, if I may make so bold to ask?" says the priest. "Sir, I am the Wesleyan preacher of the S—— district." "Well, good sir, without any disparagement to your calling, let me give you a bit of advice, and that is, if you want to

solicited the Protestant clergyman not to appear to acknowledge him as a friend, or when they met on the road, lest the greeting might be observed and reported in a quarter from whence a *coadjutor* might be sent and placed *over him.* I could mention some beautiful acts of benevolence performed by this dear good priest. By the way, I may here observe that the individual independence of the parish priests of Ireland is circumscribed, and their natural good nature and desire to promote harmony and good will kept in check, not only by the voluntary system, of which they are the victims, but also by their bishops, who have assumed the power of removing the parish priest from one parish to another, which is not only contrary to the ancient usages of the Irish Church, but to the decrees of the Council of Trent. I know of no body of men so much at the mercy of others, and so little free agents as the parish priests of Ireland.

ride a BASTE that is not given to say its prayers,
which, though very proper in a Christian, is not so
good or natural in a *baste*—preach purgatory." Saying this, while clapping his hand to his breeches
pocket, from whence jingled the sound of much silver,
onward rode the man who had had his dinner at a
station, leaving the man of method to ponder how
much the children of this world are wiser than the
children of light, to which light *he*, of course, belonged. Purgatory—this is what will make its preacher
not only well housed but well horsed—it is a most
EDIFYING dogma—and all Europe and Hindostan
know it—for the Brahmins and Budhists work wonders
with it, as well as the priests of Rome.   It has built
Tuam cathedral—a monument of the ambition, shall
I say, the taste of the Connaught hierarchy.

This temple assumes the florid gothic, and yet, after
all, it is nothing at all like any of the fine old cathedrals
I have seen in England, France, or Germany. It has a
pretending, assuming, *falsetto* look—a Brummegem
imitation!!—its immensity of windows—its multitude
of little spires, spiking up into the air, put me in mind
of a centipede or scorpion thrown on its back and claw-
ing away at the sky.   I don't know how it would look
when five centuries had bequeathed it their ivy and
their lichens, and all their time-prepared tints; but now
it is any thing but chastely gothic, or soberly venerable.   I hold it, that this edifice is, like all other
ambitious imitations of foreign models, altogether
unsuited to the place, the people, or the climate.   It

is too grand for the place or people, it is too lofty for
the climate, and so it is—there *must* be a great eastern
window, in imitation of what are seen in the well
sheltered,* city-placed cathedrals of other lands, and
this great window has been adorned with stained glass,
and, doubtless, the prince prelate of Connaught was,
not a little proud of the (not dim) religious light that
streamed from the countenances, the red and blue
countenances of the saints, who stood out so gorge-
ously in that window, and illuminated his canopied
altar—an altar, by the way, though very beautiful,
totally out of character and keeping with the rest of
the building. But, alas! there was no calculating on
the blustering winds that hurtled furiously up against
that window from the north-east—and so now it is
all broken—the stained glass has mighty gaps in it,
and these gaps and "lacunæ" are filled up with uncouth
boards instead of being properly restored; and so before
one part of this gorgeous building is finished, another is
going to decay; and *there* is this fine eastern window,
the elaborate glory of the whole building, showing its
disgraceful and premature decay. But this is not all,
one would think that fate had decreed that pride
should have a fall. It was intended that a western
tower, "reaching to the skies," should overlook the
land, and "like a tall bully," put Protestantism out
of countenance and frown it out of the province.

* Few of our ancient Irish buildings are in high places, or
are lofty erections; no doubt the old architects took account of
the stormy nature of the climate.

Antwerp, or Salisbury, or Strasburg were to be over-topped by it,* but alas! it has *not* been "founded on a rock," the foundation has given way, an awful settlement has bent out of line the courses of the masonry, crushed the magnificent western door-way, so that its strong jambs have cracked and split, and splintered, as if they had been so many laths. And there they have come to a stop, and now they dare not go up higher, they tremble lest it should *all* come down. The man who stood along with me while I inspected the building, seemed to think his own character injured, and his importance lessened, by some remark I made concerning the instability of the whole edifice, and so he was fervent and fertile in his excuses for the event, and I gave him credit for his feeling, and I myself would, indeed, be sorry that any further mishap should happen to it, for may I not anticipate that the time will come when the pure Gospel of the Lord Jesus Christ, unadulterated by human traditions, will be preached within its walls. I had not time or occasion to see the Protestant cathedral or archiepiscopal palace as I passed by; the former looked quite venerable, but neither large nor imposing in outward

* As an instance of the ambition of the Irish priests in the erection of their places of worship, I may mention, that not long ago, while on a visit at Cambridge, there was an Irish architect then occupied in taking plans, elevations, &c. of the king's chapel, certainly the finest specimen of gothic architecture in England, or perhaps in the world. His declared purpose was to build a similar church in Dundalk ; either his eye was bigger than his purse, or his faith was strong in purgatory and Irish pride; such a building would now cost half a million.

appearance; a fine old gothic door-way caught my
sight; if all were like that, it would be well. The
' archbishop, I suppose I *must* say PROTESTANT, to
distinguish him from his eminence of Rome, was
absent on his episcopal duties, for though advanced
in life, there is no prelate who is more faithful, more
intelligent, in the discharge of his high functions; so
I bid adieu to Tuam without any desire ever to behold
it again, for neither it nor its environs are attractive—
indeed, I may ask, what Irish country town is agreeable?—for a day's sojourn, not to speak of a life's residence. Here is a town, once a borough, and in all likelihood to be a borough again; an archiepiscopal see, the
residence of two most reverend lords, with a population
of fifteen thousand, and yet there is no public walk, no
library, either circulating or stationary—but* (and I
use the words of Dutton, the author of the Statistical
Survey of Galway) "there is a billiard-room, and over
it a reading-room, (that is, I suppose, a room where
there may be one or two Dublin papers, one or two
provincial, an almanack, and a racing calendar,) which
is a great relief to many shopkeepers, as it takes away
from them that great nuisance in country towns, idle
loungers, who fill their shops, and frighten away many
timid country people, especially women." Valuable
use this for a library.

The country, as you leave Tuam on the way to
Headford, is exceedingly ugly—on your left you see

* I may here remark, that in the whole line of road from
Dublin to Westport, inclusive, 184 miles, there is not one book-
seller's shop.

a low flat, with a desolate lake, whose waters flow
towards Galway. I scarcely could bring myself to
believe that a lake could be an ugly thing until I saw
some of those in Galway and Mayo, surrounded by
the dreary rockiness of the uncovered limestone
wastes, or by the brown desolation of the bog; and a
turlough is still worse, that is, a depressed basin of
the limestone district which in winter is covered with
water, but which, as there is no outlet, becomes dry in
summer by evaporation, or by a swallow (as it is
called) in the centre, leaving a whitish clayey soil,
covered with a coarse weedy herbage on which depas-
ture a flock of ragged mangy sheep, or of plucked uncomfortable geese—I don't know which would be the
greater purgatory to me, to drawl out life in a town
like Tuam, or sigh it away by the side of a turlough
in its vicinity—I believe I would prefer the latter.
Give me the "bipes plume," the goose of the turlough, rather than the " *bipes implume*"—the gallant of the billiard-room and race-course.

Indeed I cannot but consider that much of the poverty, the indolence, the ignorance, and the moral
degradation of the lower classes is owing to these
gallants of the hunt, the race-course, and the
billiard-table. This province has been from earliest
time full of such idlers. Their (I may say) only occupation, stock farming, is calculated to generate habits
of idleness and dissipation. Their absurd family
pride debars from the pursuits of commerce. The
heretofore neglect of education produced a laxity of

morals; and it cannot be supposed that when the peasantry saw their betters hunting, carousing, duelling,
and given to female seduction, they would not imitate
their betters, and that more especially when the gentry
of this province were in many instances professors of
their own form of religion.   I hope and believe that
what I have just said refers rather to past time, and
to a former generation; but what I hold is, that what
the lower classes have learned from the higher, they
will for a long time retain, and that there may now be
reflected from those below, the hideous images that once
shone forth, but may now in a great measure be obli-
terated, in the practices of those above them. Charles
O'Connor, a Roman Catholic historian, observes, that
two centuries ago "Connaught was infested with an
idle, loose-living gentry," similar to those I have above
alluded to. "It (says he) then abounded with idle
swordsmen, more numerous and dangerous than any in
Ireland—seven thousand idle fellows were therein,
fit for nothing but arms, who lived upon their friends."

Mr. Laing, in his recent very able account of
Sweden, accounts for the low state of morals in that
kingdom, as owing to similar causes, "Trade and the
learned professions are held beneath the dignity of
the Swedish noblemen—they are generally sunk in
debt and poverty.   Military service and places about
Court are the only means of living their pride and
poverty can allow them to bring up their sons for;
they dance well, dress well, and have the appearance
of gentlemen, in an eminent degree; but they are

often ignorant and unprincipled—much of the immorality of Sweden proceeds directly or *indirectly* from the want of education and conduct in this class." (Laing's Sweden, p. 243.) I beg leave to refer the reader to the Appendix for what a writer fifty years ago said respecting the Connaught and Munster gentry.

The country improves as you approach Castle Hacket. You observe here a very bold and picturesque hill to the left of the road, and a handsome house and demesne of Mr. Kirwan's to the right—there is a fine ancient cairn on the hill, and also some castellated buildings and crennellated walls. I never in Ireland saw a castle on such a lofty eminence, so I asked a man breaking stones on the road what it was—he said it was Mrs. Kirwan's FOLLY—and a folly it is—she ought to have been contented with the cairn, which was, as I may say, *natural*, and in keeping with the elevation. It was no place at all, madam, for castle building. There are fine pastures and noble fields around this gentleman's house; and, as I was given to understand, there is no hill in Connaught where there are more interesting botanical specimens. My friend Mr. Mackay, of Trinity College botanical gardens, has found some rare and beautiful plants on its summit.

But this hill, which all the world knows is called Knock Ma, is not only famous for its plants, but for what is of more good and evil, at least to Connaughtmen—it is the favourite resort of fairies—the very

place which the king of all the western "good people"
delights to honour with his presence. Here king
Fynn Varrow keeps his court, here he holds his
mushroom dance, here he comes, when after his
triumphs over other " Faery" potentates he wishes to
solace himself. Nothing at all was equal to the fun
kept up round the cairn on Knock Ma the year he
overcame Sheguy Rau Cruach, or (as it is in English)
the Spirit of Wind, dwelling at Rath Croghan, (county
of Roscommon,) in a sea battle fought in the bay of
Galway. The fishermen of Claddagh can bear witness to the gleaming of the battle array as it sparkled
under the lee of the isles of Arran before the conflict
took place, and of the turbulent rush, as it were of
two seas, when the battle came on. The end of all this
was, of course, the victory of the western king; and
this was not without its blessing, for such a take of
herrings was never before or since known on the
coast—the people actually gave up collecting sea
weed. The fish were taken in such abundance that
the fields were manured with them. Blessings, then,
are following king Fynn Varrow. Whenever his exploits
are crowned with success over the other potentates of
" Faery Land," the harvests are abundant in Connaught. But this is not all—it is not only good for
all West Connaught to have a conquering Fynn Varrow
for its patron—and sure it is that the poor Atlantic
land wants all his assistance—but it is a blessing to
live near Knock Ma, and so the Kirwans have found
it. All the world knows that this family, for genera-

tions, have been great and successful horse-racers.
The Curragh of Kildare rejoices in the name of Kirwan, and every jockey and every gambler considers
that luck is on his side when he identifies himself
with a Kirwan STAKE. Who leads on to all this
glory? who has thus fortunated the Kirwan family?
It is Fynn Varrow, the king of the fairies—nay, what
is more, and there is not a gentleman in Connaught
who has not experienced the rich results—Fynn Varrow
fills the cellars of Castle Hacket—has the port a
raciness? the Madeira a smack? the claret a *bouquet?*
Fynn Varrow is said to have been the providore and
butler of all this.* I wish it had been my good
fortune to have had Knock Ma upon *my* estate. Now
it may be that there are many who have doubts of all
this—it is very extraordinary that such should exist,
when not a person about Castle Hacket hesitates for
a moment to assert it. I myself cannot say that I
know any thing about the matter, for it so happened
that when I journeyed by that place, I could not get
any one to converse with me, and the driver of my
jaunting-car was not a Connaughtman; but a friend
of mine was lately passing by, and *his* driver was all-
out-Galway, and he told the above stories with all

---

* I hope the respectable owner of Castle Hacket will excuse
(if ever this trivial work comes under his notice) the liberty I
take with his name and household. What is said is but a report of the fanciful gossip of the lower classes, who, I believe,
(as in this instance,) never consider a family or indivdual,
favoured by the fairies, that is not at the same time, and
that deservedly, a favourite amongst themselves.

the assurance of faith—no, there was not a word of
lie in it. "And sir," says he, "I know it all to be *thrue*,
for my own fellow-*sarvent*, who was groom at Castle
Hacket, tould me this." "He was one night out at a
dance, and making haste to get home before the doors
were shut, he took a short cut through a grove, when
in the midst of the wood he saw a grey mare, one of
the breeding dams, no doubt, that produced all the
fine colts and fillies that won so many plates on the
Curragh. So the mare kept whisking her tail,
mighty kind, as much as to tell Tim that she knew
him to be one who could groom a *baste* well. So
with that Tim caught a hold of her tail, and on the
crathur brought him without harm or hap until she
left him at his master's back-door just as the house
was going to be closed for the night. But this is not all
—the "good people" have an especial oversight of *all*
in the big house. Kitty, the chambermaid, went out to
spend, and why shouldn't she, a jolly evening with her
fellow-*sarvents* at a PUBLIC in the neighbourhood."
What a stupid, sorrowful, sighing-place would a big
house be to all belonging to the servants' hall, were
there, not a SHEEBEEN at hand. "Well, after a right
jolly night there, all came home except Kitty, and no
tale or tidings were of her, though up and down she
was sought for three long days; but at the end of that
time, in her own bed she was found, and all the account
she could give of herself was, that she was brought
home and left there by Fynn Varrow, king of the
fairies." My friend, while ascending the hill where the

road cuts through the fir-grove to the west of Castle
Hacket, was told by his driver all these FACTS, and
lest there should be any doubt in the mind of his
hearer, he referred him to Tim the groom, and Kitty
the chambermaid themselves, who would make him
sinsible of the truth.   Nay more, he referred him to
Mick Lynott, the blacksmith of Claremorris, for the
following *fact*.

One day Fynn Varrow was going to do battle
with his old antagonist, Sheguy of Knock Croghan,
and it was revealed to Fynn that he would have no
success unless he got his horse shod by a mortal
smith; so off he goes to Mick, for where would
he find a better than the man who used to *plate* the
Marquis of Sligo's cattle, before they went to the
Curragh? and he knocks in the grey of a drizzling
morning at Mick's forge, and he calls him up out of
bed to come in no time and shoe a gentleman's horse
who was in great haste entirely.   So up Mick gets,
and setting his little boy to blow the coals, he fell to
handle his job.   Accordingly he shod *this* leg, and
that leg, and *then* another; but when he sought for
the fourth, not a joint of it was to be found, high or
low—"Och pillaloo," cries Mick, "here's a baste with
but three legs."—"Be asy, honest man, (says Fynn
Varrow,) and don't make a noise about a trifle—it's all
my fault, and see what it is to set out in a hurry—so
with that he pulls out the fourth leg from his pocket,
which was no sooner fastened on and shod, than off
Fynn rode to fight and conquer—and you may be

sure that when he returned home, he called at Mick Lynott's and paid him well for his job, and it is with no small pride that the merriest and queerest smith in all Connaught tells how he shod a fairy horse.

Approaching Headford from the rising ground we caught some fine views of Lough Corrib; and underneath us was the large demesne of Mr. St. George, which contains seven hundred Irish acres, and is well planted, well kept, and altogether bespeaks the residential care of an intelligent and improving landlord.

Stopping at this rather pretty village to breakfast, I took occasion to see Mr. St. George's house and pleasure-grounds, and nothing could be better kept than the whole. The house is built in the fashion of a mansion of the Elizabethan days, where some of the defences of a castle are still maintained, without the discomforts of a fortress. Accordingly here, though in looking from the house you see no obstruction, and all the well-ordered pleasure-grounds lie expanded before you, yet you are in fact surrounded by a fosse, and no entrance can be had, except through an old ivied castle, which forms a sort of barbican or outwork, in excellent keeping with all around. I merely entered the hall, for I detest the process of seeing great houses. My object was to look on the portrait of Colonel Mansergh St. George, who about forty years ago was murdered by the Defenders in the county of Cork. I remember the cruel slaughter of this brave and eccentric man. I remember also to have seen him, a fine soldier-like gentleman of the old

o

school. The picture is good—the mournful attitude of the man tells as it were its own sad story; and I don't wonder that he who inherits, along with Colonel St. George's virtues, his unshaken loyalty and Protestantism, should wish to have a fosse and ramparts round his dwelling. The person who showed me the house and grounds was the gardener, an intelligent and well-informed Scotchman—one who not only knew his own business, but seemed to have read and thought much on other subjects—he evinced that a man, to be a good and successful horticulturist, must possess much general information.

On leaving Headford, on my way to Cong, I saw about a mile to the north-west, and on the banks of the river that divides Galway from Mayo, a ruin of very considerable magnitude, which I was informed was the Abbey of Ross Reilly. These ruins appeared of such extent, and had such an imposing appearance, that I determined to visit them; so leaving the jaunting-car on the road-side, we proceeded in their direction, and indeed the approach was by no means easy, for they are nearly surrounded by the river, which makes its slow sluggish bends through bog, morass, and meadows—we therefore endeavoured to keep along the high ground, and had to scramble over sundry dry walls enclosing potato fields, where the process of either burning or planting was going on; but at length, with no small exercise of our active powers, we arrived at the ruin. It fully comes up to the description given of it in an old Monasticon

which Dutton quotes—that " this place is very lonesome, encompassed on all sides with water, and is
only one way accessible, and was not many years
since preserved entire by the interest of the Earls of
Clanricarde." It certainly is the most entire of any
of the Irish abbeys—the walls are all standing, not
a breach in any one of them. One chapel even has
its flagged roof still remaining. The whole covers, I am
sure, an acre and a half of ground—and every accommodation that any monastery ever had seems here
to be provided. It is a great burying-place, but luckily
for it the choir, nave, and transepts, comprising the
different side chapels, are, I suppose, *only* considered
as holy ground, and are therefore only used for sepulture, and consequently they are the only places that
are dilapidated and purposely dismantled—their ornaments, as usual, all torn away. There were two sets
of masons and stone-cutters repairing tombs and con-
structing vaults. We found a marble tablet, containing a large, and to all appearance a poetical inscription, for the lines had jagged ends, and this was my
only means of guessing, for the marble was turned
upside down by these tasteful artisans, who, rejoicing
in their handiwork, seemed to take with perfect *non-
chalance* the hint we suggested, that by their means
the virtues of some worthy Blake, Bodkin, or Ffrench
were to remain " to dumb forgetfulness a prey."
They most Christianly felt resigned to the wrong they
had inflicted, the thing was done, and there was no
help for it. The whole of this cemetery forms one

immense rabbit burrow.*—I think I have seldom seen
a warren that exhibited so many holes. In this uncouth habitation for conies, bones, skulls, and coffins
lay all around, that the creatures had tossed about, and
by their thus rooting up, they seem desirous to anticipate the usual short time allowed for bodies to lie entombed; and, therefore, besides the common quantity
of these remains tossing all about, there was an immense heap lying outside the church, and as these
bones seemed to have accumulated for ages, and as the

---

* It is not at all uncommon to find rabbits burrowing in the
ruined Abbeys of Ireland, and the loose soil of the nave, choir,
and transepts, hollow as it is with graves and vaults, forms
a secure place for breeding and retreat. A dignified clergyman
lately related to me a circumstance of rather striking nature, that
he witnessed in a Munster Abbey. He had entered unattended
on a fine summer's eve the precincts of the venerable pile, and
the declining sun, casting its long beams through the windows,
arches, and apertures, was effecting all those beautiful contrasts
of light and shade that harmonised so well with all that was
around. Nothing was within the enclosure to interrupt the quiet
and lounging scrutiny he was making amidst the tombs, save
the caw of the daw from the belfry, or the hum of the beetle
urging its drowsy flight through the ivied windows—when on a
sudden, a few yards off, he heard an agonising squeel, as of a
being in great pain, and then looking in the direction of the
choir, he saw a weasel mounted on the neck of a large rabbit that
was thus giving its death-note as the fierce animal was sucking
out its life's blood: when, all of a sudden, and to his utter
astonishment, he saw from under the tomb, adjoining to which
the struggle was going on, a bare human arm protruded, which
with strong grasp seized the rabbit, and dragged it into the
vault. What could this be—a ghost?—pshaw!—a miraculous
interposition?—what, for a rabbit!—take courage, oh my soul,
and let us see—and it was soon explained; a mason who was
repairing the interior of the vault, seeing the success of the
hunting weasel, took a dirty advantage of the stout little
vermin, and had the lion's share.

place from the vicinity of the river was very damp, this immense "ossarium," if I may so name it, was covered with all sorts of verdure, mosses, lichens, sedums, saxifrages, and wild strawberries just showing their fruit between jaw-bones. It was curious to see skulls like wrens' nests and thigh bones as green as cabbage-stalks; the dry bones had, as it were, assumed a new mode of existence, and again served as the basis of a new life. It really was a scene on which a person might ponder and phrenologise; and I confess no collection of human bones I ever saw interested me more— no not even that far-famed congeries which at Cologne assumes to be the remains of St. Ursula's eleven thousand virgins.

The cloisters of Ross are quite perfect—as perfect as those at Muckruss or Quin; but they have not the picturesque accompaniment, like those at Killarney, of a magnificent yew-tree in the centre. The dormitories, the chapter-house, the cellars and kitchens, are all (as far as walls go) *perfect*. There the friars, living in a damp and low situation, had need of fires, and they took care to have them. I never saw such huge fire-places. The kitchen hearth would not disgrace the largest at Oxford or Cambridge. In one of the corners of a huge apartment, which seemed to be a scullery, there is a circular excavation, cased with cut stone, too large for a well—in all likelihood a place for holding live fish, which taken out of the adjoining river, no doubt were kept *here* for ready use.

Altogether, this abbey seemed to have formed a

little town in itself, having no entrance but the one,
and its walls high and thick; it was a sort of stronghold, and, no doubt, in the lawless times before the
reformation, afforded an asylum for the weak and
persecuted, as well as a sanctuary for the criminal. If
any one wishes to see an Irish monastery in perfection,
with all its "*menage*," they will, before passing on to
Cong, and before visiting the western highlands of
Ireland, take a view of Ross Reilly, which was founded
by Lord Granard, in the fifteenth century, and was
placed under the rule of the Franciscans. It, like
many others, was repaired by the Roman Catholic
clergy in 1604.

On leaving this abbey, I could not resist the desire
I had to bring away one of these moss-bewigged skulls,
in order to show it to some phrenological friends
in Dublin; and as we had no means of secreting it,
and justly apprehended that if we returned the way
we came through the field where the people were
working, we might be ill treated, (as perhaps we deserved,) as robbers of the dead, we had to keep
along the margin of the river, and not only disentan-
gle ourselves from its windings, but leap over, as best
we could, the numerous and wide drains that lay in
our way, with no small fear of being caught, and well
beaten. We, however, effected our retreat to our
jaunting-car, and secreted our skull, which may be
seen in all its verdant beauty in the library of the
Royal Irish Academy.

CHAPTER IX.

· CONG.

CROSSING a bridge over the river, which, encircling the
walls of Ross Reilly, and dividing the counties of Galway and Mayo, is called, like many others in Ireland,
the Blackwater; it falls, after passing for some distance
under ground, into Lough Corrib. About four miles
to the north-east is the bridge and castle of Shruel—
where was perpetrated one of the most cold-blooded
massacres that disgraced the bloody and disastrous
period of 1641. Sir Henry Bingham, with a great
number of respectable Protestant gentry, and fifteen
clergymen, (amongst whom was the bishop of Killala,) being obliged to surrender his stronghold of
Castlebar, for want of provisions—capitulated with
Lord Mayo, on the condition, that he and the whole
garrison should be safely conveyed to Galway. I tell
this story, in order to exhibit not only the cruelty,
but the wanton treachery of the transaction—for the
besieged had not only the assurance of Lord Mayo,

the great leader of the Mayo Burkes—but they had
the promise of the Roman Catholic Archbishop of
Tuam, who assured them of a safe delivery at the
fort of Galway; and this was not all—Lord Mayo,
the night the convoy arrived at Shruel, made the
bishop of Killala sleep with him, in his own bed.
This was Saturday—on Sunday Lord Mayo delivered up the convoy to a relative of his own, Edmond
Burke, a notorious rebel, and bitter papist—the man
who not long before, having taken the bishop of
Killala prisoner, wanted to fasten him to the sow (a
battering engine) with which he was attempting to
beat down the walls of Castlebar, in order that the
besieged, in firing, might shoot their own prelate.

To this ferocious man Lord Mayo consigned the
Protestants; and *he* having first *received* mass, as soon
as they were a little way from the bridge, fell on the
Protestants—some were shot, others were piked,
others cast into the river—even the ladies were stabbed
with the skeins of the ferocious women, who stripped
them while lying on the wounded bodies of their husbands and trying to protect them. Sixty-five persons
were slaughtered, among whom were two women
great with child, and all the clergymen, except the
bishop, who was severely wounded, and a Mr. Crowd,
who was so beaten on the feet with cudgels, that he
died shortly after. It is but just to state, and, indeed,
it gives me great pleasure, as I have spoken of this
horrible transaction at all, to relate, that numbers of
the Roman Catholic gentry, on hearing of the horrid

act, came to the assistance of the survivors; drove off the ferocious murderers, and carried the sufferers to their houses, and took care of them. Amongst others who exerted themselves in this humane labour, it is pleasant to have to mention, that the old abbot of Ross Reilly, Brian Kilkelly, hastened to the spot, did all he could for the wounded, brought the bishop's wife and children to his abbey, and for several days entertained them to the best of his means, until they were removed to a more convenient retreat. I hope it is Father Brian Kilkelly's skull that I stole from Ross Reilly. Humane as he was amongst the sons of cruelty, I would keep it in great honour, and respect it as the honoured relic of a kind man, humane amidst bigot monsters. The Lord Mayo, who so unwisely, if not wickedly, gave up the poor Protestants to a no-torious rapparee, did not live to answer for his deed. His son, Sir Tibbot Burke, when Cromwell had con-quered all, was brought to trial as a participator in the transaction, and was shot, some say most unjustly. He had this against him, that he was possessed of fifty thousand acres; this was no weak evidence against a nocent papist.

The county Mayo is no improvement on Galway. The hills and even plains become grey instead of green, covered as the surface is with bare limestone; but you have one advantage, and it is no small one, you have now the noble mountain outline of Con-nemara and Joyce country before you; and I was put in mind of the hills of Cumberland, and West-

moreland, as seen from the plains and sandy shores of
Lancashire.

Cong certainly is a rare place—it might be called
the Irish Arabia Petræa; but there is this great difference, that our place of stones is also a place of rivers
of waters.   For here, amongst hills of stones, and
valleys of stones, you hear the rushing sound of
streams through a multitude of holes, and gullies, and
caverns, where waters are now appearing, and then
disappearing, until all at once they burst forth from
under the rock, and form a rapid river rushing to
Lough Corrib larger than the Liffey.

It certainly is a singular sight. To the left of the
village you see a strong and turbulent stream gushing
through salmon and eel weirs, as it flows with all its
turbulent eddies to the lake ; then you look to the
north, south, east, and no river is seen, nothing but the
great grey ridges of limestone; and you look closer, and
you see enormous springs turning at once great mill-
wheels with the impetuosity and force of their waters
as they rise from the earth, and while those springs
start up and boil in all directions around you, as you do
not know whence they flow, so you do not understand
whither they are tending. The fact is, Cong is situated
on a neck of land that forms the boundary between
Lough Mask and Corrib; and as the whole district is
hollow and cavernous,* the waters of the upper

* Is it the case that limestone formations are more cavernous
when in the vicinity of primitive and transition districts ? Cong
is close to the primitive district of Joyce Country. The Caves
of Mitchelstown are within a short distance of the Galtee range.

lake find their way underground to the lower; but it is not only that there is a general outflow at Cong of the waters of Lough Mask, but I believe there is a manifestation of other waters—of those that flow from the turloughs and smaller lakes to the north-eastward, for I have been assured that in many of the caves about Cong, through which streams of waters rush, the level of the stream is higher than that of Lough Mask. Be it as it may, the vicinity of Cong is very interesting, and I know not where a curious person might spend a day or two more amusingly, provided he could be prepared for the calls of hunger, for I called at three places in the village before I could get any accommodation, and when I got what was most wretched, and which nothing but strong hunger could have stomached, I was charged more than what I would have paid for good fare at the best hotel in Dublin; but enough of this, and, reader, do *you* take the hint, and fill your satchel with sandwiches when you go to Cong; but in fact it was petty sessions day here, and all were so occupied about justice matters, that they had not time to think of any thing else.

It is to be observed over all Ireland, how fond the people are of trials and all things connected with litigation. Having asked the owner of the wretched public-house where I stopped, for some person to go with me to the abbey and the caves, he pointed out a lubberly-looking fellow, who, he said, would go and show me all and every thing; so, for want of better, off we started, and we had not gone far from the inn,

when a little boy, all in rags, but with a keen eye, a
most intelligent countenance, and limbs as light as a
fawn, accosted me:

"*Plase* your honour take me wid yees in place of
that spalpeen—arrah, what will the likes o' him, the
Connemara *baste*, know about Cong—no, *plase* your
honour, I know every hole and turn in it—won't you
take me?—do, God bless you."

"Come along, then, my lad;" so off we went.

"And where will your honour go first?—won't you
come to the Pigeon-hole?" So off we set to the northward of the town, near an English mile, and calling
at a miserable hut on the road-side, out came as witch-
like a hag as I think I ever saw. Her sunken eye,
her sallow smoke-dried cheeks, nut-cracker nose and
chin—then the all-bony body, over which was negli-
gently thrown an attire altogether in keeping with the
face and form—the tattered brown woolsey gown, the
short madder-red petticoat; no shoes or stockings.

On its being announced to her, that gentlemen
were come to see the Pigeon's-hole, out she came
with a wisp of straw in one hand, and a lighted sod
of turf in the other, and we proceeded down a lane
towards the object of our curiosity, which was, in fact,
a deep chasm in the limestone waste that extended
all around, uncovered by any verdure, and which, every
where, presented rock upon rock piled in solemn and
grand desolation. All around this chasm there were
fringes of wild rose, honey-suckle, purple heath,
and the palmated lady fern, and down below was
heard the echoing murmur of rushing waters.

·· The old woman led us to some steps by which we had
an easy descent, and at the bottom found ourselves in
a cave of considerable magnitude, through which flowed
a strong stream of water that seemed alive with trout,
and across which was constructed a weir for catching
eels; the sun cast its westerly light down through
the chasm; it was finely in contrast to see the waters
in one spot flashing under the sunbeams, and then
flowing darkly on, losing themselves in the obscurity
of the caverns to which they descended, as with many
a moan. To add to the picture, (and a master of *chiaro*
scuro, some Teniers or Ostade, would have drawn a
fine study from it,) two not uncomely young women
were beetling clothes below, and as they stood in the
sun-light, with its beams sparkling from their beetles·
while with vigorous arms they struck the linen at their
feet, and their sturdy strokes sent their many echoes
through the cavern—they really formed a fine group.
And then came the old woman to perform her function,
and *it* was all-important: she had with her coal, set
fire to a wisp drawn from the bundle of straw she
carried, and proceeding down along the cavern, far
away from where the sun was sending its intrusive
beams, she tossed on high her blazing wisp, and having
given it sufficient windage, until it lit up fully the dark,
mysteriously varied roof, she cast it forth on the
waters, and on it went floating and still blazing, carrying forward its light, and discovering on and on the
vaults and passages, now high, now low, eddying and
whirling, and flashing up its fitful blaze until it was

extinguished in the far distance where the stream plunged down and was lost where eye never followed.

I think I have not seen a more picturesque sight than this;—the sun beams streaming down from heaven above—the waters flashing and foaming—all where the light extended covered with the many-coloured vegetations of moss, fern, and lichens—then the old woman, like Hecate, standing on a rock where the day-light had failed to reach, and tossing high her lurid and Stygian light, which she cast with a sort of infernal grace upon the waters—all this was a picture that cannot escape from my memory. This woman, Babby Burke by name, I hope will long live to be the appropriate accompaniment of this cave, it would be no *show* without her—she is a garrulous and self-sufficient old hag, as she ought to be, and is privileged to have the exclusive right of showing off the cavern, and of burning her wisps of straw to illuminate it. She was civil and contented with what she got, and there have been few show places where I grudged less the piece of silver I gave to the poor old woman, who really forms much of the curiosity of the place.

In returning from the cavern towards the village we took our way through a ravine which was very curious. On either side were the verdureless hills covered with the grey rocks tumbled over each other in wild confusion. This hollow seemed to have once been the bed of a great river, and through which the waters of Lough Mask and all the drainage of the country to the north-east must have flowed before it found the passage under ground. In many spots you still come upon a chasm, where, far below, you hear and see a dark stream, urging on its way. On our return to the village we went to see the Abbey, and were accompanied by the little boy, Padsey Lee, and the Connemara man. Here, also, an old woman made her appearance to show us the ruins, and ruins truly, they were. I have seldom, indeed, seen a place so dilapidated. I was not only disappointed but vexed to see it so overthrown and dismantled. It was one of the most celebrated and ancient abbeys in the island, built by Saint Fechin in the seventh century, who called it his *own* monastery, though he afterwards migrated and fixed himself at Fore, in the province of Leinster; and small blame to him, for who would not prefer the green pastures of Westmeath to the grey rocks of Mayo: yet as founded by this venerable saint of great celebrity, (and truly he was a great man, if we are to believe all that Irish hagiologists say of him,) I question if any other was so thaumaturgic. What think you, reader, of his sending water right through a hill, to turn his monastery mill? But that was not so strange—he might have got the idea here at Cong, and it was not very much out of the way to teach a Westmeath river what was so natural to a Mayo one. But what shall be said of his stopping for a whole Sunday the river Liffey from flowing over the salmon-leap at Leixlip. It was also a pleasant feat of his turning a fellow with an ugly phiz into a downright beauty; or of his causing a man who in his simplicity went to procure milk for the convent—but I think I may as well leave this *absurdity* couched in the dead language in which the friarly historian delights,

"Cum vir sanctus qui ancillas ad communia monasterii ministeria non admittebat, mandaret Pastolio Coco suo ut vaccas illas mulgerit, vir Columbinæ innocentiæ Pastolus, postquam vaccas emulsit, accessit ad TAURUM sancta simplicitate existimans Taurum uti et vaccas lac solere reddere. Quod autem Tauro negavit natura, opifex naturæ in gratiam tantæ innocentiæ benigne licessit, ita quod præbuerit tantum lactis quantum septem illæ vaccæ."—*Colgan's Acta Sanctorum.* p. 137.

And now, as I have come to look at Cong, one of the most famous, and yet wasted abbeys* in Ireland, I would make an observation or two which I may obtrude upon the reader here as well as any where else, that though the Connaught abbeys suffered less waste and demolition from those who originally suppressed them, the busy and fond superstition that turned their interior into places of much-desired sepulture, has defaced and destroyed what the avarice of Henry's courtiers and the curse of Cromwell had spared; and so as there is now no one to care for and protect an Irish abbey, it, instead of being allowed to

---

* I may as well here remark, that one of the causes (independent of inferior wealth) why Irish abbeys are not so elaborately ornamented as the English and French, arises from the difficulty of carving the Irish material. In France and England they had the oolite and new red sand-stone to work on, out of which they might with comparative ease carve any tracery; but it is not so with the stone the Irish artists could command. Our limestone, though the most permanent, is the most difficult stone to cut.

repose in the much respected solitude of a Tintern, a Bolton, or Fountains in England, it is now any thing but beautiful, it is not even decent; the "*genius loci*," outraged, we might almost personify as weeping, while all around is disgraced and desecrated. Here pigs rooting, there the village boys rioting and throwing stones, making every venerable ornament their butt; every where the rank and noisome weeds luxuriating amidst skulls, thigh-bones, pieces of coffins tossed all about—yes, the once fine and elaborated tombs of abbots, prelates and nobles, wilfully defaced, or torn away to form head-stones, and uncouth ornaments of the graves where the "rude forefathers of the hamlet sleep;" and it is not the tomb alone that is rifled, but the mullioned windows, the fanciful corbels and capitals, the curious interlacings of the groined arches—all, all are torn down with an utter recklessness of the consequent ruin, and so *now* a noble pillar comes down, and anon a fretted window, the master-piece of the most elaborate chiselling, to decorate, ay decorate, as a jewel of gold, a swine's snout, the grave of some village Paddy, who will not there be left to rot unmolested for three years, until his bones are to be tossed up to make room for some other Paddy, or Biddy, whose remains *must*, for the benefit of their poor *sowls*, find a rest in such holy ground. I say, that whoever enters an Irish abbey, let him be Protestant or Romanist, must sigh for some law appointing conservators able to restrain the ignorant and reckless hands that are, day after

P

day, obliterating the religious monuments of the island.

And here let me be allowed another remark respecting the, to me, evident difference that exists between the monastic remains previous and subsequent to the Anglo-Norman conquest. Of the former we find no remains that were devoted not to *directly* religious worship, churches, oratories, crypts, and shrines, (except the round towers,* which alone seem to have answered any secular purpose;) the old Irish monastic, in his Culdee simplicity, was contented with his little hermitage composed of wattles, his humble† cell of

* " I must here add an anecdote I met with in a Welch manuscript of the Gwydir family, in North Wales, in which it appears that so late as the year 1600 the common Welch were so wild that Sir John Wynn, when he went to church, was forced always to have a watchman on an eminence whence he could see both his house and the church. His duty was, if he saw any attack made on the former, though it was always left bolted and guarded during church time, to sound an alarm. This anecdote naturally suggests a manifest use of the round towers in Ireland ; for the castle, for such was every gentleman's house, almost always stood near a church, and consequently in a country much more wild than Wales, a watchman on the top of one of these towers must have been of the greatest advantage to give alarm. I am not singular in this opinion, both Earl Morton and Bishop Pacocke concur with me—the latter had seen a long trumpet which was dug from the bottom of one of these towers."—*Brereton's Paper on Round Towers,* 2 vol. *Archaelogia.*
Mr. Brereton is mistaken in supposing that at the period of the erection of the round towers there were any castles in Ireland. But what he says applies to the ecclesiastics dwelling around their churches. A watchman in a tower must in such a country be needful. We find that at this day in Syria and Palestine the monasteries have such towers ; having, as the Irish, high-placed narrow entrances, only accessible by a draw-up ladder, in which a watchman is constantly on the look out.

† In a lake, drained some years ago, in the vicinity of Kilmacduagh, was found at the bottom a sort of hut composed of

perishable materials; living on the milk of a few cows and the fish that the adjoining river (as at Cong) abundantly supplied; enough for him was the conviction that at the approach of the barbarous spoiler he could retreat, with his vestments and holy things, by means of a ladder, into the round tower, through its high-placed door; from thence to see his humble cell committed to the flames, there to bear the privations he was so well accustomed to, until the ravagers retreated and " the tyranny was overpast."

But to return to Cong: I had observed that this abbey is all dilapidated; here, as I was informed, was the tomb of Roderick O'Connor, the unfortunate king of Ireland, who, failing of driving out the Anglo-Norman invaders, retired to Cong, to spend the last fifteen years of his life: a fit place, amongst its rocks, and caverns, and dark-flowing streams, to sigh away a life which no longer could serve his country.

Some fellow dreamt that there was treasure buried under the wall adjoining O'Connor's tomb, and he came by night to dig for it. Instead of finding the money, he threw down the whole wall, nearly killed himself, and overwhelmed what was said to be O'Connor's tomb; what was *said*, I repeat, because I believe Roderick was not buried here at all—I was shown his tomb in two other places, at Roscommon

split oak, with the interstices filled with wattles and plastered with mud—it may be supposed that this was the place of repose of one of the religious of that establishment.

and Clonmacnoise. I consider the last as having the honour of holding his remains. My little guide, Padsey, when I expressed my disappointment at not seeing a king's tomb, did his best to console me— "Come, sir, and I will show where a great man entirely entirely was buried, and his mare also."

"And who is that, Padsey?"

"Why Macnamara the robber and his mare Moreen."

"Well, come show me his grave." So over rubbish and skulls, and through rank nettles and the roots of dwarf elder, we scrambled until we came to a corner, where was nothing to be seen but a common slabstone.

"Well now Padsey, tell me all about this Macnamara."

"Why, sir, he was a terrible man—I believe he was from the county Clare—but any how he kept in those parts, for the sake of the caves, and it's very near the mountains, where he could run to when things came to the worst with him; and he robbed the world from Munster up to Sligo; and after all it was not himself that was great, but his mare—for she was the jewel of a crathur—he'd rob a man in the county of Clare, and Moreen, the mare, would carry him off in such a jiffey that he'd be here in no time. He saved his life in that way. They swore he robbed a man near Limerick; *he* swore and proved it too, that he slept that night in Cong; the judge said it was impossible he could so shortly be in two places—

barring he was a bird—it was certainly true for him,
only that it was Moreen that carried him through. Oh,
sir, sure Moreen could lep any where—she lepped up
with Macnamara on her back, into a drawing-room
window, where a company of Galway squires were
carousing, and he robbed them all, and then he bounced
out again. But the same Moreen did more than ever
she did, one day in Joyce country. Macnamara
made the snug farmers amongst the mountains pay
him what he called his black rint; and once on a
time when he was hunted out of all the flat country
and the sodgers were after him from Tuam and
Castlebar, and Ballinrobe, and he was here amongst
the caves and rocks; so he bethought him of gathering
his rint in Joyce country, and off he set to the foot
of Mamturc mountain, and he was mighty cross all
out, and not a thing would he have but the cash, no
meal or malt would do him, and gold he must have
that was scarce; so one said, and another said, is it
not a queer thing that all of us should be paying to
this rapparee rapscallion—(not a people in the wide
world fonder of money than these Joyces)—and he,
after all, but one little man, not so big as any one of
ourselves; so they all rose, and they shouted, and they
ran at him, and one man had his scythe, and the
other his loy, and the other his stone, and they were
going to murther him, and they had him hemmed in;
on one side was Lough Corrib, and on the other
was a high rock and a big Joyce was lifting his
loy to split his skull, when Macnamara gave a

chirp to Moreen, and up she sprung, thirty feet in height was the rock, she made no more of it than she would of skipping over a potato trench; she brought him out of their reach in a thrice, and him she carried to Cong, as safe as you are, master, and safer; the marks of where she landed up on the rock are there yet—the people will shew it you, if you go that way, not a word of lie in it; but may be, your honour, I have tired you about Mac and Moreen."

"Oh, no, Padsey, have you any thing more to say ?"

"Och, then, that I have; sure he once sold his mare, for he was a great card-player, and so it was he lost all he could rap or run; the devil's child, that he was, he staked and lost poor Moreen, and if you were to see him next day when the man came to carry her away, it would make your heart sick;—so, says he to her owner, sir, would you be pleased just for to give me one ride of her before she goes, I'll be bound I'll show you what's in her. So sir, do you see yonder piers?"— and here Paddy pointed to an ancient gateway where there were the remains of very lofty piers,—" Sir, the gate was up at this time higher far than a man would reach—so Mac mounted, and dashed Moreen at the gate, and sure enough she topped it in style; but if she did, whether it was that the knowing crathur had a thought in her that her master was going to give her up or not—any how myself cannot tell, but when she came to the ground she fell down as dead and never rose again. Poor Moreen's heart was broke ! and poor

Macnamara did not long survive her; he ordered himself to be buried along with her, in that snug corner, and there they are, and never was the likes of man and mare from that day to this."

"Well now, Padsey, would you like to be such a one as Macnamara ?"

"Oh then to be sure I would, but where would the likes of me get such a mare as Moreen?"

We did not remain long at the abbey—in fact there was nothing worth seeing in it, except three beautiful windows, or rather skreens that once divided the southern transept of the church from the cloister; if the whole cloister, which is now a thickly planted orchard, were as highly ornamented as this, it must have been beautiful—the carving here is most elaborately executed, and what remains forms a fine specimen of the interlacings of a florid Gothic window.

In departing from the abbey, and giving sixpence to the stupid old woman who appeared at its gate, I asked Padsey had he any thing more to show ?

"Oh yes, plase your honour, plenty—come and I'll shew you the Robber's hole !"

" What's that ?"

" Och then come along, and when I bring you to it, I'll do my endeavour to make you sinsible."—So, accompanied by my boy and my Connemara man, we again passed through the village, and entered the wild waste of rock that lay to the eastward; and we had not gone far until we came to a chasm about ten feet long by four wide, down which, when you looked, you saw and heard below, about one hundred feet, a stream urging its course.

"This, sir," (said Padsey,) "is the Robber's hole."

"And why has it got that name?"

"Oh sir, from a great man entirely that made use of this place."

"Was it Macnamara?"

"Oh no, but one of his sort—though not with his heart—for Mac, they say, was kind of heart, but this fellow was the very divil all out—now, your honour, just give me time and I'll tell yees. He was the greatest robber and murtherer that ever was known in Connaught—'twas death and destruction to travel in those days between Tuam and Ballinrobe. His way was to seize the traveller, and then bring him off the road to this hole, and here rob and strip him, and then toss him down where no one could go look after the corpse, or ever hear what became of it. In this way he stopped a fine lady who was travelling in a shay, dressed out in a gold-laced scarlet coat—a beautiful creature, going as they say to meet her husband, a great officer, who was quartered in Castlebar—well, Davy the divil, as the robber was called, stopped her on the road not far from this town, and he brought her up here to put an end to her—here, sir, the two were—she, I may say, where I now stand, and Davy beside her; and Davy says, 'Come, mistress, strip off your finery, before you go down where I will send you.' 'And where is that, sir?' says she, mighty civil all out—for the crathur saw she was in

a villain's power—'down in *that* hole you must go,
so make haste, my deary, and strip in a thrice, or may
be it will be worse for yes ;'—'wont you let me say
my prayers ?', says the lady.—'Well, and that I wont,'
says Davy, 'seeing that I know by your cut you're
a Protestan heretic—and all the prayers in the
priest's book would do you no good.' So the lady
began to strip, but you may be sure she did it slow
enough, for still she gave a long look over the grey
rocks to see if any one would come to save her—but
there was no crathur in sight but the sheep—and no
voice but the raven croaking high and hoarse, as if
by some sense he smelled of one that was about to
die. Well, my lady had taken off her bright scarlet
gown, and her fine hat and feathers; and there was
her beautiful hair streaming in the air; and all she
had now on was a little bit of a petticoat and *she-miss*,
(as the quality people call it,) of fine linen, as white
as a snow-drift on Mamturc. And now *here*
stood the lady, and there just where your honour
stands was the robber, and at his foot, as you now see
it, this dark deep running water. Well, sir, said
the lady, 'Mr. Robber, sure you are a d*a*cent man, and
for civility sake you would not be after looking at a
lady when she is doing what you are *now* forcing her
to ?' 'Oh no, by no manner of means,' says the
robber—'I'm a d*a*cent man at *any rate*'—so, sir,
very mannerly all out, Davy the divil turned his
back on the lady, and then, as sure as you are there,
my lady gives Davy a push and down he goes, with

a crash, just as I now push this Connemara boy into this hole, down, down!" and sure enough Padsey did give the Connemara man a push, which did not actually send him down body and bones, as went the robber, but taken as he was by surprise, the poor fellow's hat went down, and I never saw a being so astonished as the Connemara man was when he saw his hat go down where, if we are to believe Padsey's story of the robber, many a good head went down before now. I could not find from Padsey what became of the lady, whose presence of mind stood her in such good stead; all I know is, that after enjoying a hearty laugh at the stolid surprise, and subsequent distress, of the mountaineer, at the loss of the hat, which he declared was nearly new—and when he, almost crying, said he could never face home without his hat, for all the neighbours would be after laughing at him, I had to give him money to buy a new one, and he and I parted; and I dare say little Padsey, when he went home in the evening, enjoyed a hearty laugh at our joint expense, being both in his view simples—one for going in the way of losing his hat, and the other in paying for an old *caubeen* as if it were a new Felt fresh from the block.

I had a longing desire to see some of the rare relics which I understood were still preserved in Cong, as belonging to the abbot of this once rich and far-famed monastery. I understood from the old woman who showed me the abbey, that Father Prendergast was the last lord abbot, and that no one had been

appointed to fill his place. I was also informed that
Sir Richard O'Donnell claimed to be the representative of these once mitred abbots, and in fact was the
owner of the property, as the lay impropriator, not
only of the tithes but the lands of the abbey. Knowing that the gentleman was a sectarian, I could not
but wonder at the absurdity of one who would consider
himself as representative of the abbots of Cong, and
at the same time renounce all clerical distinctions—
what would St. Fechin or St. Brendan say to this?
But I had heard much of the relics that were in the
possession of these extinct abbots, and was informed
that a widow-woman, of the name of Moran, in the
town, who kept a shop, had possession of them—but
I was not so fortunate as to be allowed to inspect
them. I called at the house, but met with a very
sulky reception. As I said before, all minds were
occupied with the petty sessions, and my jaunting-car
equipage was not sufficiently imposing to excite an
interest in my favour.* But though seeing is be-
lieving, and is, I may say, the only means of good

---

* I have since seen the crozier, and certainly it is a beautiful
and elaborate specimen of the advanced state of the metallurgic
arts in Ireland previous to the English conquest. The name of
the artist is inscribed in Irish characters on it, and I very much
question whether in the present day any one mechanic could be
found in Ireland capable of executing such a work. The fact
is, that all over Europe, even in what were called the dark ages,
the arts conducive to the ornament and splendour of the church
were carried on in the monastic cloisters; to these labours the
monks dedicated themselves, and though there was much barbarism without, the arts were cultivated within the church, and
for its use. Of this crozier it is needless for me to say more;
before this volume comes before the public, a description will be
published of it by a much more able pen.

describing—yet I have been consoled for my loss by
the account given me by my friends, Sir W. Betham
and Mr. Petrie, who were much better able to appreciate, describe and account for them than I am.   The
relics I allude to consist of the primatial crozier of the
Archbishop of Connaught, and a reliquary containing
a tooth of St. Patrick—both invaluable, and from
both hang tales or histories, *if you will*, of no small
importance; for the Pope wishing to reduce Ireland
to a conformity both in doctrine and discipline with
the Church of Rome, sent over a cardinal with a
piece of the true cross, the highest possible mark of
papal affection, to Turlough O'Connor, king of Ireland, who, flattered by the gift, did his best to induce
the Irish prelates to receive four archbishops from
the pope, who marked them as his subjects by *his*
sending and *their* accepting Palls, as the insignia of
their submission to the sovereign pontiff.   Turlough,
instead of consigning the priceless relic to the care of
the archbishop of Armagh, consigned it to the archbishop of Connaught, intending thereby to show that
as the king of Connaught was monarch of all Ireland,
so the archbishop of Connaught should be its primate.
But be it as it may, the pope must have had, and I think
deservedly, a poor opinion of Irish intellect, when he
tried, and that successfully, to make them his subjects
by the gift of a wooden chip, and subsequently could
raise O'Neil into a rebellion by sending him a peacock's
feather.   This primatial cross, it may be presumed,
was left by king Roderick O'Connor, in the keeping of

the abbot of Cong, when after fifteen years' residence
he departed this life in this abbey. The other relic
is still more extraordinary. It is about twelve inches
square, and somewhat like the ornamented outside
of a lady's reticule, having figures raised in relief on
it, and altogether it is a very elaborate affair. Not
long ago Sir William Betham exhibited an exact
model of it before the Royal Irish Academy, and no
doubt in the next volume of that society's transactions we shall have a print of it. But the contents
are much more important than the case, for it covers
"a tooth of St. Patrick." Now every body should
know that whenever this enlightened man opened his
mouth, out came a stream of light as from the open
door of a blast furnace which illuminated all around—
and so it was that while St. Patrick was on a visit to
St. Brone, who blessed with his abode the fertile
peninsula that is formed by the bays of Sligo and
Ballysodare, and concerning which we intend, by and
by, to say somewhat more—well, while Patrick, as
needs must, not only opened his mouth to take in and
to give out—for he eat, and taught—whether in the
act of delighting himself or in enlightening the world,
out fell one of his teeth; and as it fell to the ground
it shone like a glow-worm in the night, and St. Brone
picked up the precious treasure, had it set in its present beautiful case, and it not only served as a me-
mento of Ireland's apostle when he passed away to
bless and enlighten other coasts, but it was a means
of grace and healing ever after. But in process of

time the precious relic ceased to be in the possession
of those who would, or could, use it for gracious
purposes, and in the latter days it was in the keeping of
a layman who used it for magical purposes, and some
say he employed it in the indulgence of his bad and
sensual passions—for so it was that he who owned it
could render himself very amiable in the eyes of those
whom it was his desire to please. Now, Father
Prendergast, the abbot of Cong, hearing of all this,
determined to snatch this heavenly thing from the
hands of a child of the devil; so he calls on the man
and pretends to be mighty curious to see and handle
this wonderful relic, and the owner very civilly gave
it to him to look at, and behold you, the moment
good Father Prendergast got hold of it he clapped it
in his pocket, and no threat or entreaty could persuade
him to give it up. "This holy thing (says Prendergast)
is not yours—you can show no title to it, and I can:
for Patrick was an Augustinian monk and so am I—
what was his is mine, for our order have all things in
common—ergo, his tooth is my tooth—so, sirrah, go
about your business—with this be satisfied, that it is
now, where it ought to be, in *good* hands." We cannot
say whether the man who was thus evicted of his
property, remained content, but this is certain, that
Prendergast kept it, and as the last abbot of Cong,
he willed it to a widow woman, who now has it in her
keeping.

By the way, this same Prendergast had an old chest
in which were preserved, during the dark and dan-

gerous days of the penal laws, not only the primatial
crozier, but sundry parchments and MSS. of which
he knew not the use, for at the time he was a sorry
scholar, and he thought more of questing, station-
holding, and confessing, than of studying—and by-
and-by he had occasion to go to Rome, and amongst
other things belonging to himself and his abbey, he
left the chest in charge of his coadjutor, who was
about as learned as himself. But Prendergast, while at
Rome, observed, that in the college of the Propaganda
and in the Vatican there was great value set upon
just such old musty parchments as were at home in
his own chest, and he began to talk of his property
to some of his friends of the Irish college, and his eyes
were opened, and he longed to be back at Cong, in order
that he might inspect what he now considered to be
a treasure; and when he did return, the first thing he
inquired about was his old chest. But alas! though
the chest was there, its contents were dissipated—for,
unfortunately, the curate's brother was a tailor, and
these old parchments, though here and there a little
rotten, were found to make good measures, so one
after another they were cut into strips, the coadjutor,
all the time, admiring how such useless rubbish could
be turned by his industrious brother to such a good
and professional account. And at the same time he
was a careful soul and tasty, for while he enriched his
brother with the written parchments, he carefully cut
out all the illuminations and pictures and pasted them
in a book, just like a young lady's album, and it was

with no small self-gratification he showed this handy work to his principal on his return from foreign parts.

I left Cong with regret, for though I had seen much that interested me, yet I felt assured that had I time and opportunity I might have seen and heard much more. It is a pity there is not a good inn here; I don't know any place where a person in search of curious and interesting scenery could spend time more to his satisfaction; and to those fond of angling I should suppose no place could afford more sport. I have observed that there was held a petty session, and much people were congregated in the village. Before our departure the driver of our jaunting car overheard some men, in very passionate terms, express their determination to overtake (by making a short cut) a person who had gone in the direction of Joyce's country, and who, it seems, had got the better of them in a cause that had been just decided by the magistrates. It may be right to mention that our driver happened to be a northern Protestant, who, by some chance, had fixed his lot in a Connaught inn. So when we were clear of the village, our man made us acquainted with the conspiracy he had overheard, and suggested that it would be a humane thing to take up the poor fellow on our car, and get on so as to disappoint the men who intended to overtake him; this we most willingly agreed to, and by-and-by we came up to a little small dapper man, not at all dressed like a Connaught man, but rather like a Dublin trades-man; he was accompanied by a tall, comely, and flash-

ingly dressed female, and they were trudging along
as fast as they could, for though the man was not
aware of all his danger, yet he felt he was not very
safe; upon overtaking him he was told what was
before him, and I think I never saw a person more
alarmed, or more rejoiced when we offered to take
him up with us on the car. But then he hesitated:
said he did not like to leave his wife, (for so she was,)
and he could not ask us to encumber ourselves with her;
but though we did not reckon on this addition to our
already heavily laden vehicle, yet there could be no
hesitation; so up we took them both and pushed on.
The man proved to be a native of Tyrone, from the very
same town of which our driver was; the woman, a
Dublin lass he had fallen in love with, and married
at a short notice; and this Sally of our alley was as
unfit and as ill-disposed to rough it through Connaught as could well be imagined. She sat on my side
of the car, and her whole conversation was a sigh
after the teapots and the idleness of the alley out of
which she had been allured. Her husband was employed in a very subordinate capacity in the Ordnance
survey, and the people who had summoned him to
the sessions at Cong, had brought a charge against
him for assistance they had afforded him in measuring
by chain the side of a mountain. His defence was,
that the men being perfectly idle had offered him
their services for nothing, and that moreover it was
not *he* that was bound to pay them but his superiors;
this defence the magistrates had decreed valid, and

Q

it was decided that *he* was not bound to pay them.
Getting onwards, as we did at a brisk rate, we at
length came to the turn where the short cut from
Cong met the road, and there, sure enough, we found
four stout fellows, each with a good blackthorn stick
in his hand, and certainly had they caught the narrow shouldered Tyrone man by himself they would
have finished him.   I never saw a set of fellows so
apparently overreached, or who looked so crest-fallen
as they did when our car drove by.   The driver at
once recognized them as those whom he had overheard, but they gave us no opposition, and for the
best reason, they saw we were as many as they, and
we had good sticks too, as all should have who intend
to walk over rough and rocky mountains.   By-and-
by we came to a village where was a station of the
people employed in the survey, and there we deposited
our well escaped companions and passed on.

CHAPTER X.

JOYCE COUNTRY.

THE road from Cong to Maam Inn passes over the
ridge of high land that divides Lough Mask from
Lough Corrib, and you see the best and most picturesque ends of both waters.

Across Lough Mask you see a succession of lofty
and variously formed mountains, with all their glens
and gorges, and pushing out their great shoulders
into the lake; and you see wooded islands and grey
cliffs, and between two dark headlands a long lonely
inlet running far away amongst the hills, up which you
desire to sail and to explore, where, no doubt, are sweet
solitary vales untrodden *yet* by guides and tourists; and
then on the other side, towards the south, the broad
expanse of Lough Corrib, the second largest lake in
Ireland—a water thirty miles in length, flat and uninteresting, no doubt, in some places, as indeed almost all Irish and Scotch lakes are where their superfluity is discharged by some river—but up here to the
north, having the mountains of Connemara, and Joyce

country to the west, and very lofty hills that rise to
the east, and separate it from the Galway lowlands—
it is, in truth, a noble sheet of water, here and there
studded with islands—some large and fertile, others
rugged rocks—some embattled with the ruins of
an old fortress—some made holy by the crumbling
remains of a still older church, where some Culdee
made his desert—a disciple of Columba or Fursey, or
Fechin his retreat. If such a lake as this were in
Scotland, or indeed any where else in Europe, it would
be covered with steam boats and yachts; and there
would be hotels and accommodation on its shores—and
a country as rich, if not richer, than Cumberland
would be opened out and planted and built on—but
here all is left to nature's waste, and except a planted
island, that we a minute before saw on Lough Mask,
(belonging to Lord Leitrim, I believe,)—the whole
seems no more improved than if it were Van Dieman's
Land we were travelling through.

The drive along the northern shore of Lough
Corrib is really very fine—for looking across the
water, studded as it is with many islands, you
have before you the Connemara mountains, in all
the variety of their forms—by and by you come to
where the lake narrows and assumes the form of a
broad inlet, like the estuary of a large river; and just
at the entrance is an island covered almost entirely,
so small is it, with the ruins of a noble castle, having
four round towers as flankers. It put me in mind of
Lochleven Castle in Scotland, but it is a much finer
ruin.

It was now getting dusky, and though the lake and the mountains, and the fine island and castle looked grand, perhaps grander in their indistinctness, yet I would have been glad to have seen this scene in a clearer light. I was anxious to inquire about the castle, and therefore stopped at a range of cabins that stood in all their low dirty wretchedness on the road-side, and saluting the inmates, as I always do, with the usual Irish accost—"God save all here," out came a young woman with a child in her arms, and a better specimen of a fine Irish woman of the lower class I think I have not often seen. There was a freshness in her complexion, and a laughing lustre in her eye, that made her otherwise irregular features very comely; and her figure was so light, her step so elastic and yet firm, that she seemed admirably adapted to be the mother of a fine race of men.

In answer to many questions, she, with a sort of suppressed smile, said she did not know. The Irish never like to answer questions until they see what is the drift of the interrogator; but when I expressed admiration at the beauty of the country, and the fine position of the old fortress, and how sorry I was that I could not know any thing about it, she then said, "Och for that matter she'd tell me and welcome all she ever heard about it, but how could the likes of her know any thing for sartain? The place was called Castle Hen, and all the neighbours said that it was built by a witch, who came there one night when the Joyces were driving the old residenters, the

O'Flahertys, out of the country—and she appeared on the little island with a black hen following her, which all allowed must not be nathural; but, at any rate, before morning, up sprung that great building—and then she gave it to king O'Flaherty and the hen along with it; and she told him to take good care of the hen, for that when the Sassenach besieged him, and with their boats would be keeping off all provisions from him, the black hen would lay white eggs enough to keep him from starving; and so it was the Joyces often besieged it, and tried, when they could not take it by force, to starve out the O'Flaherty, but the eggs kept him alive. But sure enough, one Easter Sunday, after a long lent, the master, poor man, was mighty craving for a bit of meat; and indeed, I suppose, the potteen had got into his head; any how, he could'nt be in his right mind, for he takes the hen, do you see, cuts her throat, boils her for his dinner— and a heavy dinner it was for him—for, from that day forth he had neither luck nor grace; the Joyces soon surrounded the place with their boats—not a morsel of meal or meat would they let near it; and you see that as the black hen was no more, he could have no eggs, and then he had to give up the last hold of the O'Flahertys in this place—he had to quit before the Joyces, and go to the wild country beyond Mamturc, and the twelve pins."

"I suppose," said I, "as you know so much about the O'Flahertys that you are come of that people."

"No, in troth, sir, I am more akin to the Joyces— my father and mother were both of that name."

" So I thought," says I.

" And what reason has your honour to know any thing about the likes of me?"

I did not choose to say that her complexion, her figure, and her light blue eye, bespoke the Saxon cross, that had produced a finer sort of *animal*.

The road now ran along a broad serpentine river that wound through a valley, on each side of which were ranged mountain after mountain, all pretty nearly of the same height, all standing like a regiment of soldiers, of the one size and uniform, dressed as in line—right shoulders forward, guarding the deep long glen. These hills seemed extremely improvable—the sides were grassy and very pasturable—the boggy parts very reclaimable, like, though not quite so rocky or lofty as most of the sheep farms in the highlands of Scotland.

After a drive of a few miles along that fine glen we arrived at Maam Inn, where we found every attention that was possible, and very good accommodations, considering the loneliness of its position.

This house was originally built by Mr. Nimmo, the engineer, when occupied in laying out the new roads through this heretofore almost impassable district. Since his death a respectable person, formerly in Mr. Nimmo's employment, holds it as an inn, and gives universal satisfaction by his urbanity, and endeavours to afford accommodation to all that call. I found a brother of my old friend Alexander Nimmo here; a valetudinarian, whose state of health had

forced him to retire from active business—I found in
him much of the information and ability of his brother,
and he seemed intimately acquainted with this western
district, and quite alive to its great capabilities.
From him I got another version of the story of Castle
Hen, and the cause of its having that name; and also
much information concerning the immediate neighbourhood.   But for the *present* I will pass by his
matter-of-fact statements, and give the reader the
more picturesque description of a young friend who
is intimately acquainted with this country.   He thus
describes the northern parts of Lough Corrib, Castle
Hen, &c. &c. of all which he seems to have a perfect
knowledge, and is acquainted not only with the
phraseology but the turns of thought of the people.

" I never saw more beautiful scenery than this,"
were the rapturous expressions that involunta-
rily escaped the lips of a pedestrian tourist who
stopped to take breath as he gained the summit of
the last craggy eminence over which the new road
from the village of Cong passes through the mountains on its way to Maam,* the only accessible
entrance into that part of the west of Ireland denominated " Joyce Country."   The road from this
descends very rapidly over a succession of secondary
hills, till it reaches the new bridge that spans the river
of Beal-na-brack,† as it empties itself into the upper

---

* In Irish, a gap or pass.

† The river of the Trout's Mouth, one of the principal
sources of Lough Corrib.

lake of Lough Corrib, which lies immediately beneath the spot on which our traveller has seated himself, and along whose sloping bank the road leads to the white-slated house that is perched, like the end of a martello tower, at this side of the bridge, "The Corrib Hotel,"* where our traveller and his companion, who, preferring the water-view of this scenery, had taken a boat from Cong, are to meet for the night. The opposite side of the lake washes the base of Laucavran, which now throws his dark shadow half across its calm waters, giving it that peculiarly sombre tint that tells you evening is approaching; in the distance the Connemara and Joyce country mountains bound the horizon, with their blue tops accurately defined, against the pinkish sky that marks the declining sun. Although the lake was smooth and tranquil as a mirror now, yet an occasional scud would ruffle its silver bosom in long wavering lines, as some fitful gust would rush down one of the mountain gorges by which it is surrounded.

One solitary rock raises its head in almost the centre of the water, on which stand the remains of an old castle that adds much to the beauty and romance of the view, and upon which the traveller's eyes now rested, as his guide, a bare-legged gossoon from 'beyant the wather,' was making a most accurate investigation of the contents of a horn of Honor Casey's potteen from the bridge of Cornamona.

* Built by A. Nimmo, while making these roads.

Being perfectly satisfied as to the purity of the liquid, (that is, its containing no water, viteril, or parlimint,) he drew a long breath, smacked his lips, wiped them by performing a circuitous revolution round three inches of his mouth with a tongue of no ordinary dimensions, much in the same manner that a cow licks her nose. He screwed up the left side of his face into a paralytic grin, by bringing into very close contiguity the corners of his mouth and eye, and finishing by leisurely drawing the back of his bony hand across his unshorn mug, he commenced :

"Ah! then, may be your honour doesn't know that's 'Chrislane-a-Kirca?'" "No, indeed, my man, and what old ruin is it, may I ask?" "Och! then, I was just thinking as much—an' it isn't every body could tell you about that same. Sure it's one of Grania's ould castles, an' a fine antiant place it is." "I dare say it is, but what may be the meaning of that long, outlandish name?" "The manin', your honour! I'll tell you that—'tis the Hen's Castle." The Hen's Castle!! How strange—what an odd name! pray was it saved by the cackling of one, like the goose in the capitol of Rome?" "A capital room, your honour, och then there was, an' a many a room, I'm sure, an' a big bawn*—in—in—in the middle of it—'tis fine times thim O'Flahertys had of it, the murthering thieves—an' plenty of geese too, your

* A term applied to any large building, whether ancient or modern, with a court or enclosed place within.

honour, I'll be bail—though sarragh one bud it's a cowld an' a lonesome place enough now—myself does'nt know how thim lives in it at all, at all." "You surely don't mean to say that it is inhabited?" "Ah! then to be sure it is—doesn't Thomassheen Rua* and his mother live in it?" "Rather a cold, bleak place to live in, certainly," said the gentleman, in a musing tone. "Why then your honour's not far out there eather—'tis cowld enough, in troth—but she's a lone widdy, that was dispossessed jist three years agin Patreckmass nixt, by that ould curmudgeon Anthony Skinflint, me lord's agint,† a sweet bad luck to him for a nagur—because as how, you see, Thomassheen wouldn't give a day's duty to the driver futtin' the turf‡—more oetoken sarrah day's luck the same man had since, an' what's more, he never will, I'm sure an' sartin, nor any body else that had the same turn done to thim an' they in the wrong. The Lord betune us and harm this blessed evenin'—but I'm thinkin' the same stone isn't right."

The stranger's curiosity was so much awakened by these mysterious hints, and the guide's most devoutly crossing himself, that he forgot all further inquiries about the old castle to know the particulars of the driver's disaster.

* Red Thomas.
† The Earls of Leitrim and Charlemout own a large tract of country about here, but as they are co-heirs, their tenants know them but as one person under the above title.
‡ One of those abuses by which drivers and under agents make each tenant give them so many days' work.

"Wait a minit, your honour, till I kindle the pipe, an' I'll tell ye all about it, an' it's many a time I hard tell of the same stone from Cathreena na Month,* me unkle Jim's brother's shisthur, God be marciful to her sowl this night—Amin.

"Well—it's there behind ye upon the top of Ben-levi—sure, the whole country round knows the place." "Yes, but what is this place you speak of, or what has that to do with the driver?" "Asy yet, your honour, sure it's the Lac Fecheen I'm telling you of—a great big stone that's lying there, like a grave stone—and nobody yet could tell how it came, or who brought it; but there it is, sure enough, as if it fell out of the sky, for all the world—so whiniver any two factions has a fallin'-out, or the villages bees quarrelling among themselves, or any of the neighbours does have a bickerin' about the mearins, or the likes—an' that Shaun Justice,† or Shaun a Bawnia,‡ doesn't settle betwixt them, or that one of them bees a tinant, or clewin‖ of the MAGISTRATES, an' they get no satis-faction at the court, or may be it's two of the Col-loughs§ that would be belyin' other, or spreadin' bad reports of any of the little girls, an' sayin' they were

---

* Toothless Kate.

† Another " Big Joyce," as remarkable for his litigious, as John for his pugnacious propenities.

‡ Two of the Joyce Country legislators, to whom are referred all disputes, whether public or domestic.   The latter, a notori-ous character, of whom more by-and-by, of Herculean size, well known as King Joyce.

‖ Relation or follower.   § Old woman.

not better than they ought to be, or no matter what
'ud be the rason of it. Well, whin the cojutor, or Father
Mike himself, wouldn't be able to make pace atween
them, then ye see, it's the devil mysel thinks that 'ud
be a timptin' thim; but howsomdever one of thim' id
go to the Lac Fecheen an' turn it upon the other in the
name of the dioul, (Lord save us,) an' prayin' that
they might have *his* curse, an' the curse of the Lac
Fecheen upon thim afore that day twelvemonth, an'
thin he'd turn the stone upside down. An' ·as sure
as you'r a livin' man there this blessed evenin',
whoever was a-roguin' the other, eather himself or
some one belongin' to him 'ud surely die—or, if none
of the people died itself, the cattle 'ud get the dry
murrain—or the smut 'ud be on the corn—or maybe
it's the barn that 'ud take fire, or some other bad luck
'ud happen to thim for sartin—so it's two eyes worse
nor the court, or the skull,* or the priest himself,
barrin' he put out the candles upon ye."

"Did Thomassheen turn this fatal stone?"

"Entroth an' he did, your honour, for sure an'
sartin, go an' turn it upon him—an' it wasn't long
after till the milsh cow got into the afther-grass, an
was atin' it till she fairly burst, your honor, an' she
only within six months of calvin'—an' sarrah one of it
stopt there, for the shurroft† followin' his shusthur's
child—a young gorlough‡ in the cradle, died of the

---

* The swearing by a skull, a bible, and a bunch of keys, is
one of the most approved methods of solemn adjudication
among many of these people.

† Shrove-tide.   ‡ A young infant.

small-poc, that Shaun Airough, the Knock-a-latin
doctor, gave it—an' sure we all know that no one ever
died after the same man's lucky hand afore or since;
bud 'twas jist the curse of the Lac Fecheen that was
upon him—he be to go—'an that wasn't all, for he
tuck to liquor, an' grew so mortial fond of it that he
began to try his hand at the distillin', an' all the tin-
ints were aforced to give him a lock of corn, or he'd
be drivin' an' poundin' every other day*—well divil a
bit bud he was goin' on ever, ever at the whiskey, till
they cotched him in the long run—for one fine Sunday's mornin', a week afore Lint, jist as the neighbours
were clenin' themselves for airly mass, such a phillaloo-
murther-shout as we hard. An' who should be a
comin' down the Hill of Farah bud thim bloody-willi-
ans the rivenew peelers' (thim putteen huzzah's, as
his rav'rence calls thim,) an' sazed every thing he had
in the wide world, tatterin' an' tarin' every where,
t'would bring the tears in your two eyes to see thim
makin smithereens of the darlin' fine copper still, an'
dancin' upon it in the middle of the road. They took
the driver off to Galway till they lodged him in the
stone-jug, bekase as how he was so bastly drunk that
he couldn't run away like the rist of thim. An' sure
myself was med a preznor of too, and I only standin'
in the still-house doin' nothin' at all, only lestnin' to
Maurteen Brannagh, the dishtiller, tellin' about the
roocaunt that was in Gurtnaclossagh the last coort

---

* This is a well-known fact in many parts of the west.
† A disturbance.

day, an' 'tis well I ever got out of the same chaps, only the masther, long life to him, had the captain to dine wid him, when they came to swear agin us, an' he let me off."

"Well, but what became of the driver when he got out of imprisonment!"

"The driver—little good, your honour, for it's worser and worser he got 'till he was fairly on the shoughraune, an' aforced to give up entirely. He had'nt the rint, an' the land was goin' to the bad, an in the long run he had to cut his stick—for he hadn't a pin's pint in the varsal world—so comin' on harvist he wint away to England as a spalpeen with his traheens* upon his arms, an' his farleys† upon his back, lavin' the wife to keep house till he came home agin. Bud ould Anthony was too cute for them—for he wint an' sould all the poor crathurs had. Ay in troth, from the skeehogue‡ that the born infant was in to the blankit that was over thim, pots an' all—an' she had to take the bag—and is beggin' the world now—so you see what it is to have the curse of the Lac Fecheen upon a one."

"And what brought this Thomassheen, as you call him, to live in the old castle?"

"Jist this, plaze your honour. Bud I'm thinkin' that we hav' a betther be movin' on atowards the lodge§ for it's gettin' late, an' tisn't clear to me bud we'll have

* Legs of old stockings.   † Oaten cakes.
‡ An osier basket for straining potatoes.
§ The hotel is so called by the people.

a hard night of it—look at the squall that's comin'
out of the gap foreninst ye—an' we'll be talkin' along—
people say it shortens the road." It was full time to
go. The sun had sunk down behind the hills, and
the lake, that heretofore presented an almost unruffled
surface, in a few minutes became white with foam, as
the wind rushed from the lower lake thro' the narrow
pass with such fury as to lash the waves for many
feet up the walls of the old castle, while the upper
part of the lake was as smooth as when it first
struck the stranger's view—a rough white crest, like
a wall, defining the extent of the squall as it broke
upon the placid water, and already as it reached the
utmost limit of the lake at Maam it was becoming
calm and smooth, as the swell it left rolled slow and
measured to the pebbly shore at its margin. This is
no uncommon event here, the height of the hills surrounding these lakes, and the frequency of the valleys
and ravines collecting the wind and allowing it to
rush over the lake in detached squalls make sailing
here very dangerous at times. The water may be
perfectly smooth one moment and the next a perfect
hurricane. Sometimes these squalls will be accurately
circumscribed, not covering a surface of more than a
few hundred yards, driving with the greatest fury,
till they encounter one of the numerous islands, or
expend their violence across its whole breadth. It
was on one of these, rushing out of this very gap from
the upper lake, that a gallant officer, the Hon. A. B.
and two boatmen were drowned in the autumn of 1830.

The lower lake was comparatively calm, and they were making a tack across the gap with (it is supposed) the sheet belayed, when the squall struck the boat upon her beam, and she sunk within view of his brother, Lord K. But to continue our friend Barney's story of the widow and her son :

"Thomassheen, after he turned the Lac Fecheen wasn't himself for a long time. People say that no one was ever right after they had any thing to do wid it, for I'm sure it belongs to the 'gentry'—the 'good people,' you know. Bud Thomassheen was a fine, hearty, rollikin' blade, that didn't fear much for pishrogues,* or thim kind of things, an' as clane a boy as ever stood in the face of a loy,† or handled a blackthorn at the fair of Funchanough, an' that same puts me in mind of the rason he's in the ould castle to-day.

"Ye see there was an ould bickerin' betune the Walshes and the Mulligans, on account of a girl of the Walshes bein' taken off by Patsheen Gow‡ that lives at the cross-roads, an' she goin' to be married to Shamus Phaddy Shamus Brannaugh, a boy of the Walshes, your honour—an' when they couldn't get Patsheen Gow, they said they'd be revenged upon the Mulligans, for Patsheen was a clevin of theirs—an' well become them, bud at the fair of Funchanough there was a great gatherin' entirely, for the fight was expected, an' the army from Galway—bekase as how

* Fairies.   † Spade.   ‡ Paddy the Smith.

the polis was fairly licked clever an' clean out of the
pattern of Headford the Sunday fortnight afore.   So
there was a great faction of the boys, an' Thomassheen
Rua was in it too, an' helpin' the Walshes, for he had
an ould grudge agin Patsheen for swearin' to the track
of his ass's shoe that was found in Felix Mulcahy's
oats, an' there they were hoshin' and clearin' the whole
street afore them, an' darin' one of the breed of the
Mulligans to show his nose—and in the clappin' of
your hand there wasn't a tent or a standin' to be seen
in the whole fair.

"The Walshes had it all their own way, for the
others got afeard and ran away, or wint a hidin' in
the houses.   Bud as ill luck 'ud have it, they
mit an uncle of Patsheen's first cousin's, an' they
set to batin' upon him, an' sarra bit of this world's
bread ever he'd ate weren't it for so many of them
that was in it, and all strikin' together, you see they
were hindrin' one another's blows.   Bud at last the
sodgers cam up, for the polis was afeard of the
stones that was flyin' as thick as hail, an' the magistrate rid the act, as they call the newspaper he took
out of his pocket—an' whin the sogers was tould to
fire upon them, in a jiffey they all med off across
the bogs to the lake, where the army couldn't git.
Ough!! Bud it was a mortial beatin' that the same
man got.   I hard tell, he was so bad that he had to
be anointed afore night, an 'twas the opinion of
Judy Mullowney an' every body, that the priest
wouldn't overtake him alive, for he was speachless, an'

when the doctor came he took the full up of my two
fists of his skull out of him that was as small as paas,
'twas a many a day afore he was off the broad of his
back, an' troth the same man isn't right in his head
since.

"Bud, sir, to tell you about Thomassheen. There
was a woman under a cart while the strikin' was goin'
on, an' she came an' swore that it was Thomassheen
Rua that was headin' the boys: so with that same, Mr.
B. sent a warrant after him, an' he was aforced to be
on his *keepin'* for a many a day, bekase the peelers
used to be watchin' him at every wake and prin-
kim that was in the country. Bud Thomassheen
an' his mother were livin' in the ould castle there below,
unknowen'st to any one bud a couple of the neighbours. Well, at long run the sick man got better,
an' they made it up about a quarter ago; an' though I
say it, that's a cousin garmin of his aunt, there is not
a better warrant to shoot a phillaseen,* or to land a
trout upon the borders of Lough Corrib, an' there he is
livin' in the castle from that day to this, fishin' and
divartin' himself, an' sarra wan of the peelers itself
axes to mind him; though there was a summons sent
for him the other day for spearing a salmon, (an'
small blame to him, poor boy,) but that Pauck O'Neal,
the barger, is the dickins itself."

"Well, but, my man, I want to know all about this
Hen's Castle."

* Plover.

Barney's, narrative being rather disjointed, and
occasionally digressive, we shall here render it into
plain English for the benefit of those who may not
be conversant with the peculiar phraseology of the
lower order of Irish:—

Castle Hen, of which the above is a representation,
is generally supposed to have been one of the inland
castles of Grana Uaile, or Grace O'Maley, in whose
time the fortresses around this secluded spot must
have been almost unknown, if not inaccessible. Tradition says it was held by one of the O'Flahertys, who
owed fealty to this chieftainess, and it is even supposed by some that it was here the heir of Howth
was carried when stolen by the O'Maleys as a punish-

ment for the inhospitality of his parents, and only
restored upon condition of the gates of Howth castle
remaining open during dinner time. Be this as it may,
this castle, at the period of our history, was in possession of O'Flaherty—but whether the soubriquet of
"Na Cullugh," (the cock,) was applied from his
great personal courage, or his quartering a "Gallus
Gallinaceous" upon his escutcheon, history is silent:
suffice it to say, that he was known as O'Flaherty na
Cullugh, and at constant war with the Joyces, by whom
he was surrounded, each party looking upon the
other as an intruder.

As long as they feared the assisting arm of the
chieftainess of the west, O'Flaherty remained the
victor; but upon the death of that heroine, O'Flaherty
being reduced to his own resources, the Joyces began
a most fearful retaliation, and much blood was spilt
on both sides. At length O'Flaherty and a few of
his followers were surprised upon a hunting excursion
in the neighbouring mountains, cut off from the
castle, and O'Flaherty na Cullugh slain.

The Joyces now imagined the castle theirs; but
though the cock was slain, his wife defended it with
the greatest skill and heroism against all their attacks,
acquiring for her the title of "The Hen." Hence
the real origin of Krishlane na Kirca.

History or tradition is silent upon much of the
after life of this lady. Some say the Joyces made a
road into the castle, and demolished both it and its
inmates. There certainly are the remains of a rude

causeway leading from the nearest point of land towards the island, which can be easily seen on a clear day. We know that Lough Corrib has risen much, owing to the number of dams, &c. that obstruct its fall toward the sea. Besides, it differs from other lakes, in being more a congress of water from a number of rivers running together and subject to increase from obstructions to drainage and other causes; it seems more than probable that this causeway was once above the level of its waters. So far my friend.

Before I go farther, I shall narrate one or two incidents connected with the singular superstition of the Lach na Fecheen:

Peggy Griffin was as smart, merry, well-made a colleen as any in the hill country—no girl would foot it so well at a wake-dance, no one could say a smarter thing when accosted by the boys, none so kind to those she liked, none so vexing to those she would put a slight upon. Her sharp black eye, her pertly, though prettily turned-up nose, the pouting lips of her own large but expressive mouth, her red hair—all bespoke the ardent temperament that must love or hate in excess. Now amongst many admirers Peggy had but few lovers, for the truth was, the men were afraid of her. But Billy Mongan was less considerate, and more taken with her winning way, for the light of her eye was upon him, and though she was *often* saucy to others, she was ever sweet upon him. Thus the courtship went on, and though all the neighbours thought they were engaged, so it was that Will had never yet put the important question, which seemed every now and then on the point of his tongue: "Peggy will you marry me," had never yet been said.—Thus went on the time, until all of a sudden the lover's attentions ran cool. Instead of meeting at every time and turn possible, William was now never in the way; and it was soon ascertained that he had fixed his inconstant affection, or rather, it is feared, his more prudent speculation, on a girl whose father had lately died, leaving her, his only child, a farm well stocked with cows and sheep. The result was, that Peggy was altogether deserted, and the match soon made and consummated, that made William the husband of an heiress, and a comfortable farmer. The poet says, that "Hell holds no fury like a woman scorned." So it was here: Peggy Griffin was just the person to feel and act the fury; and she *would* avenge herself, and *that* at the risk of all that was valuable in life or fearful in eternity; and though aware, as she was, that if she resorted to Casey's sword, (as it is sometimes called,) and went through the terrible rite of turning the Lach na Fecheen, no petition of her's for good or evil would ever be attended to, and that God and devil would be deaf to her ever after—yet she did go through with it: she fasted three Wednesdays and three Fridays, eating nothing but barley bread mixed with sand—she performed what is called τopaꞅ τſoꞃıll, or the "backward station," that is, the creed and the paternoster she said carefully BACKWARDS, in the name of the devil, and then

she invoked every curse for time and eternity on her
false lover, his wife, and all belonging to him. The
results were terrible. Mongan's wife wasted away, the
victim of slow, withering consumption; and his property melted gradually as snow on the side of a ditch
in February; and then he died himself of a slow fever.

And what became of Peggy Griffin?

There is a poor, witless vagrant that wanders through
these hills—she is almost naked, as to the covering that
would shelter her from the elements, but she has a few
faded ribbons flaunting through her half-red, half-grey
hair—she seldom enters a house, but snatches, as it
were by force, a few potatoes that are left out for her
when she is seen to come near a village; she is observed
often kneeling beside a holy well, but her prayers are
mixed with curses, and she howls out an angry
expostulation against God and the devil, because they
must not hear her. She lodges, in summer, wherever
she can find any ivy-mantled old ruin—she speaks to
the ghosts that she says are all around her, but can
do her no good or harm—in the winter she hovels
with the cattle in some lone hut—wherever she goes
the children fly from her, and the pious cross themselves. Such was Peggy Griffin some years ago, the
practiser and victim of this horrible superstition. It
is believed (for she has not for some years been seen)
that she has gone to "where the weary are at rest."

Another circumstance connected with this dark
superstition has been communicated to me by the
young friend, Doctor Wilde, who supplied me with

the narrative concerning Thomassheen, and the Hen's Castle. There is a man living in Joyce Country, who, from the number of bullocks in his possession, is named Paurick na Mullaun. This man, though pasturing his flocks and herds on many a hill, is perfectly illiterate, and speaks no language but the Irish; he is of ungovernable passions, and has never yet spared any means pecuniary, physical, or, it may be said brutal, to attain the gratification of his desires. When attempts at seduction or abduction have failed, he has arrived at his end by means the most abhorrent. Living in the fastnesses of this district, his establishment is like that of a Turcoman Aga, and his bawn or farm-yard is surrounded by cabins which he has found necessary to erect for his numerous females, who thus being kept in separate lodges, are, in some measure, but not altogether, kept from cabals, feuds, and fightings. Scarcely a month elapses but the magistrates of the adjoining petty sessions have their time occupied by complaints laid by the respective women of this harem against their lord and against their frail sisterhood. For this strong man—strong in his position, strong in the powerful faction to which he belongs, makes no difficulty in divorcing one wife to marry another, and is in fact as great a polygamist as any moslem. A few years ago this man was accused of some nefarious deed, and on this occasion most characteristically chose not to clear himself by a legal trial, but by resorting to the wild justice of Casey's sword. He *would* turn the Lach na Fecheen

to prove his innocence. Accordingly on an appointed
day he resorted to the spot attended by a man whose
business it was to act as a sort of priest at this wild
rite, and show the adventurer how he was to turn the
stone, and what to say upon the occasion. Now so it
was that Phaurick na Mullaun's courage, when it came
to the sticking point, altogether failed, for he felt his
guilt, and knew that if he invoked the terrible curses
of the Lach na Fecheen, something horrible would
await him; so he proposed to his companion to act as
proxy for him, and offered him half-a-crown for the
job. It would appear that this substitution was not
unusual, for the man readily undertook, for the promised
payment, to repeat the necessary prayers, invoke the
awful imprecations, and turn the stone in the name of
Satan. Accordingly the whole was gone through, and
no immediate mischief ensued—the proxy's neck was
not twisted awry—his face was *not* turned round to
his back—there he stood demanding the promised
hire which Phaurick, base man, refused to pay, and
would have put the whole thing off as a joke; but this
did not satisfy the proxy, a scuffle ensued, a fierce
wrestle came on, and though Phaurick na Mullaun
was stout, yet the wild Joyce was stouter, and besides
Phaurick had on a neck-cloth, inside which his antagonist fastened his left hand, and with his four
knuckles squeezed upon his windpipe, got him under,
and then he, choking, lay, his back on the Lach na
Fecheen. To save his life then, Phaurick promised,
with an oath, the repayment of the hire, and, on being

let loose, they both adjourned to a neighbouring public-house, and it was agreed that the half-crown should be spent on whiskey: a quart of which, when produced, Joyce took up, applied to his mouth, and attempted to swallow at a draught, and in the act suddenly dropped dead. There is no doubt but that the spasm of the *epiglottis*, or trap-door of the windpipe, was the cause of the fellow's death; but all the people round attributed it to his being proxy for Phaurick; in confirmation of which Phaurick made off into the mountains, and a coroner's inquest was summoned. My friend, who as a medical practitioner residing in the vicinity was called in professionally on the extraordinary inquest, says that the scene was most imposing. The body exposed to view at a short distance from the fatal stone—the smiling lake beneath—the surrounding mountains, reposing in all the changeful varieties of light and shade—the occasional keening of the wild mountain women—loud voices, at times, of the leaders of the rival clans, as they passed their conflicting judgments on this fatal occasion; all this was calculated to fasten on the memory, and there leave a vivid impression of the Lach na Fecheen.

I was given to understand by Mr. Nimmo and the innkeeper that the people in Joyce Country were in general much more comfortable than in other parts of Connaught—that the population was not so excessive, the farms larger, and the rents not at all high—and that there was a great deal of wealth, not only

in stock, but in hoarded money amongst these mountaineers.   I also was informed that there was much
ignorance and contented destitution of all that a
better informed people would call comforts, so that a
man when he became wealthy did not by any means
exhibit it in his living, his house, or furniture.
With plenty of stock of all sorts, they never indulged
in animal food—even their own butter or pigs they
would not touch, but converted all into money,
which, when procured, was simply hoarded, hid in
some secure place—and the idea of making interest
on it was quite out of the question.   Such a proceeding was not according to their general distrustfulness,
or the determination to do only as their fathers before them did; in fact, the *only* way to come at
the hoard was by the management of the daughters,
who contrived it so, that some young fellow should
run away with them, and keep them stowed away in
some secret place, until the father, fearful of the good
name of his family, came down with the hard cash,
and that in no small measure, to make his COLLEEN
(*Anglicè*, girl) an honest woman.   From what I have
thus heard I should suppose that the people of this
district are amongst the least educated of any in
Ireland.

I asked if there was there much illicit distillation.
I was informed that there was not much at present,
but that heretofore it was very prevalent, and that
there was no small ingenuity, as well as perseverance, practised in eluding detection.   Mr. Nimmo

told me one of the best anecdotes I have heard on this rather trite subject.

A man who was known to have a large mountain farm and extensive homestead in these hills was observed very frequently to ride into the town of B———, and he never made his appearance without a woman, supposed to be his wife, jogging steadily and uprightly on a pillion behind him. He was tall and gaunt in look—she large and rotund, and encumbered, as is the mode of all country wives, with a multitude of petticoats; they always rode into the yard of a man who kept a public-house, and before they alighted off their horse, the gate was carefully shut. It was known, moreover, that this publican acted as factor for this farmer in the sale of his butter, and so for a length of time things went on in a quiet and easy way, until one day it so happened (as indeed it is very common for idlers in a very idle country town to stand making remarks on the people as they came by) that the gauger, the innkeeper, and a squireen were lounging away their day, when the farmer slowly paced by, with his everlasting wife behind him. "Well," says the squireen, "of all the women I ever saw bumping on a pillion that lump of a woman sits the awkwardest; she don't sit like a *nathural* born *crathur* at all; and do you see how modest she is, what with her flapped down beaver hat, and all the frills and fallals about her, not an inch of her sweet face is to be seen no more than an owl from out the ivy. I have a great mind to run

up alongside of her and give her a pinch in the toe,
to make old buckram look about her for once. "Oh,
let her alone," says the innkeeper, "they're a dacent
couple from Joyce Country. I'll be bound, what
makes her sit so stiff is all the eggs she is bringin'
in to Mrs. O'Mealey, who factors the butter for them."
There was while he said this a cunning leer about the
innkeeper's mouth, as much as to denote that there
was, to his knowledge, however he came by it, something mysterious about this said couple; this was not
lost on the subtle gauger, and he thought it no harm
just to try more about the matter, and so he says in
a frolicsome way, "Why then, for cur'osity sake, I
will just run up to them and give the mistress a
pinch—somewhere—she won't notice *me* at all in the
crowd, and maybe then she'll look up, and we'll see
her own purty face." Accordingly no sooner said
than done—he ran over to where the farmer was
getting on slowly through the market crowd; and on
the side of the pillion to which the woman's back was
turned, attempted to give a sly pinch, but he might
as well have pinched a pitcher; nor did the woman
even lift up her head, or ask who is it that's
hurting me. This emboldened him to give another
knock with his knuckles, and this assault he found
not opposed as it should be by petticoats and *flesh*,
but by what he felt to be petticoats and *metal*. This
is queer, thought the gauger—he now was more bold,
and with the butt-end of his walking-stick he hit
what was so hard a bang which sounded as if he

had struck a tin pot; "Stop here, honest man," cried the gauger. "Let my wife alone, will you, before the people," cried the farmer. "Not till I see what this honest woman is made of," roared the gauger. So *he* pulled, and the farmer dug his heels into his colt to get on, but all would not do—in the struggle down came the wife into the street, and as she fell on the pavement the whole street rang with the squash, and in a moment there is a gurgling as from a burst barrel, and a strong smelling water comes flowing all about—and flat poor Norah lies, there being an irruption of all her intestines, which flowed down the gutter as like potteen whiskey as eggs are like eggs.

The fact was, that our friend from the land of Joyce had got made, by some tinker, a tin vessel with head and body the shape of a woman, and dressed it out as a proper country dame—in this way he carried his DARLINT behind him, and made much of her.

As a pendant to this story, I am disposed to narrate another Connaught story about a woman and a pillion, which, if it did not happen in Joyce Country, occurred not far from it, in the county of Galway.

About the commencement of the present century, the Connaught secondary gentry, who seldom thought of going to Dublin, used, besides rigging themselves out at Ballinasloe fair, to have their common and occasional wants in the way of raiment, jewellery, and spicery supplied by pedlars who went about the country with large and strong chests stowed on carts, and which contained often valuable assortments of goods of all kinds. These persons were of such respectability that some of them dined at the tables of the gentry, and giving, as they generally did, credit, they were very acceptable, and were treated with all possible consideration. In fact there was a considerable smuggling trade carried on along the whole western coast, and in return for our Irish wool, the French silks and jewellery, and the Flanders laces, came in without the intervention of a custom-house. In promoting this traffic, many of the western proprietors were concerned, and it is said that families who wear coronets became right wealthy by the export of wool and the import of claret and French fabrics. Be this as it may, the itinerant pedlars I have just alluded to were the convenient factors of this contrabandism, and their good offices were, on all hands, acknowledged. Of these, Mrs. Bridget Bodkin* was not the least active, accommodating, or ingenious; she assumed to spring from one of the tribes of Galway, and though the gentry of the west looked down on regular traders and shopkeepers—yet Biddy Bod, as she was called, was considered as honourable and admissible, for she was very useful; and many a wedding, as well as wedding geer, was the result of her providence. But to my story: a large fleet of East Indiamen, unable to beat up channel from long-continued north-easterly winds, was

---

* I advise the reader that this name is fanciful—it is not in the record supplied by a very agreeable lady, now no more.

obliged to put into Galway-bay for water and provisions, and there these huge merchantmen lay at
anchor, freighted not only as at present with tea and
indigo, but with those delicate muslins which Man-
chester had not yet learned to imitate.   Now it was
known to Bid Bod that each officer and sailor might
have a supply of such valuable goods as a private
venture, and to make her own market she went on
board; expert as she was in smuggling, she knew
how and where about her own ample person to stow
away soft goods: for she, mind you, fair reader, was not
strait-laced as you may be—she, by nature large, still
did not care to tighten herself up as if she would be a
wasp—no, on the contrary, the poor thing became
quite dropsical—the swelling of her legs and body
was sometimes awful—what medicine she used to
get down the enlargement, whether belladonna or
digitalis, is not recorded—but she *did* now and
then keep down her dropsical distensions, and during
the low state of her intermittent "became small by
degrees and beautifully less."   But on her return from
the India fleet Bid Bod had a *full* fit of dropsy—her
body was like a rhinoceros—her legs like those of the
largest elephant of the King of Siam—she might have
got the elephantiasis from being for a time so near,
while on board the fleet, the elephant which the
Nabob of Arcot was sending as a present to Queen
Charlotte; and so she landed, in all her *amplitude*,
west of Claddah, and there she, as I may say, tapped
herself, for she unrolled all the gold and silver muslin,

the wonders of the India loom—Cashmere shawls that a lady might cover herself with from head to foot, and yet they would pass easily through her wedding ring—these she stuffed into the hollow of an immense pillion on which she rode.

Well now suppose you see Bid with her padded pillion fastened on her large black buttoned-tailed mare, and she, by help of a convenient granite stone, is mounted, and her man Luke is before her, and she has her arm *confidingly* placed around said Luke's waist, and they are jogging on slow-paced and sure —they have got clear of the town of Galway, the custom-house, the dreaded custom-house is far behind, and she is entering on the interior, the road to Athenry before her, and all seems safe. How she chuckles in her large and inmost soul over the success of her venture— when all of a sudden, at the turning of the road, out bounced a smart, dapper, active-eyed, but rather diminutive man, and caught hold of the rein of her bridle: "Madam," said he, "you must excuse me for stopping you, while I have every desire to be civil to a lady, yet having received information I can depend on, that you have just landed from the East India fleet with a quantity of run goods about you, you must submit to be searched, which I must now proceed to do in the most accurate manner consistent with my respect for your sex and quality."

Bid was at this accost, no doubt, surprised and distressed, but in no way thrown off her centre, and without any hesitation, she replied:

"Sir, many thanks to you for your civility, I am

quite aware you are but acting according to information, and doing what you consider your duty; and, sir, in order to show how much you are mistaken, I shall at once alight, but I am sure, sir, a gentleman like you will help a poor, infirm woman labouring under my sad complaint to alight with ease—the mare, bad manners to her, is skittish, and it requires all my servant's hands to hold her. 'Luke avick,' this gentleman insists on taking me down, hold hard the beast while I am alighting—I'll do my endeavours to get off—there, sir—so 'Button,' speaking to her horse. Now, hold up your arms, sir, and I will gently drop; yes, that will do;" and with that down she plopped herself into the little dapper exciseman's arms.

A summer tent pitched on a Swiss meadow might as well bear up against the down-tumbling avalanche as this spare man could the mountain of flesh that came over him, so down he went sprawling as Bid Bod intended he should do, and she uppermost, moaning and heaving over him, and there they lay, when with stentorian voice Bet cried out to her boy Luke:

"Luke, honey, ride off, never mind me—the gentleman I'm sure will help me up when he can!—skelp away 'ma boughal.'"

In the mean while, the exciseman lay groaning, and Bet moaning. I shall not attempt to describe the remainder of this scene; I leave it to the imagination to suppose that the smuggler kept her position just so long as she thought it gave time enough for her property being carried far and away, from the hands of the overwhelmed gauger.

CHAPTER XI.

JOYCE COUNTRY.

Character of Joyce Country—Its Scenery—Its Population—Discussion as to the reputed excess of size in the People of this district—A country well worth visiting and examining in detail—Facilities—Owners of Joyce Country—Road through mountain glen—A Cahir—Who erected the Cahirs—Modern house—Residence of a great man—Visit to his MAGNIFI-CENCE—In what his grandeur consists—Himself and family—Description of same—Jack, though a giant, not thick-headed—His way of keeping the peace—History of the Joyces—Of the Tribes of Galway—Joyces happy in marriage—In war—Love of a Spanish lady—Eagles attendant on the Joyces—Hardiman's History of Galway—His description of a big Joyce—Descent to the Killery Bay—Description of it—Row across the bay on a visit to Delphi—Description of it—Proceed along a fine valley—The Patree Chain—To Westport.

I WAS now in the centre of Joyce country—somehow or other I had formed a sort of emphatically romantic idea of this district. I had supposed it a mountain country (something like the border districts of Scotland,) consisting of high but green, sheep depastured hills, and inhabited by a race of tall men, dissimilar in face, form, and manners, from the Celtic tribes around. In all this I was utterly disappointed. There really is nothing strange or extraordinary in this group of mountains—nothing in the appearance of the people. As the hills are not more lofty than other groups of Irish mountains, neither are the people. It is true, that the men you see labouring in the potato fields, along the valleys, or cutting their turf in the bogs, are of a taller and comelier race than those crowded together on the

poor over-populated gravel hills of Roscommon: but
they are not by any means, as far as I could see, decidedly superior to the mountaineers of any other part
of the island. 'Tis true, I met with big Jack Joyce,
and by and by I shall describe him—but one well-fed
bacon-eating man, or family, has no right to fix un-
real magnitude on a whole people—you may see
fifty as huge men, even as Jack Joyce himself, if you
look into the tap-rooms of inns on the road between
Liverpool and London—nay, you might see just as
fine men both for shoulder, chest, and limb, in
the mountain glens of Cork, Kerry, and Tipperary.

Reader, if you cast your eye on any respectable
map of the county of Galway, you will observe that
the glen in which Maam Inn is placed, and through
the centre of which the Bealnabrack river runs into
Lough Corrib, extends in almost a straight line until
it approaches the Killery bay—in fact, the head-
springs of this river rise within a mile or less of this
fine inlet, on which they seem to turn their backs, as
if desirous, like poor mortals, clinging to human life,
to keep away, as long as possible from the immense
and awful ocean of eternity. By means of this glen
Joyce's country is quite accessible, and I know not
any position in the British isles so favourable as
Maam Inn for observing, within a limited compass,
fine lake, river, ocean, and mountain scenery. The
property in this district is mostly in the ownership
of the provost of Trinity College; and of Lords
Leitrim and Charlemont, who, as married to the

heiresses of a person of the name of Bermingham,
(I know not whether of the old stock of Athenry,) have
an undivided property here, which is strangely inter-
mixed with that of the College. Before you is a
mountain that belongs to the provost—next to that
another lifts its heathy head, and *that* is Lord
Leitrim's—and then another of the provost's shoulders itself forth—and so alternately until you come
down on Killery bay, and there ends Joyce's country.

Where the valley I had thus travelled through rises
and narrows into the character of a mountain glen,
a short distance from the road, I recognised an enclosure as one of the Cahirs or stone forts, which are, as
I consider, amongst the most ancient specimens of
human labour in the island. They are, by the people,
said to be the work of the Danes, but they do not
mean the Danes of the times of Turgesius, but the
people that Irish historians call Tuatha Danaans, an
energetic and intelligent race, whose intellectuality
was found so much superior to the battling barbarians called MILESIANS, (which name in English
means SOLDIERING FELLOWS who by brute force
got the better of them,) that they were counted necromancers. What a subject for thought and wonder,
running into distant and dreamy speculation is the
well-founded suspicion, that all over the world, in
times beyond genuine historic record,* there was a

---

* Is it not the fact that man came from the hands of his
Maker civilized; and that as the world grew older its races became more barbarized, that is, up to a certain point.

powerful and clever people—the erectors of the
Cyclopean walls, and stone circles, and cromleachs, and pillar-stones: the Stonehenges, the
Aburys, and Carnacs. The temple caves of New
Grange, and the lofty cairns on the mountain tops
not only of Europe and Asia, but also of America.
The pyramids and Cyclopean cities of Mexico—the
mighty mounds amidst the forests of Ohio, all speak
of one race superior to those who came after; and at
the same time strange to say exterminated by barbarians that seemed to know nothing of their arts—but
brutal as they were, and ignorant of the power of the
mind, supposed that what they saw was the effect of
bodily force, the work of giants.

These considerations which the sight of the lonely
Cahir gave rise to, occupied my mind until I got
nearly opposite a building, about two hundred yards
from the road, which seemed but newly erected; a
coarse, raw, ugly, unfinished edifice, that had,
amongst other marks denoting it to be a public-
house, a rude uncushioned jaunting-car, resting on
its shafts beside the door.

Considering this a rather curious place for a public-
house, I asked whose it was, and was told it belonged to " Mr. big Jack Joyce."

" Why I thought, says I, *he* lived at Leenane; at
least so he did when I passed through the country
some years ago."

" 'Tis true for you, your honour, he did live there,
but attorney K—— put him out of it last winter,

and here he is now, and he keeps a public-house, as
he always did, and as I suppose, always will do."

I was determined to go and renew my acquaintance with my big friend, whom twelve years ago I
found in all his might and glory as "mine host" at
the head of the Killery—so I drove up to Jack's door
and inquired for Mr. Joyce, and was answered by a
very tall young woman, not uncomely, who informed
me that Mr. Joyce was within, but that as he had
been out all night after cattle on the hills, he was on
the bed asleep, but his daughter (for such she was)
said, that if I desired it she would call him. I certainly did not like to go away without seeing BIG
Jack. So he was called up, and as he came, loose,
unclean, and frowzy, certainly my giant did not
appear to advantage; for some how or other, I had
let my imagination play the rogue with my judgment,
and magnify my retrospect with regard to this man.

The first time I saw him, (as I say,) about twelve
years ago, he made his appearance just as I drove
up to his door, bouncing over the wall that divided
the potato garden from the front of his house, and I
think a finer specimen of a strong man, tall and yet
well-proportioned, I could not conceive. Such do
not look as tall as they really are. The great bullet-
head, covered with crisp curls, the short bull neck,
the broad square shoulders, the massive chest all
open and hirsute, the comparatively small sinewy
loins, and pillar-like limbs all bone and muscle—
Milo of Crotona might have shaken hands with him

as a brother, and the gifted sculptor of the Farnese Hercules might have selected Jack as his lay figure. Such was my *beau ideal* of Mr. Joyce, from what I recollected of him since my former visit. But now, though I acknowledged the identity, yet, certainly, the man was greatly changed—but still, though I am sure my fancy had been playing tricks—he yet was tall, stout, and able, but I am sure I know fifty English and Irishmen just as large. Having called for some liquor—reader, I hope you will believe me not to drink, but just to put mine host in good humour—Jack and I got into chat, and to be sure he was full of the hard usage of the attorney who had put him out of Leenane; but he said he had got where he was a large and good farm, and all he wished was to see the head landlord, the provost of Trinity College, who was cheated *entirely, entirely,* by his middlemen, such as attorney K—— and others; but if he could but once get a sight of his *great reverence,* he would show him how acres, and hundreds of acres, are kept from him.

Upon acquainting him that I had the honor of an intimate acquaintance with *the greatest of all possible men,* EXCEPT LORD LEITRIM, you may suppose he was mighty civil; and taking advantage of that desire to please, I endeavoured to get from him an account of his family, but he really could not tell any thing about them; he seemed to think that size was not so much the characteristic of the tribe or name as of his own immediate family; and to show me that he had not been the means of any degeneracy, he whistled to his son who was in a distant field, who came at the call, and certainly a taller and more comely stripling, of about twenty years of age, I have not seen. He was at least six feet four inches in height, and I am sure if fed on animal food as an English farmer's son would be, he would prove a grand specimen of the human race. I left *big* Jack and his *big* family, receiving from them a thousand thanks for promising to introduce him to the notice of the new provost.

On my road towards Leenane, I met some persons with whom I entered into conversation about the neighbourhood, and about Jack Joyce. I found that he was not a favourite, that he was too apt to resort to his strength to settle disputes, when the *fist* he threw into the balance made the scale descend in his own favour. Indeed, he acknowledged to me on my former visit, that, as a justice of the peace was a great way off, he used to settle differences amongst the neighbours by taking the parties at variance by the nape of the neck, and battering their heads together, until they consented to shake hands and drink a pint of *potteen* together, which, of course, it was Jack's office to furnish for a *consideration*.

Before I go farther, I may as well tell all I know about this tribe of Joyces, that have given their name to this part of Connaught.

They were a troop or band that came over from Wales or the West of England, under the command of

Bermingham of Athenry, in the reign of Edward I.
their name was Joyes or Jorse, and they were said
to be descended from ancient British princes. Transplantation improved them in stature, for certainly the
Welsh are not a tall race. This people not only settled
in these western highlands, so very like those in Wales,
but they became important in Galway town, and
formed one of the thirteen tribes of that ancient and
extraordinary corporation,—the *merry* Joyces!!! For
all tribes had their *soubriquets*, and perhaps a Blake
is positive, and a D'Arcy stout, (quere, fire-eating
duellists,) and a Martin litigious; and so on respecting each characteristic whereby they were formerly
designated. Only this I think I have heard say, that
however a Martin loved litigation in the good town
of Galway, he allows no writs or issues of law to
extend beyond his gateway at Oughterard, just twenty
miles from his mansion-house.

Of the Joyces many were mayors and bailiffs of the
capital of Connaught, and not only the men bustled
and battled away against the rough-riding rogues,
the O'Maddens and the ferocious* O'Flaherties, but
even the women were sometimes of *big* note; amongst
others, I may mention, Margaret, the daughter of
John Joyce, who one day going down to wash her
household clothes in the broad transparent stream
that runs out of Lough Corrib, and as she stood in

---

* As part of the litany of the Galwagians it was piously inscribed on the town wall—" From the ferocious O'Flaherties,
good Lord, deliver us."

the current, as did the daughters of Grecian kings in the time of Ulysses, who should come by but Don Domingo De Rona, a Biscayan merchant of great wealth and note, who had arrived at Galway with a carrack of Benecarlo wine, which was much in demand for doctoring* the claret, the Galway merchants were so famous for concocting.

Now, as fair Margaret beetled away in the stream, and as with ruddy legs and untrammelled toes, (as straight and fair as her fingers, not a corn or bunnion on one of them,) she trampled the linen, the Don was captivated with the maid; he made love as Spaniards do; produced proofs of his pedigree, and his cash, and in due time they were married, and proceeded to Corunna; but not long after he died, (as old cavaliers are apt to do who marry late,) and Donna De Rona came home a sparkling and wealthy widow, and by and by her hand was solicited by Oliver Oge Ffrench, one of the heads of that tribe, and in due time they were married, and after the marriage he became mayor and one of the greatest merchants of the city. He traded much to foreign ports, and as it was no shame to smuggle in those days, and as the good town of Galway never was allowed to be

* It is very well known that the wines of Bourdeaux are not adapted to Irish, or, indeed, English palates; therefore, the claret that a *squire* drinks is quite a different thing from the Vin de Bourdeaux that a *monsieur* drinks. The Galway merchants were in the habit of pleasingly doctoring the imported wine to the taste of their customers; hence it was said that they *made* wine in France, but they *made* claret in Galway.

lighted by night, in order that smuggling might go
on and prosper, so Oliver Oge was often on the sea,
showing a good example of enterprise and free trade—
exporting wool and importing brandy and wine.

In the meanwhile the Donna was not idle; she
was the greatest improver in the west; she had particularly a passion for building bridges. She might
have made as good a pontifex as Pope Joan, and
heaven's blessing was on her for her good works; for
one day as she was superintending her masons, an
eagle came soaring from the ocean, and balancing
itself with poised wing just over the dame, it dropped
at her feet a ring formed of a single stone, so strange
and outlandish in its make and form, but yet so
beautiful and so precious that, though the most skilful lapidaries admired it, and would have given any
price for it, none could say of what kind it was, or
of what country or age was the workmanship: it has
been kept in the family since. I wish I could tell
the reader which of the Joyces now owns this precious
relic. All I can say is, that it is *not* on the finger
of big Jack, or his wife. But indeed the Joyces seem
to have been a favoured race; it is a favour that they
should be named and known as merry; for he who
has "a merry heart hath a continual feast." I assume
it to be a favour also that they were under the especial
patronage of eagles. One of the family in the religious and valorous times, when men went to fight for
the love of Christ against the Saracens, a fine, tall,
stalwart fellow, a fair specimen of a Joyce, had gone

to the wars of the Holy Land, and there he was taken prisoner by the Paynim, and there the dark, gazelle eye of an Arab maid fell on him, and she loved *his* blue eye and MERRY countenance, which even captivity could not sadden, and also his large proportions, and she set him free, and followed her Irish cavalier through Egypt, Barbary, and into Spain; and there they were wandering as pilgrims in sordid state and apparel, just favoured with food and lodging, because returning from Palestine, when the guardian eagle of the family, as they were winning their weary way over the Sierra Morena, came fluttering over his head, and gave such signs as led him along a certain path until he reached a spot where a Moorish king had deposited, after a defeat, all his treasures. How the stout Joyce contrived to appropriate and make his own these heaps of gold, history does not inform. All it says is, that he came (I hope not unaccompanied by his Arabian true love) to Galway, there lived and died, and showed his gratitude to God, and his love to his country, by building churches and strengthening the town wall.

I must conclude my remarks on the Joyces by observing, that Mr. Hardiman, in his excellent History of Galway, says that he has heard and witnessed many instances of the size and strength of the Joyces. "I saw," says he, "an elderly man of that name of uncommon stature and strength, who, (as I was informed,) when in his youth elevated by *the*

native, never was satisfied until he had drove every
man out of the fair green; those who knew his
humour, and also his strength, generally retired
beyond a certain small bridge; when his caprice was
satisfied by submission, he permitted them to retire
quietly; resistance would not only have been useless
but almost certain destruction, for nineteen in twenty
were of that name and all related; when I saw him
he was the remains of a noble figure, remarkably
gentle and kind to every one, and heard, with great
regret, the pranks of his youth mentioned." So
much for the Joyces; yet still, I say, that I do not consider that (take them *now* as a tribe or race) they are
superior in strength or stature to the well-fed mountaineers, who are *not* pressed on for the means of
subsistence, in Connemara, Clare, Tipperary, or Kerry.
I have a mountain farm in Tipperary, and I will
engage (leaving Jack Joyce and his son out of the
question) to produce ten men off that farm as tall
and well-proportioned as those of any district of
the same extent and population in Joyce's country.

The descent is very rapid from the high grounds
on which Jack Joyce's new farm and public-house is
situated, to the Killery Bay, and the inn of Leenane.
As you descend by a very good road, there are noble
mountain views, and the long Killery stretching its
dark and deep cut line through the mountains, was certainly a fine sight, and very unlike any thing I have
seen elsewhere in the island—not, perhaps, presenting so grand a prospect as either Bantry Bay or Lough

Swilly, but it has features all its own. About either of these fine estuaries there appears something that man has done—man has *some* share in the decoration, or even grandeur of the scene; but here at the Killery man and his works are out of the question; no sail upon the waters; no cultivation along the shore; all as rough nature has left it; even trees seem out of character with the place; and *there* is the deep bay, and *there* are the high mountains all around, the same, we may suppose, as when the first sea-rover turned inwards his prow for shelter or curiosity, and sought, and that in vain, for something that marked the occupation and dominion of man.

Some have said that Killery Bay is like a Norwegian fiord. Never having been in the Scandinavian peninsula I cannot decidedly contradict, but it certainly does not meet *my* idea of a fiord, which supposes pine-crowned precipices hanging and frowning over the deep blue wave; but this is not the case here: perfectly bare of any timber, the mountains, though rising all around, and assuming all manner of outlines, yet shelve gradually down to the shore, and I would say that the character of the place is not *sublime* but *savage*.

We arrived in good time at Leenane, and found the new owner, or rather renter, a civil but inexperienced woman, who had lately taken possession, and who complained bitterly of her landlord, who had promised to put the house in good repair, and make it sufficiently decent to induce travellers to stop with her.

This, it was evident, he had *not* done, and I was ready
to partake in her vexation on observing the nice furniture and other accommodations intended for a good
inn, stowed away in such a truly uncomfortable and
dirty house. Having bespoke our dinner, we expressed
a desire to go by boat to see Lord Sligo's sporting
lodge at Delphi; and here it was well that we asked
the price before engaging it, for the landlady, in order,
perhaps, to compensate, as she might, for her, *as yet*,
unsuccessful speculation, demanded more for a vile,
dirty, leaky brute of a boat, than we would have paid
for the hire of one of the gayest and best appointed
cutters in Kingstown harbour. However, by appearing to care little whether we should go or not, we,
by-and-by, agreed on more reasonable terms and went
afloat. It was also well that the water was smooth,
for the boat was not only leaky and heavy, but the fellows that undertook to row us seemed any thing but
expert. They were uncooth, savage creatures; the
elder of the two knew *but little* English, and the other
none at all, and they both seemed discontented and
very much out of humour at being obliged to leave
their potato planting to go rowing a pair of idle Sassenach fools, as they evidently considered us to be.

I consider myself well paid for this boating excursion. Nothing can be finer than the mountain scenery all around. When you are in the middle of the
bay you seem locked in on every side, and were it
not for the smell and colour, and vegetation peculiar
to the sea, the incomparable sea, you would imagine

T

you were on a mountain lake; but there is scarcely
any lake that has not a flat, *tame* end, generally that
where the superabundant waters flow off and form a
river; but here nothing was tame; on every side the
magnificent mountains seemed to vie with each other
which should catch and keep your attention most.
Northwards the Fenamore mountains—the Partree
range to the east—Maamturc to the south—a little
more to the south-west the sparkling cones of the
twelve pins of Benabola—then a little more to the
west, the Renvyle mountain—and off to the north of
that again, the monarch of the whole amphitheatre,
Muilrea, with its cap of clouds that it has caught, and
anon flings fitfully off, as much as to say, I am the
great cloud-compeller of Europe, and not one of you,
ye proud rangers of the sky, shall come from the
banks of Newfoundland without paying me tribute,
and, no doubt, ample tribute they *do* pay, and we had
every reason to be fearful of partaking in the results
of Mr. Muilrea tapping the American—but the alarm
was false; the clouds only slowly rolled their huge
masses along the topmost ranges, and we could see
in their clear glory all the inferior hills as they rejoiced in the lights and shadows of the uncertain day.

After a row of more than an hour we landed at the
little pier at the entrance of the river of Bondarragh,
and passing a small fishing village we went along the
river for about a mile and half, until we reached this
much-talked-of lodge of Delphi. Was it called so
from any fancied resemblance to the oracular moun-

Muilrea—Entrance to the Killery.

tain in Greece? As far as a picture can give an idea
of scenery, I have some notion of the far-famed throne
of the solar god, but I could trace no similarity. I confess, altogether, I was greatly disappointed in this place.
I think the mountains fine; I consider the sides of
the hills, as they rise from the little lake, singularly
picturesque and beautiful; for, as the ranges of rock
ascend, they assume a tortuous and wavy form, and
between each wave of the uprising stratification, the
fresh green grass of the young summer seemed to grow
luxuriantly—there were then before you, as in mani-
fold variegations, the green and the grey tinting the
whole sides of the mountains. There are two lakes
in the valley, one close by the lodge, and the vale a
little above the small pleasure-ground, taking a turn
at nearly right angles, contains the other. By ascending a green eminence you can see both lakes: the upper
and larger one, drawing its waters from the magnificent Muilrea, must present sublime views of the gorges
of that noble mountain. I greatly regret that I had
no time or opportunity to proceed along its banks.
Having seen earls and dukes' improvements in the
Highlands of Scotland, England, and Wales, and what
wonders in the way of planting have been done by Lords
Fife, Athol, and Breadalbane, I expected that this Irish
nobleman, having this great mountain district* to

* The district in ancient topographies is called *Partrigia
de Monte;* it is now called the barony of Morisk, and of
it there is a very curious, ingenious, and instructive model,
with all its mountains, lakes, rivers, and vales executed by Mr.
Bald the engineer, who has also executed the beautiful map of

himself, would have filled the glens and clothed the
sides of hills with his plantations, and that I would
have seen masses of timber, becoming the purse and
great mind of a most noble marquis; but it was no
such thing—I think that if a Dublin pawnbroker had
got possession of this valley he would have stuck
down about as many firs, and larches, and alders, and
erected about as tasty a cottage, and decorated it with
about as ornamental a verandah, which, by-the-by, is
going fast to ruin, and that is not extraordinary, as
the most "puissant" owner every year sets it to certain
sporting lodgers, and perhaps in imitation of some
Italian Marchese, makes the fishing and shooting of
this place a means of increasing his revenue.

Altogether respecting this *show place*, I may say
nature's work is grand and man's doings pitiful, and
I think it is worthy of the *improvement*, that it should
be set *furnished, with the grass of a cow!!!* year after
year.

I have heard it said that in certain hot summers
residence here is made almost intolerable by insects
larger than midges, but not quite the size of musqui-
toes, that bite bitterly, and make you wish by night
for gauze curtains.

Having got as good a dinner as hungry tourists
need desire at the inn of Leenane, we proceeded in
the evening to Westport, going along the valley

Mayo, which is not more remarkable for the fidelity of its details than the beauty of its execution. The model I allude to
is in the Royal Dublin Society's House.

through which the Owen Erive river runs, and falling over many pretty cascades feeds the head of the bay. This road is well laid out, is in excellent repair, and presents, I think, a succession of as fine mountain views as are in Ireland—here dark and deep gorges—there a bold, bare bulwark of a hill, presenting his huge shoulder—and now a long, deep, quiet glen, with its green sides covered with flocks, and the bleating of the lambs as they seek their dams along the ravines and precipices, breaks sweetly on the lonely silence of all around, and gives a pastoral character to the district. The evening was peculiarly serene, the Partree hills, (and indeed it is a noble chain of great and singular variety,) were covered with light, flocculent clouds, that under the tintings of the declining sun seemed as intended for a clothing of wrought gold, a raiment of heaven's own panoply, and so transparent was it, that every grey precipice and every beetling quartzose rock smiled in its turn under the sunshine as they were now revealed, and again veiled, by the golden-fringed clouds that moved so gently, so gracefully up the hill sides, and then passed away in splendid masses eastward.

We just got out of this fine mountain country, and the sun was setting as we descended into Westport. It is not to be expected that I should say much of Westport, I leave it to topographical works, such as the recent and excellent one of Mr. Fraser, to do this; but this I may notice, that it is a good and rather a clean town, that there is a linen-hall almost unused, for the manufacture has, as elsewhere, almost gone to nothing; that there is an excellent hotel, where I was treated most civilly and satisfactorily, and that the stranger, with great liberality, is allowed to walk in the fine demesne of Lord Sligo, whose entrance-gate is within a few yards of the hotel. Altogether I do not in the west of Ireland know where a family travelling for health or pleasure could spend time more agreeably and cheaply than at the hotel of Westport.

CHAPTER XII.

LOUISBURG AND CLARE ISLAND.

Visit to Clare Island—Proceed to Louisburg—Holy Well—Holy trout—
Its changeful story—Introduction to the Rev. Mr. S——r—Hospitable
reception—His character—His usefulness—His preaching—His servant-
man—A character—A Giant's skull as big as a potteen still—History
of Grana Uaile—Her lover's courtship, and interview with the Queen
of England—Her treatment of her husband—Anecdotes of the O'Mealeys—Extraordinary and dangerous superstitious practice—Not confined to Louisburg—Practised in other places—Bible readers put a
stop to it in Innismurry—See note—Voyage to Clare Island—Appearance—Visit the Abbey—Robbing of bones—Skull of Grana Uaile—Its
fate—Take care how you chew a Scotch turnip—Description of an
Irish Coast-guard—Return to Westport—Accident at sea—Providential
escape.

AND now, as I have arrived at Westport, and must
repeat that my stay in it was altogether too short, I
will endeavour to make up for it by summoning the
recollection of a longer stay twelve years ago—a stay
which will always be accompanied by pleasant recollections, connected with the dear and estimable friend,
with whom I then sojourned, and with whom I often
afterwards took sweet counsel, until it pleased the Lord,
in his own inscrutable ways, to remove him from his
useful field of labour and take him to himself,—I
allude to the Rev. Thomas W. who was at that time
the senior curate; the rector, from sickness and old
age, being allowed to be an absentee.

While sojourning with my friend, he proposed to
me an excursion, which, as it accorded with my
strongest propensities, I joyfully acceded to, and it

was to proceed to Louisburg, there to visit a man I had long desired to be acquainted with, the Rev. Mr. S. and having taken a breakfast with him to proceed to Clare Island, and inspect Grana Uaile's realm, the castle, cliffs, and monastery in which she lies buried. My friend had made all due preparations for the trip; the days were at the longest; the weather settled, and he not only engaged the captain of the coast-guard to come along with us, but he also made interest with the commander of a gun brig, which was cruising off the bay, to take us off shore near Louisburg, bring us to Clare Island, and back again. So we set out early on horseback from Westport. About two miles from the town we stopped at a holy well; there a very civil and officious man, whose duty, and, I believe, livelihood it was, put his hand under a bank that overhung the clear water and brought forth, lying on his palm, a trout somewhat less than a herring, which he said was holy, and gave us to understand that there was some mysterious connexion between the saint and the fish. He told a story how some Protestant had carried the fish home and placed it to fry on a gridiron for his dinner; but that the fish bounded, and why should it not ? *off* the iron, *out* of the -kitchen, *over* the fields, and néver stopped until it was safe and *cool* swimming in the well. As corroborative, he called on us to mark how the creature was quite blind, and how he had two cross lines upon its sides, the *evident marks of the bars of the gridiron.* Who could resist such attestations as these ?

Clare Island.

We then proceeded over the hills that form secondary ranges of Croagh Patrick to Louisburg, a poor and out of the way village, and were soon in the humble but hospitable dwelling of M. S. where we breakfasted, and it was not his fault that we did not dine. I think I now see before me the shining joy of the old man's countenance, when, as we were at breakfast, a salmon was brought in just caught and a present. " Dear friends," says he, "when you arrived I had nothing to offer you but such lowly fare as I would not wish you to partake of, but now I am doubly thankful to my good neighbour who enables me not only to give you a welcome, but plenty along with it." It was no small disappointment that our arrangements were such that we could not stay; and indeed it was worth while making his acquaintance, for he was quite a character. He was one of the few in his day (for he was at the time I saw him nearly seventy years of age) who, being master of the Irish language, so as to be able not only to speak it fluently and correctly, but also to read and write it, took advantage of this gift to preach and speak to the people, and to this duty he devoted himself with a singleness of purpose and a felicity of power, that were attended with the happiest effects; possessed of a highly imaginative mind, and familiar with the modes of thought and turns of expression of the people, and participating in their taste for humour, fun, and anecdote, he actually amused the most bigoted until they with pleasure listened to him;

and he had the singular power of being able without force, and by the readiest transition, to turn any
conversation, however light and trivial it might at
first seem, to a religious purpose. This I hold to be
a rare gift, and many I have known attempt it and
fail painfully; but not so with S——. Of all men I
ever met he knew best how to suit his discourse to
his hearers, and therefore he would venture to adapt
his images to the habits and comprehension of his
audience; and certainly what he said with great effect
to a congregation of Connaught peasants, would have
been exceedingly offensive to the tastes of a city
audience. Oh! if Ireland had had half a century
ago many such coarse, quaint, but at the same time,
faithful preachers in the Irish language as S——,
what a change, under God's blessing, would have
come over the face of the country. S—— was de-
signedly a coarse and homely preacher; he dwelt in
images and illustrations that came home to the
daily habits and modes of thinking of the people.
He was also a Calvinist. Preaching one day on the
doctrine of final perseverance, he set about making it
comprehensible, by comparing God's dealing towards
one of his chosen people to a father's conduct towards his child. "If one of your little ones were to
stray away from the cabin door, and if it should fall
down and dirty itself, would you not take it up, wipe
its little frock and say, '*stas ma bouchall*,' that's
my good boy, stand up again; but come jewel,
don't be after falling any more." I am rather afraid

I injure the good man's memory by giving this specimen of his familiar method with the people; but
bear in mind his language was Irish, and he was
addressing the ignorant and the unpolished. Mr.
S—— was a man of great shrewdness and presence
of mind, and his opinion was, that it was more expedient to open out to the people in a way capable
of striking their apprehension the plan of redemption,
as laid down in the New Testament, than engage in
a controversy concerning the differences between the
Churches of England and Rome. If, therefore, he
could at any time use the *argumentum ad hominem*—
touch the people's common sense, without wounding
their prejudices—if he could make them ashamed of
their superstitions, without giving personal offence,
he thought he was best doing his work. Watchful
thus of his opportunities, he was one day passing near
the holy well of Kilgeever, which is west of the Reek.
It is a place of much resort, and stands in a romantic
dell at the base of one of the secondary hills that
slope away from Croagh Patrick, and commands a
fine view, not only seawards, but also of the Old
Head and the entrance of the Killery. Adjoining it
are the remains of an old oratory, and altogether so
wild and yet so beautiful is the spot, that superstition
has "the wisdom of the serpent" in making it her own.
S—— was passing by at that season when pilgrims
from all Connaught resort to the Reek and its secondary holy places, and he observed a man wheeled
along in a sort of barrow by the labour contribu-

tion of the people, who, for the love of God, passed him on from house to house. The appearance of the person so franked along, is not unusual in *any* part of Ireland. Assuming to be a helpless cripple, he reclined on his go-cart, enveloped in a multitude of stitched-together rags, which were full of pockets, in which he stowed the potatoes and broken victuals which he here and there received, and on which he did *not* feed, for such take care at convenient opportunities to exchange the quantities they gather of these miscellaneous matters for smaller portions of food and liquor more agreeable to their fancies. The fellow now before us was broad shouldered and huge; he had an extravagance of carroty-coloured beard that flowed in wavy lengths over his bosom; there was a healthy, laughing, leer in his grey eye that betrayed how much more fun and joke than achings or disease were his concomitants. Such a person is in some places called a boccagh, in others a shouler. Carleton, in one of his well-drawn stories, has described such another to the life. Mr. S——— with a glance of his eye saw that this fellow was a trader on the compassion and superstitions of the poor people, and he immediately accosted him : " Where are you going, my poor fellow ?" " Och, then your honour, where would I be going but to the holy well of Kilgeever, and from far and away I have come, blessed be God, Patrick, and all the saints, for I am tould and believe that if I am but washed in the blessed well, I will get strength not only to

stand, but also to do my stations at the Reek."
Assuming at once an air of authority, S—— cried
out to a man dressed in the uniform of the coast-
guard: "Come here, sir, and take this man into cus-
tody; I know him to be an impostor; he can walk as
well as you or I, and he *shall* walk without help of
barrow or crutch to the Bridewell of Westport." The
fellow was taken by surprise, he supposed he was in
the presence of a magistrate, who by some means
had got information of his roguery, and he actually
bounced up, started off from his go-cart, and made
for the face of the hill, with the activity of a mountain sheep. This was exactly what S—— wanted;
he immediately addressed the people in Irish,—
showed how *he* could perform a miracle more satisfactory than the holy well, and took ample occasion
to show how much better was "the fountain of living
water," than these idle idolatrous wells, where superstition enabled knaves *to thrive on fools.* "Boys,
would it not save your faith very much from being
abused, if I were always here to try my hand on
every cripple, before he washes in the holy well of
Kilgeever ?"

Mr. S—— is now gone to his reward; he died as he
lived, a holy believer in the all-sufficient work of his
Saviour; and while living he gave an evidence of his
singleness of purpose, and his conscientious feeling
that clerical *emolument* should not be enjoyed without the performance of *duty*. He had given him the
large benefice of Connemara,—a parish larger than

an English county; he resigned it to a younger man, considering himself unequal to its duties, and lived contented with the very small means that a perpetual curacy afforded.

Departing from Louisburg in order to embark for Clare Island, Mr. S— sent his servant-man along with us to show a short cut to the shore, and a curious fellow he was as ever I met; it might be well said here, like master like man; for wearing as he did an old rusty black coat, that once graced the worthy minister, he seemed to derive an assimilation, not only in the outward, but inner man, and the similarity was as caricaturish in the one as in the other. He was full of legendary lore; knew all about Fin M'Coul, Gal M'Morni, Cunan Miul, and Osgar; had the polemic conversations of St. Patrick and Oisin by heart; was acquainted with all the great events of the Reek and Patrick's triumphs over the diabolic serpents there, and the history of Grana Uaile was at his fingers' ends. While sitting on a green bank overhanging the southern cliffs of Clew Bay, the sun warm, the winds still, the ocean placid, and nothing to interrupt the stillness of the grand and yet beautiful scene, except the gentle tossing of the complacent ocean on the ranges of rock below, we talked of Fin M'Coul and his Fions, and he told me the story of the origin of Lough Derg in Donegal, which I have narrated in my sketches in Donegal. He spoke of these Fions as giants, and as a proof of their existence, that he saw some years ago a man's skull raised out of a morass near Louisburg, that was as large as the head of a potteen still ! !

" And how large might that be Paddy," says I, " seeing as how I may not be acquainted as well as you with the gauge of a still." `

" Why, plase your honour, it might hold five gallons or thereabouts."

" Why," says I, " such a head as that might be too large even for a horse."

" Troth, yes; but don't all the world know the Fions were giants ?"

As Clare Island lay before us, and it looked beautiful in its raised outline, stopping up, as I may say loosely, the mouth of Clew Bay, we talked of it and of Grana Uaile and the O'Mealeys, of which noble race she was.

The following is what I could gather from my present informant and other sources respecting this heroine of the west:

Grace O'Mealey, which has been corrupted into Grana Uaile, was the daughter, according to him, of Breanhaun Crone O'Maille, tanist or chieftain of that district of Mayo surrounding Clew Bay, and comprising its multitude of isles. This district is still called by the old people the Uisles of O'Mealy, and its lord owning as he did a great extent of coast, and governing an adventurous sea-faring people, had good claim to his motto, "TERRA MARIQUE POTENS." Breanhaun Crone O'Maille dying early, left a son and daughter—the son but a child—the daughter just

ripening into womanhood, seemed to have a character
suited to seize the reins of government and rule over
this rude and brave people. Setting aside then at
once the laws of tanistry that confined the rule to the
nearest male of the family, she took upon her not
only the government but the generalship of her sept,
and far exceeded all her family in exploits as a sea-
rover; and from her success, whether as smuggler or
pirate, as the case might be, she won the name of
Grace of the heroes. Acting in this wild and able
way she soon gathered round her all the outlaws and
adventurers that abounded in the islands, and from
the daring strokes of policy she made, and the way
in which she bent to her purpose, the conflicting
interests of the English government and the Irish
races—she was called the gambler. As a matter of
policy she took for her first husband O'Flaherty, prince
of Connemara, and there is reason to suppose that
the grey mare proving the better horse, so the castle
in Lough Corrib, of whose traditionary history notice
has been already taken, was nearly lost to the Joyces
by O'Flaherty the Cock, but was saved and kept by
Grana the Hen, hence it got the name which it still
keeps of Krishlane na Kirca—*the Hen's Castle*. Be
this as it may, Grana's husband, the prince of Connemara, dying soon, she was free to make another
connexion, and in this also she seems to have consulted more her politics than her affections, and
became the wife of Sir Richard Burke, the M'William
Eighter. Tradition hands down a singular item of

the marriage contract. The marriage was to last *for certain* (what said the Pope to this?) but one year, and if at the end of that period either said to the other, "I dismiss you," the union was dissolved. It is said that during that year Grana took good care to put her own creatures into garrison in all M'William's coastward castles that were valuable to her, and then, one fine day, as the Lord of Mayo was coming up to the castle of Corrig-a-Howly, near Newport, Grana spied him and cried out the dissolving words—"I dismiss you." We are not told how M'William took the snapping of the matrimonial chain; it is likely that he was not sorry to have a safe riddance of such a virago. We shortly after this find Grana siding with Sir Richard Bingham against the Bourkes and doing battle with the English. The O'Mealys, on this occasion, turned the fortune of the day in favour of the President of Connaught, and most of the M'William leaders being taken prisoners, six of them were hanged next day at Cloghan Lucas, "in order to strengthen the English interest." It is probable that it was in gratitude for this signal aid afforded to her lieutenant, that Queen Elizabeth invited Grana over to the English court; and it certainly confirms the Irishwoman's character for decision and firmness, that she accepted the invitation of the Saxon, of whose faithfulness the Irish nation had but a low opinion. Accordingly Grana sailed from Clare Island, and before she arrived at the port of Chester was delivered of a son, the issue of the marriage with M'William

Eighter. He being born on ship-board was hence named Tobaduah na Lung, or Toby of the Ship, from whom sprung the Viscounts Mayo. It must have been a curious scene, the interview at Hampton Court between the wild woman of the west and the "awe-commanding, lion-ported" Elizabeth. Fancy Grana, in her loose attire, consisting of a chemise containing thirty yards of yellow linen wound round her body, with a mantle of frize, coloured madder red, flung over one shoulder, with her wild hair twisted round a large golden pin as her only head-gear, standing with her red legs unstockinged and her broad feet unshod, before the stiff and stately Tudor, dressed out (as we see her represented in the portraits of that day) with stays, stomacher, and farthingale, cased like an impregnable armadillo—what a "tableau vivant" this must have been; and then Grana having made a bow, and held out her bony hand, horny as it was, with many an oar she had handled, and many a helm she had held, to sister Elizabeth, (as she called her,) sat down with as much self-possession and self-respect as an American Indian chief would now before the President of the United States. Elizabeth observing Grana's fondness for snuff, which, though a practice newly introduced, she had picked up in her smuggling enterprises, and perceiving her inconvenienced, as snuffers usually are when wanting a pocket-handker-chief, presented her with one richly embroidered, which Grana took indifferently, used it loudly, and cast it away carelessly: and when asked by Sir Walter

Raleigh why she treated the gift of her Majesty in such a way, the answer of the wild Irish girl was of that coarseness that ought not to be read by eyes polite. Moreover it seems Elizabeth was not happy in the presents which she proffered to the Vanathess: she ordered a lap-dog, led by a silken band, to be given to her. "What's this for?" says Grana. "Oh, it is a sagacious, playful, and faithful little creature, it will lie in your lap." "My lap!" says Grana, "it's little the likes of me would be doing with such a thing—keep it to yourself, Queen of the English, it is only fit for such idlers as you—you may, if it likes you, fool away *your* day with such vermin." "Oh, but," says Elizabeth, "Grana, you are mistaken, I am not idle, I have the care of this great nation on my shoulders." "Maybe so," says Grana, "but as far as I can see of your ways, there's many a poor creature in Mayo, who has only the care of a barley-field, has more industry about them than you seem to have." Of course Elizabeth dismissed her soon—she offered, at her last audience, to create her a countess. "I don't want your titles," says Grana, "aan't we both equals; if there be any good in the thing, I may as well make you one, as you me; Queen of England I want nothing from you—enough for mè is it to be at the head of my NATION; but you may do what you like with my little son Toby of the ship, who has Saxon blood in his veins, and may not be dishonoured by a Saxon title— I will remain as I am, Grana O'Maille of the Uisles." It was on her return from England, and when driven by stress of weather into the small harbour of Howth, that the often told circumstance occurred respecting her abduction of the young St. Lawrence. Landing from her vessel, she and some of her followers proceeded to the castle and demanded admission, but were refused, on the grounds that the noble owner was at his dinner and could not be disturbed. "Oh, the Saxon churl," says Grana, it's well seen he has not a drop of Irish blood in his big body—but he shall smart for it." And so he did, for Grana on her return to her vessel, entering into a comfortable cottage, and finding therein a beautiful boy, the eldest son of the baron, (who was out at nurse, according to the Irish fashion,) she carried him off and brought him with her to her western land, where she kept him many a day, and did not restore him, until besides receiving a large ransom, she made the stipulation that whenever a Lord of Howth sat at his dinner, his doors should remain open for the admission of all strangers. It is said that the St. Lawrences have kept to the covenant ever since; if so, the observance in its spirit of open hospitality may explain why the lords of Howth are not the wealthiest of our nobility. Grana continued on her return to strengthen her power, and had strongholds guarding all the harbours along the coast of Mayo, and so active and vigilant was she, that it is said that in her castle at Clare Island, where her swiftest vessels were stationed, the cable of her chief galley was passed through a hole made for that purpose in the wall and fastened

to her bed-post, in order that she might be the more
readily alarmed in case of an attempted surprise. At
her death it would appear that the power which was
but concentrated by individual vigour and ability
dissolved with the spirit that gave it energy. The
O'Mealys kept their share, and the Bourkes theirs.
Grana lies interred in Clare Abbey—more of that by-
and-by. In after days Grana was made the subject
of song, and the disaffected to the British connexion
made her the personification of Hibernia, determined,
at all hazards, to resist the Saxon rule. It does not
appear that this heroine deserved, *in any way*, to be
made the goddess of disaffected adoration, or the
model of Irish hostility to British rule. Her siding
with Sir Richard Bingham, the President'of Connaught, shows that she was no *Boadicea*. The political song that was made the watch-word of party in
the early part of the last century, called Grana Uaile,
is to be found in Hardiman's Irish Minstrelsy, and is,
perhaps, the most trashy thing in that collection.

My communicative companion told me other anecdotes of the O'Mealys, one of which I recollect.

The sons of William O'Mealy, who flourished, I
suppose, in the early part of the 16th century,
were two of the stoutest, and bravest, and most expert swordsmen in all the west—and it seems they
had procured swords, brought from some distant
country, perhaps from Toledo or Damascus; and
they were so well tempered and so trenchant, that
it was supposed they would cut through any thing—

and so it happened, on a day, as they were walking
along the coast, not very far from where we are now
sitting, that one says to 'the other, "I have a great
mind to try my sword against yonder rock, and see
if I can't cut a slice off it."

" You had better let it alone," says the other—
"the sword was got for you not to cut rocks but men's
heads."

"I'll have my sport," says the other, (very obstinate!) "who shall hinder me to do what I will with
my own?" so with that he gives the rock a skelp,
but, as if in order to punish his pride, the sword
broke in two, and there the glory of his life lay useless; this made him very angry, and he challenged
his brother and cast it in his teeth, that he was
neither generous nor strong if he would not try HIS
sword also; and HE put to his mettle, lifted up his
good sword and actually cut the stone in two, as *clane*
as if he was after cutting a cheese; and there it is to
be seen, the two halves lying side by side to this
very day.

But the matter did not end there—the brother
whose sword had failed (mighty angry) began to say
bitter words, and all as one as hinted that his brother
dealt with the devil, or otherwise he could not make
such a cut as that; whereupon they fell to fighting,
and he that held the sword wounded the other; and
then, he snatching the sword before it fell from his
brother's hand, wounded him mortally in his turn—
and so they both died and were buried in one grave,

the two swords being thrown in over their coffins,
and the opinion is, and all the country believe in it,
that whenever the earth about this grave is stirred
the head of the O'Mealys dies.

It was from this very amusing man that I first
received an account of that dark superstition of the
people, the Lach Fecheen spoken of in the preceding
chapter. I was surprised at what he told respecting this fearful indulgence of the spirit of revenge,
which I never had heard of in any other part of
Ireland, but which, from subsequent inquiries, I have
found to prevail along the western coast of Ireland
from Connemara to Sligo. It appears to me to be
decidedly of Scandinavian origin, and convinces me
that the northmen had settled very early along these
shores, and it is a decided corroboration of the circumstance that the Danish professor, Rafn, has lately
stated, in his communication to the secretary of the
Royal Irish Academy, that the coast of Mayo was
peopled in early times by Scandinavian and Icelandic
tribes. My Louisburg informant (as I say) made me
first acquainted with this abhorrent superstition, and
adverted to a place not far off, called the stone of
Duac M'Shaun—this was a flag on the sandy shore
south-west of the Old Head, in the direction of the
Killeries. He told of a blacksmith who had a man
convicted at the sessions for stealing cabbage-plants out
of his garden—the fellow turned the "Lach" upon him,
and he died of a bloody flux. He also said he knew of a

Leitrim man who turned it in anger against the clerk of Louisburg, and the following night a church window was blown in. " You may be sure," says he, " that during harvest this flag is well watched—good care is taken that nobody shall PLAY THE DEVIL at that time." I have since heard some additional circumstances besides what I have related in my account of Joyce country, with respect to the " Lach " near Louisburg. It was some time ago stolen away by a man notorious for his evil deeds, and thrown by night into the deep sea; he thereby thought to avoid the ruin that those whom he had injured might bring on him by turning the stone, and invoking its curse against him. The ruffian, however, did not escape; his victims went, and when they found the flag gone, they turned the sand, and the fellow died like a poisoned rat. The superstition is still in operation. Reader, you remember, no doubt, the 6th of last January; if you are a householder or tree owner, you have hàd good cause to remember it. Maybe you won't believe that the raging of that cruel night was all owing to a devilish old woman, residing in the barony of Morisk, who turned a " Lach na neeve" with a fearful malediction on her neighbours. I suppose she did not consider how much GOOD she was about to do with her ill wind when it brought luck to all the slaters, sawyers, glaziers, &c. &c. in Ireland. But I must not, even at the risk of fatiguing you, gentle reader, pass over one interesting fact for which I MAKE MYSELF ACCOUNTABLE re-

specting this superstition. It has been in full operation in the island of Innismurry, off the coast of
Sligo. The society established for spreading the
Holy Scripture in the native language through the
islands surrounding the Irish coast, not long ago sent
their Scripture readers into this small isle, which is
extremely difficult of access. There the most primitive manners prevail, and there the inhabitants have
had the good sense to submit to the patriarchal
sway of a venerable man who lives as much in the
hearts of his subjects as any potentate in Europe.
Well, these Scripture-readers had not been long in
the island until his majesty of Innismurry issued a
decree that his subjects should sow no more barley,
because with barley they made potteen whiskey, and
that was not only illegal but a mischievous manufacture—bad for the body—worse for the soul. "Children," (says he in his Edict,) "you must cultivate
wheat in future—nay more, you must never again
turn the fatal flag—it is a devilish thing that God's
Holy Word, which is now *for the first time* read
amongst us, tells us, no follower of Jesus should
practise—for Jesus tells us "to bless and curse not."

The Scripture-reader, whose letter I saw, announc-
ing these good tidings to the secretary of the institution that employs him, further says, that his majesty
of Innismurry informed him that the last man who
turned the fatal flag on his island was drowned, and
that it was the opinion amongst his people, as it is
indeed every where that rite is practised, that any one

who ever got a request granted by turning the stone never after has a prayer heard by God.

Reader, don't you think that a society deserves something more than mere approbation, that by sending the Word of God into this lonely isle has succeeded so far in destroying the works of the devil.

While thus conversing, I was not sorry to see the boat arrive which was to take us to the brig that was in the offing, for the day was shortening, and the wind so light, that it would be some time before we reached Clare Island, and I took my leave of my poor communicative friend, never to see him more ! !

It was but too true that our voyage to Clare Island was to be tedious—it was not till nearly sun setting we arrived there; but the time was not lost—the commander of the brig was an extremely intelligent man, and being devoted to the study of natural history and geology, had made a good collection of all the minerals to be found on the western coast, and his conversation beguiled the time very pleasantly.

At length, however, we got into the small harbour on the eastern side of the island, and landed on the little pier that has been erected immediately under Grana Uaile's castle, of which nothing remains but a square tower, little differing from those that are to be found all over Ireland, but standing in a very picturesque position. There seemed a rather populous village in the vicinity of the little bay, and

Grana Uaile's Castle, Clare Island

the land all around was as green and fertile as possible.
My friend and I immediately started off to visit the
abbey, which lay on the western side, and we had to
make our way through a rich valley producing as
abundant crops of potatoes and corn as I think I ever
saw. I at once perceived that Clare is the most fertile of all the isles that surround Ireland,—containing
2500 acres. In skilful and tasteful hands it might
be made a paradise. On our right hand, as we were
on our way along a very 'difficult path, arose a lofty
hill, that should be called indeed a mountain, but
which might be cultivated almost to the summit. To
the north-west of this eminence are fine cliffs, which,
on this occasion, I did not see. Afterwards, and on
my recent visit to Achill, I observed them rising like
a wall, and presenting a fine bold front to the ocean;
but on the south and south-west the island is low and
tame, especially in the neighbourhood of the abbey,
which is poor and mean, with an ugly barbarian looking village near it. I confess I was surprised that
that part of the island which immediately fronts the
south-west, and which looks directly towards the
nearest land in that direction, namely, America,—
should shelve so gradually to the sea.

There was little worth seeing in this building once
belonging to the Carmelites—two things and two only
struck me,—a man that accompanied us into the
church, pointed to a window which seemed to me a
very good specimen of Irish art, of which the accompanying wood-cut is a representation; but this was

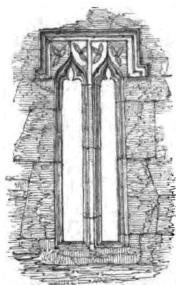

not of half the interest in my eye, as what the man took down from said window, where it seemed to have been very carefully placed, a skull, in the sides of which where the ears once were, holes had been made, and therein were inserted a pair of plain gold earrings —and this I was told was the skull of Grana Uaile. I observed it with reverence, such as was evidently expected from us all by the people; and why should not this relic be respected, and why, when looking at what once contained the thinking part of this singular and resolute woman, should I not ponder on how little difference there is after all, (let phrenologists say what they will,) between that skull of this sea queen and the brain-caps of the nameless multitude who lived and died and rotted—heirs of a common lot.

But alas! before I have done with Grana Uaile, I must narrate a melancholy event, which reached me from what I thought good authority. Not very long

after I had visited Clare Island, bones becoming daily
more and more in demand as manure—some specula-
tive Scotsman chartered a vessel in the Clyde, for the
express purpose of rifling all the churchyards along the
western shores of the Irish coast, of their loose bones,—
of which he had reason to know there was abundance.
In this way he ranged along, from Malin Head to
Cape Clear—wherever there was an abbey at all accessible, his men landed by night, and with as little
noise as possible, carried off the bone-heaps; amongst
other places they landed at Clare Abbey, and swept it
of all its bones, and with the rest they sacked up the
jewelled skull and cross-bones of Grana. I had
rather they had gone up the Rhine, invaded Cologne,
and carried off all the skulls of the 11,000 virgins.

The people when they found in the morning that
Grana and all their grandmothers were gone, were
outrageous—but what could they do—or what think,
but that as Grana Uaile had often run up the Clyde
and robbed and plundered, so now she was abducted
herself with all the gold she was possessed of,—her
violence had often perhaps crushed the heart of some
Scotchwoman, her own bones are now crushed to
make large an Aberdeen turnip, and thereby fatten a
highland heifer;—and allow me, reader, to repeat a
story that has been told—it is rather apocryphal, and
good sir, you need not give any credit to it if you
don't like.

Not very long ago as a farmer in Ayrshire was
eating his slice of a boiled yellow turnip, the garniture

of a leg of Cheviot mutton, he found something hard in his mouth and rattling between his teeth, which rather than swallow, he cast into his hand, and lo! and behold you! there was a hind tooth, certainly not one of his own, for it was smaller than any of his identical huge grinders, and what was more extraordinary, a little gold ring, evidently such as women wear in their ears, kept it company;—all Scotland could not account for such incongruities being found within the heart of a yellow turnip,— an Irishman might have come to the decision that they were all that remained of Grana Uaile.*

On our return to the little port where our brig lay, the sun was near setting, and we made haste to get on board—but before I did so, I was witness to a SCENE.

I have before observed that the commander of the coast-guard was along with us, and he took this opportunity of inspecting the party stationed on this island. While we were getting on board, there was a strange uproar—a number of the islanders who could speak nothing but Irish, were vociferating most furiously, and with threatening gestures pointing to one of the coast guard—a fine, able, but rakish, ruf-

---

* From information I have lately obtained, I am disposed to consider that the robbing of Grana Uaile's skull by Scotch bone dealers, did not take place at all; for, to this day, the heroine's skull is exhibited to admiring pilgrims, ornamented with its gold ear-rings, and decorated with ribbons. Either then the theft did not occur, or the pride or love of profit of the villagers has induced them to substitute another skull; for pilgrims resorting to the abbey, of course, call for whiskey.

fianly-looking young man, who seemed defending himself as well as he could to his commander, against the charges of the people. It was sometime before the matter could be adjusted—but at all events we set sail, and when clear of the island, the captain said, that the man the country people were accusing, was one of the most troublesome fellows he ever had under his command,—the rest of the men were all either Englishmen or Northerns, and were regular and trust-worthy,—but this fellow was a Tipperary man—an excellent seaman, and able and willing *at times* to do as much as any two others,—but of no principle, and so pugnacious, that he never was stationed any where, he did not kick up a riot; on the present occasion he should be obliged to bring him to trial, for the people accused him of what he was sure he was guilty of, taking their provisions from them and not paying them; and what was worse than this, of taking liberties which neither fathers, husbands, nor brothers would suffer, and that this had caused all manner of heart-burnings on the island.

Strange! how such characteristics should, under so many various circumstances, belong to the natives of Tipperary ;—strange ! that birth and breeding in spite of all discipline and training should give such an idiosyncrasy for mischief.

We were not long at sea when, under the little wind that attended us, the night came down, and there was neither moonlight nor starlight—and as under these circumstances the captain of the brig

could not venture into the shallows of Clew Bay, and
as my friend must needs be in Westport before morning, (for it was Saturday,) we were consigned to a
four-oared boat, manned by five steady Englishmen,
and thus in a night almost pitchy dark we were to
find our way up to Westport, through the intricacies
of this bay, beset as it is with its 300 islands. Onwards we went rapidly and yet steadily through the
calm and silent sea which lay in deep repose, and
thus we went, fondly anticipating our safe arrival and a
good supper—when all at once we struck the ground,
and there we remained immoveable, in spite of all
the exertions of the sailors—and there we were likely
to stay, for the tide was falling, and it must be some
hours before it would rise again and lift us off. It
seems, the men, all English, were not aware of the
intricacies of the navigation, and we had got on some
shallow bank, or on that curious natural break-water
that extends across this great estuary from Newport
in a diagonal line, until it terminates under Croagh
Patrick.* At all events, we were aground, and could
not be pushed off; and it was a consideration that
forced itself on every one present, that had the wind
risen, and the sea came in as it generally does from
the west, nothing could have saved the boat from

* Mr. Bald the engineer, in his valuable evidence before
the Committee on Public Works in Ireland, thus speaks of the
breakwater on which we got aground :
"The bar which forms the harbour is a natural breakwater of
a mile and a half in length, on which is situated the Isles of
Doreineb More and Doreinch Beg. This natural breakwater

being stove to pieces, and every one in her being lost.
But it was not so, and we did, as we had great reason,
thank Him who commandeth the winds and the
waves! for all remained as quiet and as genial as
summer's night could be, until the morning sun and
the morning tide both rose to guide us and help us
on our way to Westport.

slopes seaward, in some places one in thirty ; but inside, facing
the harbour, its natural slope is one to one. It is formed of
boulders. This breakwater is, perhaps, one of the most remarkable hydraulic works that exists in Europe, and is well
worthy of the attentive study of professional men. Its mass is
greater than that of the breakwater at Plymouth, or that of
Cherbourg in France. To form such a work would cost more
than two millions of money.

x

CHAPTER XIII.

CROAGH PATRICK.

THE desire to visit Clare Island hindered me on my former visit to Westport from ascending Croagh Patrick. I was determined to do so now; in fact, it was to visit this mountain and Achill that I came beyond Athlone.

I remember, more than twenty years ago, seeing Croagh Patrick from the plains of Sligo, near Bally-moate. I was there for some days, and as is but too often the case in the month of August, the weather was wet, cold, and muddy, and you could not see ranges of hills or mountains five miles off; but all of a sudden, as if by magic, a change comes over the

Croagh Patrick.

atmosphere: up stand before you two magnificent conically formed mountains—one massive and at the same time lofty, and apparently not very far off, and that I was told was Nephin; but far away to the left, blue and distinct, rose a magnificent elevation, so mathematically exact, that it might be said that nature had placed it there to work a problem in conic sections.

"That's the Reek, sir," says a man that stood beside me.

"What do you mean?"

"Why the holy mountain of St. Patrick, where all Christhens do be goin' to do penance."

"Oh I understand you, that is then Croagh Patrick, from whence the saint drove all the serpents and poisonous reptiles into the Atlantic."

"You just have it," says the man, "blessed be his name for so doing."

I have often seen Croagh Patrick since, but it was never until now my convenience to ascend it.

I have always had a passion for ascending mountains. I never have been near one of any elevation that I did not attempt to mount his back, and I am sure I have been a fool for all my pains: the fatigue and danger, in almost every instance, overbalance the amount of knowledge or pleasure you attain. In this way I have been on Ben Nevis, on Mangerton, Helvellyn, Slieve Mis, Muckish, &c.; but there are more reasons than one for going up the REEK. It's a holy mountain. There must be, independent of the view from it, something curious on its top. At any rate as I am now grown old, perhaps it will be a good resolve that, whether satisfied or not, I will never venture on another ascent. So taking a rather early dinner, my friend and I set off on a well-appointed jaunting car, which our good hostess furnished us with, and soon got to Morisk—a village, close to which is a ruined abbey, directly under the mountain. Soliciting a little boy to come with me, (previous to ascending the hill,) I went down to the abbey, which lies close to the shore. It was not much worth seeing, a small nave and chancel, with few or none of the usual accompaniments of a monastery. The friars of the Augustinian rule, that the O'Mealeys placed here, were not as disposed to make themselves comfortable as the Benedictines or Cis-tercians. I am inclined to suspect that the Culdees or hermits that formerly had fixed themselves on the top of the Reek, removed here when the rule became less strict, or perhaps when ejected from it by the Roman Patrick. The walls of this building are crenellated, which is not usual with sacred buildings. Where once was the altar in the choir, is a stone, on which is sculptured the Saviour on the cross. The stone is broken in two. My little companion took care to tell me that that wicked deed was the act of a Protestant, who broke it out of pure devilishness; but, says the little fellow, casting up his eyes in a pitying mood, "God help the blind heretics, they have no religion at all at all." I may here remark that, in almost every religious ruin I have ever visited, the neighbouring people, besides telling you of the original destruction by bloody Bess or cursed Cromwell, with his copper nose, always have some more recent instances to narrate of Protestant mischief-doers. The children have got these stories at their fingers' ends: it seems part of a system, by these means to pre-occupy the minds of the young Roman Catholic with deep and hateful prejudices against their Protestant countrymen, and in this way, alas, how easy is it to lead the young mind, whether Protestant or Romish, to *hate*.* May the day come, and that soon, (and then, for the first time, Christianity may be said to flourish in the land,) when children are taught certainly that more difficult lesson of mutual forbearance, exculpation, and love.

The owner of the public-house, with great readiness and civility, provided us with a person who said he knew the mountain, often attended gentlemen when ascending it, and could speak English—so we started. Of course Croagh Patrick (though like every lofty mountain, when seen afar off, seems one great mass) has its secondary range, which you must ascend, and from which the cone itself springs. Our party on the occasion consisted of my friend and I, the guide, the waiter of the hotel at Westport, who

---

* The ballads and stories of a people are accurate tests of their feelings and disposition. In no country are they made use of with such bad effects as in Ireland. I am aware that much art and industry have been used to teach the young idea how to·hate.

had driven us to Morisk, I believe for the pleasure
of the excursion, and a little boy, the son of the
publican at Morisk, who certainly was not more than
nine years of age.

This range, which you first ascend, is very rough,
high, and toilsome to overcome; the way, to be sure,
is before you not to be mistaken, perhaps not so
beaten a mountain track in Europe—but here its very
difficulty is its virtue, and your fatigue is part of your
merit. Just as you arrive at the summit of the
secondary range is a fine spring well. Human nature
cannot withstand the desire to take a drink here; and
here, as cold water is not good for panting temples and
a palpitating stomach, many a bottle, flask, and blad-
derfull of whiskey have been broached. Indeed I don't
know how the stations would be gone through at all
without the CRATHUR; and it's true as you are there,
reader, that if St. Patrick drove down DEVILS from
this mountain he has brought up multitudes of
SPIRITS—ay, spirits seven times more dangerous and
devilish; and the latter state of poor Pat, in spite of
the Roman Patrick, is worse than the first.

Here our Westport waiter left us—religion did not
require it, and glory had no stimulus to induce the
serving man to toil further. It was here at this well
that not long before a *scene* took place between a
guide and a gentleman of the legal profession from
Dublin. This person, a little puffy, barrel-bodied
attorney, came to Morisk and sought for a guide to
lead him up the mountain, and up they started, and

the little man grunted, and panted, and perspired—
"larding the lean mountain" as he ascended. The
guide did his best to alleviate his difficulties, and
showed him the easiest paths, and where best he
could plant his foot—at length they came to the
well—I believe it is called Glass-well—here St. Patrick made his first stop when he came to achieve
the disenchantment of the mountain; hence it was
that one of his two boys, Meeniune, was sent before
him to prepare his way, while Fiechus, the other, staid
with his master. Not far from this, I say, Meeniune
was attacked by the serpents, and crushed to pieces in
the entanglements of their tails, but he was put together again and restored to life by his master. Here
came the fat little tourist, and he was in a pretty
plight, like a tallow candle in a hot tavern. "Well,"
says the guide to himself, "this dacent man is certainly
doing penance for some great sin, and the poor simple
sowl doesn't know that I could put him out of pain
for a few shillings; it is a wonder all out that some
one, even if the priest hadn't the good nathur, would
not tell him that there's many a one about here that
would do the DHURRUS for him. So it's myself
that'll have the innocent* fellow out of his trouble in
a jiffy." So with that the guide came up to him where
he sat wiping with his silk handkerchief his reeking,
steaming head and neck. "Why then, your honour,
I wonder you'd be after thinking of going up yon

* Innocent amongst the Irish always, with a grown person,
carries the force of simpleton.

mountain, and working thro' all its stations, when
you know that I'll go up for you and do DHURRUS
with all the veins in my heart."

" What do you mean?" says the attorney, " YOU
go up for ME!!!"

" Yes, plase your honor, and that I will, and you
may sit there quietly until I come back, not a one I'll
miss—look at my knees when I return and see if they're
not battered and bleeding enough to *plase* yees."

" Why what, honest man, do you mean? can you
see for me—can you *admire* for me—can your going
up enable me to say, when I go home, that I have
been at the top of Croagh Patrick?"

" Ah then," says the guide, " is that ALL that
brings yees to the Reek—myself thought ye were a
religious man, and that yees were undher vows or
orthers to perform stations here, and sure all the
world knows that I could do all *that* for yees, and
chape enough—ay chaper and just as well as ever
Bob of the Reek did, ' rest be to his sowl, and the
heavens his bed.' "

Our guide certainly did not commit the mistake of
supposing us to be VOTEENS instead of tourists.
After leaving the well we soon got to the ridge of the
first range, and after walking along a comparatively
level and easy path, at length came to the real Reek
itself, and making a little *detour* towards the south,
we came on the " Kessaun Cruagh," or " the footway
of the Reek," which is a pass that ascends up the steep
side of the cone and is worn deep into its side,

partly by the winter torrents and partly by the feet of the multitudes that for a thousand years have thought they were appeasing an angry God by making this difficult ascent. "Here, sir," says the guide, "is the first station of the mountain, called the station of the Kid."

"Why is it called the station of the Kid?"

"Troth then myself is not *sure*, but I think I have heard them say that it was a devil's child, as all souls that the devil owns take the shape of goats before they go to their last place; and this was a young one that was left here to watch and give notice when Patrick their enemy was coming, for they were mighty much afraid of him; and here upon the top of the Reek was the last retreat of all the serpents and venomous things of Ireland, and here they were commanded by one great snake or land fish—he was general over all, and had terrible strength and power. And now was to come the *tussle*, for up come Patrick and his boy Fiechus, for Meeniune had to stay behind—he was so bruised in the heel he could not walk; and down came the serpent, hissing out fire, and thundering down rocks, and the saint had nothing in his hand but a bell, which every now and then he rung, and as the sound arose, the serpents turned tail and fled: but just as Patrick was going to give a loud ring, and a rush at the same time up the hill, Fiechus his boy supporting his arm when it was tired shaking, the big general of the serpents gave a lash with his tail and smashed the bell, tore off the

clapper, and it fell to the ground not worth a whistle;
and what now could Patrick do?—why he first began
to cry like a child and give over—but again, good
thoughts came on him, and he did this—he made his
prayer to the blessed Virgin. In the turn of a hand,
holy be her name, the bell came back as sound as
ever, with a new clapper, and it did ring so
loud, and had such vartue, that the serpents all left
the side of the mountain and took to the top, and
Patrick pushed on, as we are now doing, until he had
his foot fixed as we shall do by and by on the summit. And now, master, for fear I would not be able
to show you above, for don't you see that a cloud has
gathered there like a cap, and more is coming from
the sea, and I fear it will stay there all the evening,
look off there to the south—don't you see a lake—that
is Lough na Peche, the lake where Patrick sent the big
serpent, after that with bell and book he drove him
from above; but the lake was too small, he splashed
all the water out of it in a jiffy with the lashings of
his tail; so finding that was no place for him at all,
Patrick began to ring his bell again, and sent him off
to the large lake you see yonder to the east, some
call it Lough Derg, others Lough na Corragh; there
the serpent is fastened alive to the bottom, but in the
time of storm, when the thunder is rolling, and the
lightning flashing and frightening away the dark night,
then the serpent is allowed to rise and take its sport
on the surface; and when by any chance men at this
time pass that lonely water they see the serpent

riding the waves like a wild horse with a flowing mane; the froth boiling away from his sides, and all is terrible entirely."

With this description of St. Patrick's struggle with the venomous creatures the poor simple fellow amused us while we followed him toilingly up the path, and many a time had we to stop and take breath—many a time wipe the moisture from our panting foreheads, as with hands as well as feet we attempted to win our way upwards.   Just near the top was a little flat— "There sir," says the guide, "just *there*, a poor woman and her two childer perished not long ago— the crathur's husband had died of a decay, and left her desolate, and it was not her low state, without any one to do a hand's turn for herself and her children, that grieved her—but it was that she had no means to get masses said for his poor sowl; and she thought of him every night suffering away in purgatory, and crying out in the middle of the flame, 'Oh, Biddy jewel, can't you help me out of this torment.' So she thought of coming up here to the Reek; it was not the season *at all* for such a work, it was long after Hollantide, and not a pilgrim had passed up for many a long day; but poor Biddy was resolved to set out, for why, her dear Darby was a suffering; and as she was a lone woman, and had no one to leave her two children with, she took them with her and faced the mountain; it was, as I said, a bad season; the day wet and windy, and some of the neighbours who saw her going up, shook their heads, and wished

that God would get her safe over her blessed work—
nobody can tell whether she went through all her
stations or not; the crathur any how tried her best,
and night came down on her; and such a night—the
storm set in from the north-west, the ocean came
tumbling in from the head of Achill—the rain that
poured thick, soft, and sweeping below, was all hard
driving sleet on the mountain.

"To this spot poor Biddy retreated for shelter,
and nothing had she to save herself and her little
ones but her poor threadbare cloak. To make my
story short, the neighbours fearing for her went up
next morning in search of her, and here they found
her and the little things beside her all stiff and
huddled together; the cloak was wrapped round the
childer—the poor fond mother (heavens be her rest,
and sure it is she is there, dying when doing such a
holy work) had stripped her own body of its covering
to save those she loved better than her own life, and
all to no purpose."

A piteous tale this of the strength of superstition
and of fond woman's intense love—*what woman's
intense love will do* for her husband and children.
Love divested of selfishness—love 'reaching beyond
the tomb, and fastening on eternity.

Passing on from the platform of the scene of this
sad perishing, we shortly after entered into the cloud,
and leaving below the clear lustre of the cheerful
evening, took our standing on the summit of the cloud-
capped Reek, which, although on every side from

below it has the appearance of terminating in a pin-
nacle, yet in fact has a flat of near half an acre on the
summit. This is the case with all mountains I have
ever been on:* let their summits appear ever so
steep from below, there is a comparatively level spot
on the top.

I must now attempt to describe the top of this
singular elevation; and here I may observe that I
was not sorry to be enveloped in the clouds, and
be there, as it were, abstracted and shut in above
the world on one of the high places of the earth, for
centuries dedicated to a gross and barbarous superstition, a thing only fit for darkness and dreariness;
a palpable obscure—a gloom like that of the cloud
that hung and shed a chilling moisture on us that
could be felt even in the heart.

I entered on the platform on the top of the Reek
about an hour before sunset, while all below was
smiling in the gentle light of evening—around us
was the dripping curtain of cloud which made all seem
saturated with wet and look cold and dreary. The first
place pointed out was where the whiskey-sellers sit
who supply the pilgrims with cordials between the
different rounds they take on their bare knees. How
thus Satan peeps out here and administers his own
peculiar specific—his destructive "opus magnum," as
a sort of interlude to the other *spiritual* proceedings
that he rejoices in here. You next come to what is

* Except Slieve Croghan in Achill, and that is only half a
mountain, the other half being submerged in the ocean.

called the altar, not very far to the right of where the
money-changing and whiskey-drinking go on.   This
altar where mass is said is nothing else but an
enclosure of stones, built on three sides, about five
feet high, with a sort of ledge or table, on which
the holy candles and other things that belong to
the altar and the saying of mass are laid out;
on the interstices of the wall are stuck a number of votive offerings of the rudest and meanest
sort—iron nails, buttons, rags, and bits of broken
earthenware—where I picked up a little crucifix on
which our Saviour is attempted to be represented,
carved out of a piece of sheep-bone. Here, of course,
St. Patrick said mass. A little further on is Patrick's
bed, a trench somewhat shallower than a grave, in
which the Saint is said to have slept, and prayed,
and fasted, like Moses in the Mount, forty days,
before he altogether drove the venomous vermin
from the mountain; further on to the right of this
is a little low wall just at the edge of the precipice,
which is called Lug na Naimh, here St. Patrick
stood, bell in hand, and every time he rung it, and
he was not content with ringing it the common way,
but strong in faith of the angels that were around him,
he flung it away from him, and it, instead of plunging
down the Lug, was brought back to his hand by minis-
tering spirits; and every time it thus lustily was rung
thousands and thousands of toads,* adders, and

* For Colgan's account of St. Patrick driving the serpents,
see Appendix.

noisome things went down the Lug, tumbling in confounded mixture, neck and heels, one after the other.
And here, reader, you may desire to know what a Lug
is : there is no lofty mountain without one—it is a
sublime precipice that is generally found on the north-
eastern side, and which goes down plumb many
hundred feet, and generally at the bottom is a tarn
or lake, whose depth from the surface is, perhaps, as
great as the height of the precipice above. Ben Nevis
has such a Lug, down-descending above fifteen
hundred feet. The mountain of Lug na Quilla, the
lord of the Wicklow range, and the second highest in
Ireland, has, as its name denotes, a noble one—
so has Mangerton—so has the Keeper—and so
has Galtee More, and perhaps the grandest and
most picturesque Lug of Irish mountains is that of
Nephin. Down the Lug, on the north-east of
the Reek, nothing now was to be seen—imagination
might fill up the whole chasm with the bones and
exuviæ of all the venomous vermin that Patrick sent
a packing—there now, at any rate you might fancy any
thing filling the great depth, with the clouds sweeping from the west, and tumbling and rolling like
cumulative wool-packs over the side and into the
fathomless abyss.

Turning in a northerly direction to where the
mountain looks to the north, and presents the longest
face of its summit to Clew Bay, I was surprised and
gratified to find along this whole range of the platform
a low wall, built of large, uncemented stones evidently

of the most ancient construction—a Cyclopean monument raised ages before the Roman Patrick ascended,
if ever he did ascend, built by that ancient people
that have erected their solemn monuments in every
land, and have left behind what proves, that however
unaccountable their remains, they were created by
men of intelligence and great social power. The low
wall which, I believe, has never been before noticed,
a wall that has borne the Atlantic tempest of thousands of years, I observed, and considered it afforded
me a clue to unravel, as I think, the mystery of this
mountain, and explain the traditional story of St.
Patrick and the serpents. It is very well known that
there never were any venomous creatures in Ireland;
long before Patrick, Solinus, and Festus Avienus
called Ireland the sacred Isle, because the gods had
kept it from serpents and other venomous things—
Patrick then only *allegorically* fought with, and drove
these animals* out of Ireland into the ocean; (by the

*'As I have before observed, Ireland was stated by writers,
long before the period assigned to St. Patrick, as free from serpents. It was also free from frogs, as appears from the following
saying: " Ranæ in Gallia et Italia Clamosæ, in Britannia mutæ, in
Hibernia nullæ." Colgan says, that after the English conquest
frogs were seen first in Ireland; they appeared in Waterford
when the English landed; they then disappeared, and were not
seen until William the Third came with his Dutchmen from
Frogland. What shall be said now, when, since the union,
toads!!! actual toads, have been found in the county of Kerry?
Reader, I have actually seen a box-full brought from that district; and, at this moment, a Doctor of Divinity keeps an Irish
toad as his quiet pet, in his apartments in Trinity College: it
has borne Dublin air these three years; no doubt he will die
when O'Connell brings back our Parliament to College-green.
Nay, more, I am informed that lately a snake was caught in
the woods of Curraghmore, county of Waterford.

way, if he wanted to send them down into the sea, he ought to have driven them to Slieve Crohan in Achill, or the Cliffs of Moher in Clare, for the Lug down which he is said to have tumbled them is not in the direction of the ocean.) Well, I say all this in an allegory. The serpents that the Roman bishop dealt with were the doctrines of the Druids, and it was on this eminence that the Druids had one of their great religious establishments. Croagh Patrick is, as I believe, very like Mount Carmel, a lofty mountain impending over the ocean, visible from all parts.

Here a sect misapplying some true religion and mingling it up with much superstition and will-worship, made a sort of leader or demi-god of the prophet Elias, and from him arose, according to their own statement, the order of the Carmelites; now it is well ascertained that the Druids were very similar to, if not actually the same, as Carmelites. The historian of the Carmelite order calls the Druids "Sanctos Druides, Eliæ filiæ, fratres nostros et prædecessores." (Hist. Carmel. Ord. 1. 1. 4.)—that is, holy Druids, sons of Elijah, our brethren and predecessors. Another author says, "If you examine the mode of living and regular observances of the Druids, you will find them to be true Carmelites." Now, what I want to show is, that the Druids* had fixed on this sea-over-

* Some one has observed, that as Augustine the Monk came to England to put down the Culdee religion, so Patrick came to Ireland for the same purpose. Were the Culdees Christianized Druids?

Y

hanging mountain as their Carmel—this they had enclosed with their Cyclopean wall, and, no doubt, there were also their circles, and pillar stones, and other monuments, until they were destroyed by their Roman enemies; and it is of little consequence to my position that the Carmelites have now joined the ranks of all-conquering Rome—Rome, that has absorbed and assimilated every former superstition, as Rome civil did every Pagan rite and polity. It does not weaken my argument that the provincial of the Carmelites, now in Ireland, is as little like Elijah as he is like a Druid. Still I maintain that the conquest Patrick achieved was over the "Sanctos Druides," and their rites and place—their Carmel—the high place where their honour dwelt.

I have a good deal more to say about my sublime half-acre. Coasting along this remarkable wall, I turn again to the westward, and come to a lofty heap of stones, somewhat like a cairn, which my guide told me was the Virgin's station; this seemed the most knee-worn of all the rest—the very hardest of rocks, the primitive quartz, was worn smooth by superstitious flesh, and all round this mount of Mary were little heaps of stones, generally about a bushel full. These were the memoranda of Aves, said in rapid succession by the votaries of the scapular,* who make Mary their great goddess.

---

* It seems that when the Carmelites, or Druids, were evicted from the Reek, they have made a re-entry and reprisal as the inventors of the scapular. So it is again the Carmel of our Lady.

On the Virgin's heap lay a large, rude, red stick—
"What's that ?" says I.

"Oh sir," says the little boy, who, fine child as he
was, had still attended me and without any apparent
fatigue, would every now and then put in his word
and give out the legendary information he was possessed of—"that is a part of the bier that bore up
Bob of the Reek when they brought him to be
buried."

"And who," said I, "is Bob of the Reek, and why
is he buried here ?"

"Oh, in troth, sir," said the guide, "he *desarved*
it, for of all men living he spent the most time *here:*
there, sir, is where he lies, throw a stone, as I do, on
his grave, and my blessing go with you, for Bob is
worthy of it." So I threw my stone on a little cairn,
and then inquired about Bob.

"Oh then, sir, Bob was the boy for doing penance,
or *dhurrus*, for others, and he used, day after day, to
be coming up here, and going the rounds here on his
bare feet, and then upon his two bare knees, for any
poor sinner who either was unable, from want of
health or other means, of coming themselves to the
Reek, and he did it so chape, and so he might, for
he got in the season so many jobs, that he could
afford to do them for less than another, and he was
honest entirely; entirely, not one round would he
wrong a poor sinner of, and he has his reward, poor
Bob, heaven's light be round him as he rists."

" And how did Bob live in the winter season when no stations are kept?"

" Why, he lived amongst the neighbours, ay, with the gentle-folk themselves, and a merrier, pleasanter, happier companion there was not in the whole country round—oh, master dear, it is he that would have tould ye all the outs and ins of the holy well, and about Patrick and Fiechus and the bell."

" Well, now you talk of the bell, what's come of it?"

" Why, then meself never saw it, but I am tould it's to the good this very day—a family descended from Fiechus, meself forgets their name, but they keep it for the good of the country; for when the bell, Patrick's own bell, is brought out, let the man swear what he may upon Gospel or Breviary, when he comes to lay his hand upon the bell he would turn black in the face if he swore any thing but the truth."

It was now time for us to think of descending; the cloud on the top was getting darker and more dripping, and though our watches assured us that the sun was not yet set, the gloom was so dense that we thought it better to descend. We, of course, went down by another way, which, if I spell right and understand my informant's Irish, is called Scolpa na Aigle, or the Eagle's Road. The reader should recollect that before Patrick took all the honours of the Reek it was called Croachan Aigle, the Eagle's Mountain. Now this descent is on the north-west side, and looks towards the mighty Atlantic, but, as yet, we were still in the cloud, and I could not but observe one thing which calls for speculation: there was on the surface, as we descended, a thin coating of bog not more than a foot thick, covering the silicious rock; now this bog, or rather what centuries ago was bog, exhibited a singular appearance— the whole minute and moory matter was washed away by the continual rains that fall *now*, at this great elevation; and nothing is left but the fibres of bog-plants that run in a ramified net-work in every direction. It is thus: Suppose I took a square foot of turf, or peat (as the English call it), and poured from a height, a stream of water so as to wash away all the soluble and powdery matter, and left nothing but the skeleton of fibres behind. Such was the state of the bog near the summit of Croagh Patrick; it assured me that some great change had taken place in the climate since this bog was formed, and that as it once *grew*, so now it has died and become a sort of anatomical preparation under the increasing rains and storms that characterise our present climate;* perhaps, when I get to Achill, I may give my explanation of all this, but for the present no more need be said by one professing to be no meteorologist.

* My friend, Lieutenant Larcom, of the Ordnance Survey, who, in my opinion, knows as much of Ireland—its history—its antiquities—its capabilities of every kind, as any Englishman existing—informs me that he has seen on Sliemish, in the county of Antrim, the same washing off of the ancient bog surface of the mountain.

And now we had descended so low as to drop from out the cloud—all at once we entered "the precincts of the cheerful day," and what a transition. We were yet high enough to have a magnificent prospect, and that at the most genial of moments, just as the setting sun was gilding with its long glories earth and ocean; and all the lesser eminences that lay below that "Cumulo stratus," that was supported, as I may say, by the pillar of Croagh Patrick, sparkled with the brilliancy that shone from the radiant throne of the setting sun. All the three hundred islands in Clew Bay sent their long shadows in beautiful contrast over its elsewhere silver surface; and then off to the north-west the mountainous head of Achill, and *it* had its canopy of clouds, and so had the far away retiring ranges that ran towards Nephin; but Clare Island, the beautiful western isle, reposing, in form like an Egyptian Sphynx, along the line of the ocean, its inferior heights were all gilt and sparkling with the glories of the orb that was fast descending behind it.

I never saw such a contrast from the gloom of that superstitious place, covered as it was with its own genial cloud, to the golden splendour of a sun-setting in the month of May: it was, as it were, to leave the temple of some demon god where all was melancholy and cruel, to enter the church of the true Deity where all is beauty and benevolence—all light, love and glorified gladness.

The sun had now gone down, the golden path that lay along the placid Atlantic had vanished, the

crimson-fringed throne of clouds,* behind which the
orb had retired, was beginning to lose the intensity
of its lustre, and all over land and sea came that soft
and drowsy repose, that hinted broadly, that night
must soon spread her universal curtain, so we hastened
to get down, and as Miss Botherem says, "exerted
our energies."

While half running, half leaping, I kept up to the
guide, and still insatiable as to knowledge about the
Reek, was questioning him and the little boy; I
asked the man had he ever been up as a pilgrim; he
said that while his mother lived, and while God gave
her health, he and she every year went up twice for
the good of the soul of his father; he did not remember ever to have seen *him*, for he died early, leaving
his mother a lone widow with himself, and another
who died early, to take care of; and that ever since
he could recollect, and he was able to follow her,
they went up to make their stations for the good of
his father's soul. The thing, I know, is all false—
Christ is the sinner's purgatory, and as he has done
the work *alone*, so he *alone* is able to save; but
though purgatory is a fable, only fit to gull the ignorant and fatten priests, yet how touching is the resting place it affords for filial and conjugal piety, when

* It has been often remarked, that Ireland is superior in its
CLOUD SCENERY to almost every other country. More than
one English tourist has noticed this; and none so truly and so
prettily as Lady Chatterton, in her recent ramble through the
south of Ireland; a very agreeable, *nice*, and ladylike work
indeed.

grasping at a fond superstition like this, and even beyond the tomb catching at the hope it holds out, still
would serve, and still would watch, and still hope for
union and communion in those everlasting mansions
where all graces cease except charity: This guide
was, while believingly devout, so as to accept all that
he had ever heard, however monstrous, as true, was
provokingly ignorant. Attempt to reason with such
a man, you might as well argue with the grey rock
on which his foot was planted—the Gospel is a
simple thing, it is adapted to the poor, and while hid
from the wise and prudent, it is often revealed unto
babes—yes, but not to babes that have been sucking
in poison will its sincere milk be acceptable. I
tried it with this stolid but kind creature; but it was
all in vain—he could not be brought to understand
how if Christ had finished the work, and made the
atonement for sin, there was no necessity for penances, expiations, and the merits of Mary and the
saints.

I asked him did many priests come up the Reek—
he replied not as many as used to come; he said he
saw seven going the rounds there together once, but he
was sure he would never see such a holy sight again.
I said I thought so too—the schoolmaster is abroad—
light is breaking in—Protestantism is reforming
Romanism whether it will or not. I think I shall live
to see the day, old as I am, when the schoolmaster,
the Bible schoolmaster, (and oh, for our common
country's sake, stand back ye schoolmasters of Lord

Brougham and of Mr. Wyse,) when the schoolmaster, not with Patrick's bell, but with Christ's
holy Gospel in his hand, shall ascend this mountain,
and as Patrick drove away the Druidical and Carmelite
serpents, so will he, with the light of truth, drive
away all the fond, dark, and profitable superstitions
that disgrace the Irish as a nation, and lower them
in the scale of intellectual existence.

I asked the guide did ladies ever ascend the Reek?

" Yes, *plase* your honor, Lord Sligo's daughter
did, and what's more than that, she rode up—yes,
your honour, and if you don't believe me I'll just
bring you to where the very colt that carried her is
now grazing."

It would have been no proof to me, that a young
lady had ridden up the Reek, to see a horse grazing
in a field; but 'the story, though difficult to give'
credit to, was so decidedly asserted, that I was fain to
believe it, and actually did go over, in the twilight,
to see the horse that performed such a feat. If ever
these trivial *sketches* reach the eye of the young
lady who rode the Kessaun Cruagh—she may see
how an old tourist admires the spirit and activity
that could back a horse where strong men find a difficulty in scrambling—honor be to the horse also as
well as the rider—he is now a poor spancelled thing,
altogether too active for the work he is put to; he is
like a wild country boy, fastened by hard fate to a
scrivener's desk, writing so many words for a shilling.
If I were Lord Sligo I would have made him my own,

or rather my daughter's—the good, sure, and active creature that carried my fair child over the Reek.

I cannot conclude my descent from the mountain without saying a word concerning the little boy between eight and nine years old, that of his own free will, and without his parent's knowledge, accompanied us the whole way; and when on our return my companion and I were allowing that we had enough of it, actually in going down skipped before us like a fawn, and seemed as gay and untired as if he was just let loose from school.

It appears that he never was up to the top of the mountain before, and he seemed of that unrestrained and self-willed character which is so common amongst the children of the lower classes ; who seem in a very unhappy, and I may say, dangerous way to themselves and others, permitted to take all manner of licence; and their parents appear not only to allow but to set them the example of giving full sway to all their appetites and passions. The boy stated that his mother allowed him to have a glass of whiskey every morning before his breakfast; what an infernal dose to send into the stomach of so fine a little creature; what a first and downward step towards making him a sensual devil hereafter. The boy's intellect seemed unusually precocious; could this constant stimulus have the effect of exciting him too soon? I shudder at the thoughts of his mental and bodily rottenness hereafter, and could not help sighing as I parted with this interesting child, never to see him more on this side of the grave, that it was his hard lot to be born·the son of a whiskey seller. So good night to CROAGH PATRICK, which afforded us a pleasant evening, and gave us a good appetite for the supper that awaited us at our very good inn in Westport.

CHAPTER XIV.

WESTPORT TO ACHILL.

Road from Westport to Newport—State of country tillage—Manure for potatoes—Burning soil—Sea-weed—Advantages and disadvantages of this manure—Newport—Appearance—Different from reality—Comforts of a Newport breakfast—Unpleasant position of Irish landlords—Sin of father visited on children—Beggar woman—Monument of a spiritual man—Friary of Borishoole—Enter the isthmus of Corraan—View of Clew Bay—View northward and westward—State of bogs in this district—Capabilities—A civil welcome—A great mistake—Ferry over Achill sound—Meet an archbishop.

I STARTED from Westport for Achill without eating breakfast. Don't attempt, reader, if ever you take this road, to follow my example, as you shall see by-and-by.

The road to Newport is through a hilly country, not unlike some parts of Ulster; the people were all busy, having the opportunity of fine weather, drawing sea-weed and putting it out on their fields as manure for potatoes. Ever since the burning of kelp has been given up, which, in a great measure it is here, and along the whole Irish coast, sea-wrack is now applied for manure, and it has wonderfully increased the growth of potatoes, and, consequently, the population. From the coast, thirty miles inland, it is brought on cars and drays, and when that is not practicable, on horses' backs, and not seldom on human backs, in panniers. The only boats I saw on Lough Corrib were employed in landing sea-

wrack; and in order to make the carriage more
convenient, it is dried like hay, and when put
out on the land it again swells out and dissolves. It
is a happy and singular circumstance that the farther
the wrack is brought inland, the less is required to
produce a crop of potatoes. I have heard some say,
that it takes four times as much on the sea-shore,
as it does for the same quantity of ground in the
interior. It may be questioned whether the great
dependence of the people on this comparatively novel
species of manure is not conducive to evil. In the
first place, because it is a precarious supply, depending much on the state of the weather* in the spring
months; in the next place, because it induces the
people who depend on it, to put off the potato-plant-
ing until they procure (and that often not until very
late in the season) a sufficiency of wrack. Besides,
I believe that it does not at all answer in very dry
seasons; and what I deem to be more 'objectionable,
it discourages other modes of procuring manure,
and the people have in a great measure given up the
practice of making manure by housing of cattle, by
composts, or other modes resorted to where sea-weed
is not to be had. At all events, it is the case, that
scarcity oftener occurs, and crops fail along the
western coast than elsewhere; and though this may

* I am informed that a stormy winter is prayed for in some
places along the coast, the tempest sending in a large quantity
of sea-wrack. It may be well said here at any rate, " it is an
ill wind that blows nobody luck." These prayers of the western
Irish must be allowed to be but selfish.

be mainly owing to the extreme wetness and uncertainty of the climate, I think it may also in many cases be accounted for, from their entirely depending on sea-wrack as a manure. No doubt, multitudes of people are employed in the cutting, gathering, and transporting it, while the season lasts; and many a life is lost, and many a severe sickness incurred in the rough and perilous labour of cutting the wrack off the rocks, sometimes many miles off shore.

Newport looks well, as many other bad towns do, at some distance. A river, a few ships, a bridge, some trees, and a long fronted mansion, belonging to the landlord, Sir Richard O'Donnell; and then the town, rising from the river up the opposite side of the hill,—all this looks well, and I was in good humour with the place, anticipating my breakfast; but when we passed the bridge, and made some inquiry for the inn, and were directed to an ugly, mean-looking pot-house, just near said bridge, as the only place where breakfast could be got; and when we entered this vile den, redolent of sour beer and effete whiskey punch, when we were sent up a tottering thing, half stair, half ladder, and into a room, small, frowzy, and unclean, wherein were two beds, out of which some persons had but just unnested themselves, in order to give us room for our repast—good English reader! don't you think it must have been a strong, sturdy appetite that could stomach a meal in such an apartment as this. Well, all I can say, good Mr. Englishman, is, that if you had come

eight miles of a sharp morning in the month of
May; if, moreover, many miles more were before
you, without any inn at all, and Achill at the end of
your day,—Achill, where you were not certain that
you could get a place to lay your head; why, you
would have done as we did, that is, eat away and be
glad, always assuring yourself that things are worse
in a Portuguese Venta or a Spanish Posada.

And now, reader, as I am upon economicals, allow
me to recommend my practice to you, which is,
always to take with you a pound or so of good tea,—
you will generally get plenty of fresh eggs and pretty
good bread; and provided with these, what great
reason have you to complain ?

Walk up the street of Newport, and you will see
that it was intended to be a better town that what it
now is. There are some large houses, which undoubtedly were built by those who anticipated more prosperity. But sundry tenements are in decay,—altogether
the place has a poor, starved, sickly look; and why
should it be so ?   Here is a quay just at the end of
the street, at which a vessel of 400 tons can unload.
Here is a fine bay easy of access,—the channel
deeper and with much fewer obstructions than that
of Westport—and yet all here is dull and unthrifty :
wherefore, I have no right to give a decided opinion;
perhaps it may be explained as owing to the incapa-
bility of the landlord to give any encouragement;
perhaps, like many other Connaught landlords, he
has inherited an immense estate, with proportionably

immense incumbrances, and has found the vexatious
position entailed on him of acting the landlord, without the power of doing so adequately or beneficially.
No wonder that men placed in such cruel positions
by the improvidence of their forefathers, should seek
to hide their heads in a foreign land. Alas! for
those in such a predicament, when the new tithe law
and poor law allow the mortgagee to go free, while
the poor nominal possessor of acres (even suppose
reckoned by tens of thousands) must discharge the
whole, scot and lot. I have said it before, and I
don't care how often I say it again, that I think the
extreme poverty of the lower classes, and the awfully
increasing state of our population, are mainly owing to
past improvidence and present embarrassments of the
landed proprietors. Sir Richard O'Donnell, I am
informed, is the nominal owner of 80,000 statute
acres. It is very likely that this gentleman has the
desire, the strong desire, to improve this immense
territory, which, for the most part, is one wild, unprofitable waste; but what can he do?—why the
poor rich man is walking with a millstone about his
neck and his hands tied behind his back,—it's a very
uncomfortable cravat!! No doubt you feel it, Sir
Richard,* and so do your tenantry; and it is very

* All that I have said about Sir R. O'Donnell is only my
own surmise, which may be as impertinent as unfounded. The
gentleman may be very unembarrassed, and the state of his
town and property may arise from altogether different causes.
I can only say that there are landlords in the predicament I
have *supposed* for Sir Richard.

hard, you know, to untie a cravat made of a mill-stone.

While sitting on the bridge waiting for our jaunt-ing-car to be harnessed, I was asked for charity by a woman, not very badly dressed, and who was accom-panied by a fine intelligent-looking little boy. She said she was a widow, and had three children at home, besides the little fellow along with her. I asked her why she did not send that fine boy to school? She said that the priest's school was no good, and that she dare not send him to the minister's. I asked her did she know the minister? She said she did, that he was a dear good man, and that if the people were let, they would love him.

" Does he help you ever ?"

" Troth, sir, I believe if I went to him he would, but I dare not go for fear of the priest, for he has warned us to have nothing at all to do with him."

I shall not here repeat the contemptuous expres-sions that this poor ignorant and, no doubt, preju-diced woman lavished on the religious opinions and practices of the landlord; she could not possibly un-derstand why he should have introduced into the town a *new* minister, and he such a poor, sorry, sad-looking man, that lived *on him* at the Big House,— when he had such a darlint clever man living ready made to his hand in the Glebe House. Enough of Newport,—I wish I may never see it again, until there is more industry, unity, charity, and, of course, prosperity amongst its people.

z

About a mile outside the town, on the road to Borishoole, I was shown a sort of monument on the road-side. I asked was that the record of some untimely death or murder. I could get no information. The man whom I asked, evaded my question, by asking in his turn, how would the likes of him know, seeing he did not live near hand? But on my return, the person travelling with me gave its history. It was erected over the place where a priest was found dead in the morning, after lying there all night. He was a friar, who got his living principally by saying offices. For what? For souls. No, guess again, reader,—you can't,—well, to put you out of pain, I'll tell you,—for saying offices, for spirits; yes, he went about blessing *potteen stills;* and according to his vocation he could not, as a *spiritual* person, avoid partaking of such blessed liquor, and it was on his return from such a sanctification as this that he fell down on the road-side, and was found dead in the morning.

Having passed over the bridge across the Borishoole river, I observed an ancient building some distance from the road, which I knew to be the Dominican friary, where there is a great patron on the fourth of August, St. Dominick's day. As it appeared neither large nor beautiful in ruins, and as I was extremely anxious to get early to Achill, I did not visit it. I am sorry now I did not spend some time there, for I have since heard that there are some very curious and large artificial caves in the vicinity,

whose character and position I should have liked to
examine.

Passing through two or three villages, (for the
country along Clew Bay is populous, thanks to
the sea-weed,) we began to ascend into the mountain isthmus that divides Clew Bay from the great
estuary that separates Achill from the main land.
There is a large tongue of it that runs up near Clew
Bay, and forms a peninsula of that tract of mountain
country called Corraan, which is immediately opposite to Achill.   Across this isthmus the road leads,
and an excellent road it is; and, reader, if ever you
travel it, just before you enter the pass that leads
by a turn of its direction, close to the estuary I have
just alluded to, give a long, large look at Clew
Bay;—I hope you will have as clear and sunny a day
as I had, and I think you will allow that it is scarcely
possible to behold a finer land and sea view.   Directly
under you, and to the left, the noble bay with its
multitude of islands, Innishmore, Innishma, Innish,
Crushna, Innisheougha, and I don't know how many
other Innishes—all green and fertile, some tilled,
some pasture.   No bay in the British isles has so
many islands; and then the large Isle of Clare, forming the great breakwater barrier against the Atlantic;
and from this quarter Clare really looked sublime; for,
on this side were its beetling cliffs, against which the
wind, that came not ungently from the north-west,
was sending the long Atlantic billows, which, meeting this iron wall, sent up the white foam on high,—

foam, which indeed was tossing and boiling and
surging on every rock around; and then the magnificent Croagh Patrick, the most beautiful of all Irish
mountains. There it stood to the south, overlooking
our bay, with its multitudinous isles, and it had
flung its cap away; its top acuminated to the sky,
"facile princeps;" the acknowledged superior, not
only in form, but in height, of every mountain within
the line of vision.

I had now entered on the peninsula of Corraan,
and mountains on the left shut out Clew Bay;
but we had a fine sheet of sea water on our right
that flowed up a sort of deep gully or ravine, and
seemed to have been intended to make an outlet here
into Clew Bay; and now, decidedly, we were within
that wild bog-covered district, that extends far away
to the north, comprising the district of Achill, Ballycroy, and Erris, and which, on inspection of the map,
the reader will see extends from Killala Bay southward
to Clew Bay, and from Mount Nephin, on the east,
until it meets the Atlantic. Along the sea-shore, and
especially in that comparatively low and sandy peninsula, called the Mullet, there is much cultivation; but
inland,—townless, roadless, treeless—one wide waste
of bog covers all. But it is not to be supposed that
this bog is like the great flat flow bogs in the centre
of the island, such, for instance, as the Bog of Allen.
No; the Bog of Erris, as well as of Connemara,
covers mountains, hills, champains, and vales.
Nature's universal brown vesture—it fits all; and

this is what, in my opinion, makes the reclamation of these wastes hopeful. Really the more I know of the great central red flow bogs of Ireland, the more I see the difficulty of profitably reclaiming them; but it is quite different with the western wastes; the shallowness of the boggy covering, which is seldom thicker than five or six feet, and the great inequality of surface, affording rapid and ready falls for drainings; the gravel that is invariably found underneath the bog, and what is best of all, the general proximity of limestone, and of coast, affording sea-wrack. These are capabilities which I am astonished are not, in this speculating day, taken advantage of; and that they are not taken advantage of, bespeaks not only the pecuniary difficulties of the landlords, but general conviction amongst monied men, that Ireland is as yet an insecure place for the investment of capital. When I have said so much, I think it is right to state some of the natural difficulties attending a speculation of the nature I now allude to; and the first great difficulty is the climate, which, though mild, as respects absolute heat and cold, is so very wet and stormy, that there is no certainty of the ripening or harvesting of any corn crop. Potatoes, it is true, may be grown, and very abundant crops produced, but then, as I have said before, this crop is extremely liable to fail, and a too wet or too dry season is equally fatal to it. There is another obstacle,* and that is, the comparatively small quantity

* Another obstacle to improvement speculation in Ireland is the want of industrial expertness and honesty amongst the

of dry land that can be procured for the pasture of
cattle. For, I hold it, that the moment a person
commences the drainage and consequent improvement
of a bog, no beast larger than a sheep should ever
be allowed to walk on it. It is only, then, on the
system adopted on the Continent, of housing the
cattle, that these wastes can be made good grass
lands. But if, by raising rape for seed or soiling; by
growing rye and hardy and early ripening kinds of
oats; by selecting a hardy race of sheep, and by
folding them, always at home in winter, and the
black cattle all the year round, I think a system of
profitable farming could be carried on in these now
desolate wastes, that would make a patriot Irishman's heart, when he saw it, sing with joy.

As I travelled along towards the island of Achill,
and saw the fine swells of land all around, not more
than fifty or one hundred feet elevated above the level
of the sea, when I saw the drainage so feasible, and
the manure on the spot, I set about castle-building,
and made myself (what indeed I am not, and more's
the pity,) an active young man, and with ten thousand pounds at my command, and with intelligent
and trustworthy stewards (and where are they to be

people. To get the wages and not do the work is the general
desire.   Sundry well-contrived and well-meant speculations
were broken down under these discouragements, and the cheap
labour of the Irish has been found, like other cheap things, to
be a bad commodity to trust to.   But the Irish may, and I
expect will yet be educated up to self-respect and trustworthi-
ness.

got?) Oh what great things would I not do before I came to the bottom of my ten thousand pounds. While castle-building in this way, my baseless bog enterprise was cut short by two men, who, hastily quitting their potato planting, and jumping on the road, came, and with hats off, and bodies bowed to the ground, wished my lordship welcome to the country, and long might I reign. I, in my turn, was *mighty* civil, but could not help asking them why they were so glad of *my* arrival, and why they called me a lord?

" Och, thin, don't we know your lord's reverence, and ain't you going over the sound to the island, and ar'n't they watching for yees, and looking out for yees this many a day."

Here I suspected there was some mistake—so I said, " Boys, I believe you mistake me for some one much greater than I really am?"

" Why, ar'n't you the Protestant archbishop going into Achill?

" Why 'tis true I am, as you see, going into the island, but I am no archbishop, as you may very well see by my travelling on a jaunting-car."

" Och then, sir, whoever you be, at any rate, we have done you no harm—so God speed you, whoever you are, but ar'n't you at any rate going to the settlement?"

Upon my informing them that I was, they retreated back to their work, convinced that they had not yet seen a Protestant archbishop; and I, no doubt, complacent at being taken, even by a Mayo spalpeen, for a prelate. I busied myself, on leaving these poor fellows, about divining what object they had in accosting me so civilly, supposing I was the Protestant archbishop: when there had gone forth such a command from the priests against any one in these parts speaking to a heretic—this, I confess, I could not explain so easily as their after anxiety to know whether I was going to the settlement or not, for they might have been anxious to ascertain that we were Protestants, lest it should come to the ears of their priests that they had saluted a Protestant prelate.

On arriving at the Ferry, where there is rather a comfortable little inn, I found that the Archbishop of Tuam had been in Achill for the last two days, and that this day he was expected to return. I moreover ascertained that I could not, in the present state of the tide, get my horse and jaunting-car into the island—that if I did get across myself I would have to walk ten miles to the settlement; and the inn-keeper, a very civil and comely woman, gave me the disinterested advice to go back the road I came, about five miles, when I would meet the boats that were bringing the archbishop back from the island, that these boats belonged to the coast-guard, who were stationed within three miles of the settlement, which I could then reach early in the evening, and that my horse and car might follow me next morning, when the tide allowed them to pass on. This advice I at once adopted, and returned back; and just as his

Grace was landing, hit the opportunity, and got from the officer commanding the coast-guard a most cordial invitation for me and my friend to accept the accommodation of his boat. Having the honor of a personal acquaintance with the archbishop, I received the pleasing information from him that he was quite satisfied at what he had seen in the island, was satisfied with the number and appearance of the children brought to confirmation; and indeed I do not think I ever saw a countenance lit up with more gratified good humour than was that of this fine and venerable old man, when he recounted all he saw and heard in this new field of Protestant labour. A Protestant prelate had never before been on these wild shores—and for him now to return in peace and safety, after confirming thirty persons, and seeing one hundred and twenty attend worship on an island where five years ago there was not a Protestant (except, perhaps, half a dozen of the coast-guard;) this was to this good man* a subject of gratulation, and his fine eye sparkled with almost youthful brilliancy as he described the settlement he had just left.

---

* I little thought, when I here saw this admirable Christian prelate, that before my book would pass through the press, he should have gone to his eternal rest. It is not for me to pass any detailed eulogium on this singularly faithful and pious bishop. My friend the Rev. J. D. Sirr, one of his own clergy, and one who knew and could appreciate all his fine qualities of head and heart, has published the funeral sermon, which he preached to a sincerely mourning audience. It is no flattery to say, that the sermon, warm as it came from the heart, is worthy of its subject.

CHAPTER XV.

ACHILL.

WHILE the boats were preparing to return I had
occasion to observe on the sides of the hills surrounding the cove in which our little fleet was moored, the
strongest heath I ever saw—some of it grew six feet
long, and though, perhaps, a cudgel could not be cut
out from any stem, sufficient to arm a faction leader
in a fair, yet I am sure I could have dressed up a
very pretty walking-stick stout enough for a city
dandy. This heath was splendidly in blossom, and
really was a beautiful covering for the sides of these
otherwise dreary hills—a fine covert also for game—
here a fallow, or even a red deer might have had its
lair, but this the country people will not allow, to the
great annoyance of sportsmen; for they are in the
habit of setting fire to these heath-covers, in order
that the cattle may, in the following autumn, find
browsing from the fresh, tender, succulent sprouts
that spring up from the burnt surface.

We soon set out—there were three boats, each as

well as possible appointed for either sailing or rowing, and as there was an emulation between the respective crews who should get on quickest, and as two of them had before night to go along the coast nearly twenty miles, it really was a beautiful and interesting sight, to see with what dexterity the respective crews would hoist or take in sail, and take to or lay by oars, according as the change in tide, current, or position required the different expedients for getting on. The estuary we were in, bounded on one side by Achill, and on the other by the mainland of Erris, and surrounded by mountains, was, on this clear and beautiful evening, a fine scene for such a boat-race. It was pleasant to see the good-humoured emulation which (as allowed by the commanding officer) prevailed, and as it more than once happened, by a rapid change from sailing to rowing, a point was turned by the boat in which I was, and so nearly half a mile was gained a-head of the others. It was pleasant, while getting on thus gaily, to look down into the clear, translucent water, and see the tide currents sweeping along with all the force of a river flood, and to observe the beautiful vegetations, the star-fish, the medusas, and all the, to me, singular productions of this land-locked sea-lake. Then, when tired looking down I had plenty to occupy my upward vision: to the east, the long ranges of the Ballycroy mountains trending towards their massive master, Mount Nephin; but it was to the west that my eye was attracted by the lofty and singular peaks of Achill—no where do

mountains look so lofty as when you view them from
a boat at sea—the smallness of the little skiff you are
in, and your low position contrast with the loftiness
of the hills. And here was one, singularly curious in
the form which it assumed, it was not a conical point,
but like a tall, square tower erected on the very
summit of the range, it was not unlike the Devil's
Bit in Tipperary, but infinitely loftier; this was Slieve
Croghan, that impends over the Atlantic; this curious
elevation which looks like a gigantic hill fort, is a
part of the face of the great precipice that overhangs
the ocean. I asked the chief of the boat's crew, who
sat beside me, was this a good place for fish; he said
not at all, that sometimes, but not often, herrings
came in, but that he was sure of the fact, that within
these last few years the fish of all kinds had, in a
great measure, deserted these shores; I suggested to
him the possibility of *this* being owing to the every
year increasing cutting of sea-wrack from the rocks,
for it appears almost evident, that if the places where
the fish-spawn is deposited, and where the fry in
their early life resort, are disturbed by the weed-cut-
ting, it may be as sure a way to destroy fish, as by
burning heath on the mountain to drive away game.

We were now approaching where this sea-lough,
which was hitherto a fine expanse of water, narrows
to a strait not more than a furlong across, dividing
Achill from a small island of about three hundred
acres in extent, called Innisbeagle. This is called the
Bull's Mouth: I suppose when tide and storm urge

on the ocean from the north-west, this narrow pass
roars like a bull. Here is the coast-guard station, at
which we were to land and make the best of our way
to the settlement.

Whenever you see a coast-guard station on any of
our coasts you may be sure to find something like
comfort, and here I found not only comfort but civility,
for I was invited to go in and get refreshment, which I
declined, because as the sun was now fast descending I
was anxious to get to the settlement before it set; so,
accompanied by one of the coast-guard who was going
further on in the island, we started on our walk of
four miles.

Immediately about the Bull's Mouth the land in
Achill seems green and good; there was some tillage
along the shore towards the north, and within a range
of sand hills there were on green pasturable uplands
some sheep grazing; and altogether this tract seemed
to be under the management of a thriving and rather
improving man—I understand he has a long lease
under Sir R. O'Donnell;* but you soon leave this,
ascend somewhat higher on the island, and come on
the wide waste of brown bog that covers the whole
interior, whether hill or vale; and here I may observe
that the general character of this bog-surface is different from that of the bogs in the interior—its colour
is of a lighter brown, or rather approaching to grey,

* Until lately, I was under the impression that Sir Richard
O'Donnell was the owner, in fee, of Achill; I have since heard
that his tenure is a lease for ever under the Marquis of Sligo.

and consists of an aggregation of vegetable fibre in an inert state, neither living nor yet decomposing. This is a state of bog, in my opinion, much more capable of holding gravel and retaining manure when drained, than the softer and less fibrous stuff of which the inland red bogs are composed; here, on all sides, I repeat, is a wide field for the outlay of capital; but this must be brought about by a landlord who can alter and will alter the state of farm tenures in this island, consisting of thirty thousand acres, of which he is the sole proprietor.

The person who attended me on my walk to the settlement was a very intelligent man; I won't say that he was without his prejudices, but I believe him to be a person of truth, and that he was much interested in the prosperity and improvement of the poor natives of the district. Though not a native, he had been resident in the island for some years previous to the coming of Mr. Nangle, and I was glad I could receive information from one *not* belonging to Mr. Nangle's settlement, and who, it might be supposed, was not imbued with the "*esprit de corps*" inseparable from one of that *religious* colony. This person gave me a very sad picture of the state of the island five years ago: there were about five thousand inhabitants dwelling in villages, and though the population was not at all in proportion to the size of the island and its great capabilities, yet it was in excess, as compared with the means of subsistence, for, according to the long established practice of the

people, though there was no check upon population,
there *was* upon the means of support, in consequence
of their village regulations. All the occupiers of the
villages held in *common* from the landlord; there was
a portion of the ground nearest to the village enclosed
from the rest for the growth of potatoes and oats,
and a wild range of boggy and mountain land outside
was commonage, on which each family had the right
of pasture for a certain number and quality of cattle;
the enclosed land was also, in a measure, in common,
for though each family had its own ridge, no family
had a field to itself; this was somewhat like the
ancient Rundale system in England, and it was the
system, I believe, which, before the English conquest,
prevailed all over Ireland;[*] indeed I consider that
any one who had the curiosity to become acquainted
with the habits, the manners, the superstitions, the
vices, the virtues, and the rural economy of the
ancient Irish, would find Achill the best place for his
inquiry; for I am convinced, the people five years
ago were there in the very same state they were one
thousand years ago, and *that*, let bards, senachies,
and poetical historians say what they will, was
barbarous indeed. Reader, pardon this digression, I
was speaking of the Rundale system—each family, I
said, had their respective ridge in the enclosure; a
family might have more ridges than one, but it did

---

[*] As each householder had his ridge in the enclosure set
apart for tillage, so the church had its ridge, or ridges, called
Patrick's ridges.

not follow that they should be adjoining each other;
therefore the same ridge must be tilled in the same
way, and according to the same practices as were in
use years ago. A man, if he wanted more tillage ground,
could not go beyond the old village enclosure and
take in a new spot for himself. No such thing: if he
brought in any new piece to cultivation every householder had a right to his ridge therein, as well as the
man who made the improvement. This, of course, raised
a bar against improvement, unless the whole population joined in what it was not easy to get them to do, a
concerted enclosure. It may be thus supposed how
much faster mouths would increase than the means
of filling them. Then there was no such thing ever
seen in the island as a plough or a harrow; there
might have been a car, or two, that went on *slides*
instead of wheels. The only instrument used in
cultivation was one peculiar to the district, called a
gowl gob, or two-bladed spade, constructed unlike any
thing I had ever seen before, having two long, narrow
blades pointed with iron, fixed on one handle—this
seemed light of use and suitable to the working of the
boggy and sandy soil. The dress of the people was
as primitive as their husbandry; very few of the
men wore hats, their long glibs were their protec-
tion from the weather—the woman, beside the russet-
brown* woolsey gown, and the madder-red short

* It is curious to see how this western people assimilated the
colour of their clothing to the brown and dingy-red of the bogs
amidst which they lived ; all wild animals, in this way, have the
colour of the glebe on which they lie. The grouse and the
Connaught woman are attired in nearly the same colours.

petticoat, with the yellow kerchief tied down close to their heads; then their houses were very like a Hottentot's kraal. An Achill village consisted of a congeries of hovels thrown indiscriminately together, as if they fell in a shower from the sky, and their construction was as follows:—a dry stone wall was built of a form like an obtuse oval, for they had not arrived at the art of making a square quoin, or erecting a gable end. Outside this wall, and at about a foot distance, another loose wall was run up, and the space between the two filled with sea sand, and then this was roofed, generally with timber washed on shore from wrecks, and covered with heath, which covering did not reach over the outside wall, and form an eave, but rested on the middle between the walls, and the moisture from above passed, as it should, through the intervening sand. Well those people, though perhaps as healthy and long-lived as any other, must sometimes be sick, and how were they to manage then?—no doctor or apothecary within thirty miles. Why there was an old woman resident in one of the villages, looked on as half witch, half doctress, and she, indeed as decided, and, no doubt, successful in her treatment, exceeded even Doctor Sangrado himself in the simplicity of her practice. She administered one dose—handy it was, but heavy. What do you think, reader, it was? Paracelsus himself could not match this " *opus magnum*"—this mineral specific—why in the morning, fasting, she

2 A

made the Achillian open his mouth wide, and down she sent a musket bullet!!!

How *this* operated, whether mechanically by its weight, or whether some charm accompanied it, I cannot venture to declare; neither shall I venture to answer a question put to me by a grave and dignified doctor, namely, when informing him of the Achill medicine, how many bullets the administratrix of this dose was possessed of.

I am sorry to have further to record that the morality of the people (according to my informant) was at a low ebb; that infanticide was not uncommon, and the intercourse from which it resulted still more frequent. In one instance, certainly, the Achillians had caught at an invention not known a thousand years ago, that was potteen distilling and drinking— the former is in a great measure suppressed by the vigilance of the excise service, but the latter still goes on, and as much is paid for ardent spirits by this very poor people, as would maintain four Protestant missionaries, twelve schoolmasters, and twelve Scripture-readers on the island. But the priests would rather have the former than the latter, for in their estimation, as all the world very well knows, the one are only *merry-making spirits*, while the other are downright devils. I would not have it at all understood that it was the intention of my sensible companion to say that his poor neglected people were without good qualities—quite the reverse: there could not be a more kind, civil, and obliging people, grateful for any kindness shown them, and sensible enough to see that they wanted instruction, and exceedingly anxious to ensure its advantages for their children; in short, these people had all the virtues and vices of semi-barbarians: gentle until their passions were roused—kind until they expected to receive injury, and ready to believe more of evil than of good respecting a stranger, and his motives for coming amongst them.

CHAPTER XVI.

THE SETTLEMENT.

Village of Dugurth—Its contrast with the Settlement—Appearance of
Settlement—Reception—The principals—The physician—Better at least
than the bullet doctress—Garden—Cultivation—Fruits and vegetables—
Strawberry better than bilberry—People will be cured though cursed—
Infant school—Is such an institution fanatical—Economy of settlement
and distribution—A printing press in Achill ! !—Only think of it—And
done by jumpers—This a jump, and that a large one—Trait of barbarism—
Discovery of a Protestant bed of limestone—*Timeo Danaos et dona fe-
rentes*—So say priest-obedient Catholics, and won't use it—Morning worship
at the settlement—Cultivation of farm—Profit and loss—Settlement, in my
opinion, not happily located—Effects of storms—Innisbeagle—A reach of
priestcraft—Opposition of Roman Catholic clergy—Placed in its true
light—The penal laws of the pitchfork and boghole exercised against
Jumpers—Will they continue in force—An argumentum ad hominem.

[☞ Those whose desire is to establish the sway of the Roman Catholic
Hierarchy in Ireland may skip this chapter, unless disposed to read what
they won't like.]

WHILE thus conversing, our length of road was
beguiled, and just as the sun sunk behind the
western range of Slievemore, but while all the hill
tops were bright with its departing light, we entered
the village of Dugurth. Just such a village as I have
above described, but certainly containing some houses
that *had* gable-ends; but for the most part of the
construction I have alluded to, a dirty, dreary, uncouth place; and then, turning a corner of the road,
and ascending an eminence, "the Protestant settlement" came into view, and truly it was a contrast to
the congeries of wigwams called Dugurth; it consists of a long range of slated buildings fronting
the south-east, and with its rere to Slievemore,

that rises in great loftiness to the north-west,
ornamented by a sort of pedemented building in the
centre, having a handsome broad esplanade in front,
on the other side of which extend some well-culti-
vated, well-ordered gardens.   All this formed a *tout
ensemble*, peculiarly striking and satisfactory, as connected with extraordinary contrasts that presented
themselves on every side.

Having the pleasure of an acquaintance with both
Mr. Nangle and Mr. Baylee, the superintending
clergymen of the settlement, I soon found myself at
home, was most hospitably entertained and lodged,
and had for the rest of the evening a pleasing and
truly instructive conversation with these gentlemen
and their admirable consorts.   The next morning I
also had the pleasure of meeting another friend, Dr.
Adams, a physician who left his practice in Dublin,
where, besides his professional income, he was in the
possession of a good private fortune.   Yet this man,
having come down out of curiosity to see the settlement, was so taken with the great field of usefulness
lying here before him, that he gave up his practice
and comfortable house in Stephen's-green, built himself a dwelling here, laid out a pretty garden, now
producing abundance of vegetables and some fruit,—
the first fruit, except a bilbery, that ever ripened in
the island; and what is better than all this, he has a
well-furnished dispensary, where he spends two days
of the week, from morning until evening, and where

he instructs a young native in the compounding of medicine.

Now, though some may be inclined to doubt whether Dr. Adams's doses are better for the stomach than the old woman's bullet; yet all must allow that, though a bullet may *cause* it cannot *cure* broken arms, legs, or heads. It does not let blood so neatly as a lancet: and, after all, even Dr. M'Hale, and his men of might, Fathers Hughes and Dwyer, cannot but allow that Dr. Adams's dispensary is better than the old woman and her ball. So the people think at any rate, and they *do* come to be cured and will come, though the priests say it is better for them to die and go to heaven, than come to be cured by a devil's child and go to hell hereafter. Alas such is the love of life, that they run even *that* chance.

Dr. Adams, besides his medical efficiency, has made himself extremely useful in the conducting of the infant school. The dispensary is his *business*,—the infant school his *recreation*. What a fanatic this man is: may be so; but of all the forms and phases of fanaticism I ever met or heard of, this is the least objectionable. The pope himself, however he may wish him out of Achill, would admire him. I am sure the venerable old Italian priest *would* praise him. Yes he *would;* and only think of the sovereign pontiff beatifying the doctor, and making him a second St. Luke, as far as a pope could do so.

I rose early in the morning and visited the whole range of buildings of which the settlement is com-

posed. The first of the line to the north is Dr.
Adams's house; next the infant school; then the
boys' daily and Sunday school, which has a communion table, and reading-desk and pulpit, and answers for
the present, as the chapel; then come the two central
houses, forming the residence of the chaplains; next
the female school; then the printing office; then
the house of the steward; and next the houses of
the schoolmasters and Scripture-readers. Pleased,
as indeed I was, with all this, I took advantage of the
time which was to elapse before morning prayers, to go
down to the sea-shore, which lies about a quarter of
a mile to the left; there to see the cliffs, and inspect
the fine bed of limestone that has been lately discovered, and which promises to be of such advantage to
the vicinity. Why, if the Protestant settlement had
done no other good to Achill, the finding of this
TREASURE would have proved a blessing. The whole
island is one great primitive formation, and gneiss is
the prevailing rock. The Rev. J. D. Sirr, who, besides being a truly pious Christian pastor, and an able
writer on religious subjects, is a good geologist,
walking along the shore for his recreation, while
spending some time at the settlement, detected this
immense mass of limestone. As it belongs to the primitive formation, it, of course, contains a great deal
of silex, and like that of the similarly circumstanced
districts of Connemara and Donegal, is white, flesh,
and dove coloured; and it was a pleasant lounging
hour I spent amidst these sea-cliffs, admiring, not

only the curious sea vegetations* and animals, but
also the curious inroads that the pholadæ and other
marine animals of that class were making in the
limestone, while the gneiss and granite remained
untouched.

Taking care to return to the settlement in proper
time, I of course joined those who were from all sides
approaching the house of prayer. All persons belonging to the settlement, before breakfast and supper
attend public worship at a stated hour; about
forty persons were present on this occasion. The
service was as follows : first a hymn, set to some
simple but sweet popular tune; the air chosen for the
day was "Old Lang Syne," and all joined, and it
was sweet and interesting; and then was a chapter
read in Irish, and briefly commented on by the minister in English; and then there were some of the
beautiful collects of our Church Service read, and we
were dismissed.   After breakfast I went forth to see
the gardens and the farm; there were good and
thriving vegetables in the gardens, and some few trees
of the poplar sort that were venturing on a little
growth; about thirty acres are reclaimed, and there
were promising crops of artificial grass-oats, and
potatoes. The houses of the settlers were scattered
up and down through the improved land, and on con-

---

* It was stated to me that the people had no estimation for
this limestone because it was discovered by Protestants. They
made no use of it.   This won't last long.   The schoolmaster
and printer have got to Achill.

versing with the steward I found him an intelligent and business-like person. The shortness of my stay precluded me from making any inquiry as to the economics of the farm. In the present up-hill state of the work, embarrassed as the conductors are with all manner of difficulties and opposition, I think it would not be fair to object, even suppose the expenses far exceeded the profits—my conviction was, that all concerned in the oversight of the whole settlement were honestly and vigorously doing their duty. But here I may observe, that I think the settlement has not been happily located. The take consists of one hundred and thirty-three Irish acres, the greater part of which extends up Slieve More, one of the loftiest mountains in Connaught, the rest of it is situated in a valley, or rather gully, that crosses the island from north-east to south-west, and it is in a direct line with the gully that the buildings of the settlement range; the consequence is, that the winds, the terrible winds of this climate, rush through this valley and sweep all before them.*

The settlement, therefore, though it may look very well on a fine summer's morning or evening, must be a fearful place for a winter's residence; but independent of its unhappy position, there is not enough of reclaimable land to support the people, and were it

---

* The finest field of oats (says Mr. Nangle in the seventh page of his third Report,) ever seen in Achill, growing on six acres of our reclaimed land, was almost totally destroyed by the rain and storms; our potato crop also failed.

not that Mr. Nangle has been fortunate enough to obtain from Sir Richard O'Donnell a lease of a fine improvable island, called Innisbeagle,* I really do believe that the priests would have been successful in their attempt to starve them out of Achill. But getting possession of this isle, containing three hundred acres of comparatively level ground, all improvable, and having along its shores an inexhaustible supply of sea-weed, the colony may now bid defiance to the priests, and may grow even more than is required for their own subsistence. I had for my dinner, both days I staid on the island, as good beef, stall-fed, from the produce of the farm, as could be desired. I am sure wheat can be grown on Innisbeagle, and as a mill is being built to grind it, I expect that in a very few years this colony will show a smiling and thriving, as well as a religious aspect.

And here I must speak somewhat at large of the

---

* Amongst the many companies got up in London, one has been set on foot for cultivating the waste lands of Ireland. Now the moment it was known that such a company was in being, the Mayo priests determined to make it a cat's-paw, and aware how essential it was to the overthrow of the Achill settlement that the island of Innisbeagle should be snatched out of Mr. Nangle's grasp, it was made evident, such is the power of Jesuits!!! that no part of the west of Ireland was so advantageous for the new company's operations as this little Innisbeagle—out of a million of acres, this island of three hundred acres was the only spot fit for a commencement of operations. It could not possibly be done without. Accordingly application was made to the landlord, Sir R. O'Donnell, and a handsome offer proffered ; to his credit, it is to be said, that as he had promised it to Mr. Nangle, nothing would tempt him to recede from his agreement.

opposition which this settlement of Mr. Nangle's has met with from the Roman Catholic clergy of the diocese of Tuam. It must be allowed that it was not in human nature for them to see a Protestant, a decidedly Protestant and polemic settlement made in a place where never Protestant had slept one night before, (except some of the coast-guard, who though *quartered* were not *settled*, and who, when they departed, left nothing behind.) A fair, honest, open, uncompromising hostility, Mr. Nangle had a right to expect, and was prepared for; an opposition similar to what we might suppose would have been made to a convent of monks or friars, if they had chosen to settle in the exclusively Protestant Isle of Man or Anglesey. But here the priests have actually gone beside themselves with rage and vexation. Mr. Nangle set up his schools—he provided good masters, and a system of instruction commenced such as never was seen in Achill before—for the priest, and indeed the parson who drew tithe from the island, never troubled their heads about the teaching of the people; no matter how the flock fed, so that they could be fleeced. But now the raging priests came in and cursed the parents if they did not take away the children from the heretic schools. " Give us something then in their place (said the people) and we will do your bidding." The National Board here was ready to help the priests in their necessity, and funds were supplied—houses procured or built—masters, such as they were, provided, and Romish education began;

and the people of Achill have to thank Mr. Nangle
for *this*.　Well, as yet the priests had done nothing
very outrageous; they acted like conscientious men in
doing their best to keep the children away from the
danger of imbibing false doctrine; a Protestant clergyman should and would use his influence in the same
manner if he saw his young parishioners induced to
go to a convent school.　But the priests did not stop
here, and their commands were, " have nothing to
do with these heretics—curse them, hoot at them,
spit in their faces—cut the sign of the cross in the air
when you meet them, as you would do against devils—
throw stones at them—pitch them, when you have
opportunity, into the bog holes—nay more than that,
do injury to yourselves in order to injure them—don't
work for them, though they pay in ready money every
Saturday night—don't sell them any thing, though
they provide you with a market—ready money and a
good market at your own doors—nay, don't take any
medicine from their heretic doctor, rather die first."
This was exacting great sacrifices, and that to please
men who seemed never to care for them, until this terrible Nangle and his jumpers came into the island. Have
these anathemas, these directions to do bodily injury,
these self-denying ordinances, succeeded? Not quite: the
children of Roman Catholics come *yet* to the schools:
the colonists can still get potatoes, oats, and Keem
mutton to buy.　The people are beginning to look
foolish on finding that Roman Catholics from Westport can be hired in the spring and autumn to do the

extra labour of the settlement, and they think, and that justly, that it is carrying self-denial too far to let others, and they of the Church of Rome, carry away the hard cash that they are not allowed to pocket. It is not in human nature for such opposition to succeed. The Romish arch-prelate may come into the island, as he did lately, with mitre on head, and vestmented in all pontifical splendour, and he may set up a cursing stone, and call all true to Rome to come and there covenant to have no dealings with the hateful heretics—but the thing won't do—some will even on selfish grounds break through the absurd TABOO that the priests have drawn, and others will begin to think daily better and better of the Protestants who have provided them, however indirectly, with schools, and a more active and circumspect priesthood; have given them a sight of a bishop and introduced cultivation, order, sobriety, and decency, into the island.

But what an audacious set these Romish priests are—I declare I have no patience with them—here are they assuming in Dublin, and all over England and Scotland, such a bland, and soothing, and liberal aspect, and they come and even ask our Protestant bishops to give them money to build their chapels; yes, and conservative lords and squires are found giving sums, and those large ones, to build chapels. A Protestant landed proprietor has given a large territory to the monks of La Trappe. Moreover, if a man refuses to aid them in building schools, chapels, and convents, he is pointed at as a bigot—may be he is ?—

well, but look at the proceedings of these most exacting and expecting, and very bland priests in the west.
Here comes a Protestant clergyman, altogether un-
connected with church property of any sort, not
drawing one penny from the " blood-stained tithes,"
but depending on the voluntary system, as much, and
infinitely more than the priests themselves; and he
takes from a *Protestant* landed proprietor a piece of
ground in a totally neglected island, and there he
opens schools, into which he don't *drive*, he merely
invites children, he sets about an improved system of
culture, encourages industry, discourages drunken-
ness and disorderly conduct, as far as possible
requires that all within his influence should abstain
from violence, injustice, or breaches of the peace, and
lo! because he has the *impertinence* to molest the
priest's *owlish*, silent, solitary reign, they are to
be cursed, hooted, stoned, pitchforked, and thrown
into bog-holes, and a man calling himself a priest of
Jesus is found, and that openly, saying, that he has
encouraged his followers to do these things. I really
consider these such unwise proceedings on the part
of the Romish clergy, that I might suspect, if I did
not know the singleness of purpose of Mr. Nangle, and
those associated with him, that the Most Rev. Father,
Dr. M'Hale, was bribed by him, to resort to such absurd opposition, to serve the cause of the settlement,
and at the same time bring their own intolerant system
nto disgrace with all sober men. At all events
the arch-prelate has given Mr. Nangle the benefit
(and it is a great one) of a persecution.

And now, gentle reader, I will give you a bit of advice, which you may follow or not just as it pleases you—when next a pair of bland, glozing, supplicating faces, stand at your door, asking you for some aid to build their chapel, school, hospital, or convent, just put a report of the Achill mission into their hands, and ask them how their church can carry thus two faces under one hood; the face of a ramping roaring lion, in the west, and elsewhere that of a pretty playful lamb, wagging its tail, while it is sucking you and fattening on you?*

I am glad I have done with the subject. It would have given me pleasure to record liberal rather than illiberal acts; it would have pleased me more to have to say that Popery, where it can, is not that cursing, banning, biting, inquisitorial thing that it was in the dark ages; but when I see the logic of the cudgel, the stone, and the bog-hole resorted to at present, I cannot, even if my book never sold, forbear expressing my indignation.

---

* I would willingly, if I could, confine my accusation of intolerance respecting the Achill settlement to Dr. M'Hale and his subordinate clergy, but I *cannot* do so, when I find not one single Roman Catholic voice raised through the empire against the penal proceedings of the Achill priests. Suppose, for an instant, that a Romish settlement were commenced in the Isle of Anglesea, and that the bishop of Bangor and the clergy of his diocese issued forth such commands and curses as have been promulgated against the Achill Protestants. What a commotion would not this raise—how the Protestant press of the empire would sound, and *that* justly, the tocsin of reprobation.

CHAPTER XVII.

TOUR TO SLIEVE CROGHAN.

I CAME not to Achill for the sole purpose of seeing this settlement, planted as it is purely on the voluntary system, asking tithe from no man, and proposing to put money into, instead of taking it out of the pockets of the natives. If there never was a Mr. Nangle or his colony, I would visit this curious and hitherto unnoticed district. So, as I had a day freely at command, and had inspected all the economy of the settlement, I determined to make an excursion to the western end of the island, where Slieve Croghan lifts its bold perpendicular front, and breasts, as the great bastion of Europe, the Atlantic ocean. I felt obliged to my much esteemed friend, the Rev. Mr. Baylee for undertaking to go with me, and to bring two or three companions, who would not only add to my information and amusement during our long excursion, but also give such a strong appearance to our party that there was no danger of bodily injury; for though on our onward journey we were to pass through or near villages where no priests dwelt, and therefore would, in all likelihood, be treated with civility and respect, yet as on our return we should pass villages where the priest, schoolmasters and confraternity men reside, there we might chance to receive some salutations, harder even than hootings. We therefore were attended on our excursion by a schoolmaster employed under the mission, not exactly at Achill, but on the adjoining mainland; by a Scripture-reader, and a cottager of the settlement. All these men were, not four years ago, Roman Catholics; all different from each other as much as men could be, and yet *all*, in their way, exceedingly interesting. The two former were of unquestionable talent and energy of mind; indeed, their daring to come out from Popery bespoke the latter quality; but there was moreover, an "*esprit*" an "*abandon*" in their character, which peculiarly belongs to the Irish, the excitable Irish—when breaking loose from the trammels of the priests, they fly high, like wild hawks, unhooded and disregarding the old lure.

The schoolmaster was once the peculiar protegé of the priests; he was from the neighbourhood of Ballinasloe, and was thought so much of, that he was sent to Innisbofin, there to keep the natives steady to their duty to the priest, and discourage and discomfit

any audacious swaddler that should venture on their
shores. I wish I had time and space to describe in
his own ardent language, the way in which he saw,
renounced, and fled from his former bondage. The
man is decidedly a man of talent; if he has a fault,
and it may, when over indulged in, be a great one, it is,
that he is too polemical and disposed to dote about
questions. The Scripture-reader is a quieter man;
he is admirably adapted to his work; he has Scripture, as they say, at his fingers' ends; he has it also,
I deem, at the ends of his heart and brain. I never
saw a person apply it better, or more timely. The
labourer seemed to be a dark, though not a dull man.
It is likely he has learned enough to believe that
what he formerly trusted to was wrong; but he had
not yet, I think, had his eyes opened to see clearly
what is right. The fact is, the man was and is yet
but a semi-barbarian. I believe he was born on the
island.

We set out along the valley leading to the southern
face of the island, and then taking a turn to the
west, kept along the southern side of Slievemore, the
second loftiest mountain in all this district. We had
not gone far until, I may say, tired of discourse on
religious polemics, I asked were there any ancient
buildings, or caves, or cairns on the island. " Oh !
yes," says Mr. Baylee, "we are just in the vicinity of
some;" so my attention was directed to some more
than usually grassy slopes on the side of the hill,
where I at once recognised a whole assemblage of antiquities, a Druidical circle, two cromlechs, an artificial

cave, and what all over Ireland, wherever I have met one, is called, a giant's grave. The circle of pillar stones was not large. One of the cromlechs was perfect; the top stone of the other was thrown down. The cave was torn open, and its covering removed, and the grave was as much destroyed as the people could afford, without expending more labour than was convenient.

What curious, what unaccountable works, especially these long Kists,* composed of upright stones, about four feet high, five feet asunder, twenty or twenty-five feet long, and covered at top by massive flags; they generally are found adjoining cromlechs. There is one I lately visited, it is near that noble cromlech, a few miles north of Dundalk. I also saw one adjoining that wonderful congeries of Druidical circles and cromlechs near Sligo. In the Transactions of the Celtic Society of France, there are an account and plans of two such, one near Tours and the other in Brittany. Both are called, "Les Roches aux Fees;" they also have cromlechs near them. They are certainly the unaccounted for remains of the same great people who, it would seem, have, though powerful, scientific, and universal, left no literary records, and who, as is supposed, existed before the introduction of syllabic writing.

We asked the natives of the adjoining village (who were quite civil) who it was erected these monuments? They said they were put there by the Danes; by the

* See Appendix.

way, the greater part of these Achillians are said to
be descended from these Danes, who, I am sure, were
not the sea-pirates of the ninth and tenth centuries,
but that very ancient race that is known in Irish
story as Tuatha Danaans,*—a people so clever and intelligent, that they were counted by their more savage
conquerors as necromancers. I think I have before
remarked, the strange circumstance of an intelligent
and more civilized race being conquered, and if not
extirpated, at least enslaved and degraded, by a more
numerous, but an inferior and more ignorant people.
I dare say, had I time and opportunity, I should find
many more remains of remote antiquity in this island.
I think I could observe a marked difference in the
countenance, the eyes, the formation of the head of
the Achillians. Their eyes are generally dark, their
faces flat, and their heads large. I would say they
are like the Welch.†

Having passed along the roots of Slievemore, we
arrived at where Achill narrows to about three miles
in breadth, and upon a ridge of comparatively low
mountain that connects Slievemore with Slieve Croghan.
Where the ridge is highest, stands a square building,
lofty and slender, which was erected during the

* Since writing the above, I think I have reason to believe
that, though there may be descendants of the Tuatha Danaans
on the island, yet, that there has been a Scandinavian settlement in more modern times.

† The distinctions are still kept up between the two races in
the island. Those who suppose themselves Milesians, speak
with contempt of their fellow-islanders of Danish descent.
When wishing to mark an act with reprobation, they say, " None
but a Dane would do that."

French war as a watch-tower. It is well adapted for that purpose, for the eye sweeps from it the whole north-west coast, up along the Mullet, south to Innis Bofin, and the coast of Connemara. Here an officer of the navy was quartered with a few men. What a lonely spot!—what a horrible solitude!— when the driving tempest sending *up* the spray of the Atlantic billows, and sending *down* the almost incessant rain from the clouds, roared in wrath, and, as it were, said, "I want to wash away these fellows;" and yet there is no account of any of these weather-beaten men committing suicide. No—that is left for the sated sensualist to perpetrate, as he sits in cushioned indolence, and feels that he is tired of a world, out of which he has extracted all its joys, and left not even the dregs of hope behind.

Keeping to the southward of this lonely tower, a large tract of moorland lay before us, rising with a gradual ascent until it closed upon the loftier ranges of Slieve Croghan, to which we were tending.

This moor was now dry and passable, both for man and cattle, in consequence of continued dry weather. Coming towards us was a group of men and women, driving before them a small herd of cattle. The cows, some red, some black, and some white; the women with scarlet cloaks, and deep yellow handkerchiefs tied round their heads; and the men in their dark sombre frize—all presented those contrasts and positions that form the charm of colouring and grouping; and moving as they did slowly and compactly along the face of the wild moor, over whose wide surface the shadows of the light clouds coursed after each other, and presented those varieties of light and shade that make you exclaim, how lovely in all its changes is the face of nature!

Upon my remarking what a fine effect the moving group had upon the moor, one of the company said that the yellow kerchiefs I was admiring had been, not long ago, the cause of exciting, in no small degree, the wrath and almost malediction of the great Dr. M'Hale, on the occasion of his coming *first* to Achill, for the gracious purpose of cursing and putting down "THE SETTLEMENT." Of course the priests exerted themselves that his *Grace* should be hailed, on his arrival, by a multitude of people. Accordingly all were commanded to be in attendance, in their best attire, to welcome the greatest man that ever was seen. Accordingly the people, and especially the women, flocked in from all the villages of the island; and, as for centuries the Achill beauties have rejoiced in tiring their heads with deep yellow* kerchiefs; when the touchy prelate, who was no doubt in a chafed mood from the force of his excommunicating offices, saw what he conceived to be the ORANGE *colour* exhibited all around, he raged. Reader, did you ever see a scarlet coat or handker-

---

* The ancient Irish were partial to yellow ; even their undergarments were of this fashionable hue ; and a yellow *chemise*, consisting of some 20 yards of narrow linen, was the indispensable integument of an Irish belle.

chief shaken at a turkey-cock, and then observe the strutting wrath—the purple passion—the blue swelling neck, gills, and face of the irritable creature—how it at length erupts its ire in a loud and dissonant gobble, gobble ? So did the great Titular of Tuam. He burst out upon the Achill priests, and said he did not understand being thus insulted by that hateful and Protestant colour; and supposed that these *base* women had been taking *orange* handkerchiefs as their SOULS' BRIBE from that pestilent Nangle. With great difficulty (says my informant) was the noble rage assuaged of this great prince prelate, by the assurance that this was a YELLOW,* and not an orange colour; that it was in vogue amongst the Achill beauties 1000 years before Luther came to trouble the world.

And now we began to ascend Slieve Croghan, whose top, I was sorry to see, had caught the clouds, and was hooded in mist, while all below was clear. But I was thankful for the day even as it was, and had no right whatever to complain; and here, before undertaking the ascent of this very lofty mountain, we sat down to take some refreshment, and it was needful. While sitting here we had a

---

* There is no word expressive of orange in the Irish language. Accordingly, when the hated Dutchman introduced his orange symbol, the Irish were at a nonplus. And, therefore, when a Jacobite song was composed abusing John Orangeman, they had to call him SHAUN BUIE, which signifies YELLOW Jack. If the reader desires to see a song, as bad as it is bitter, entitled Shaun Buie, he may consult Hardiman's Irish Minstrelsy.

fine view to the southward, including the outer part
of Clew Bay, Clare Island, in the distance Innisturk
and Bofin Island, and directly off shore, the Billies
Rock, which rose pyramidically out of the sea, about
two leagues south-west of where we sat, and against
which the heaving billows were vexing and tossing
themselves, as if angry at their own ineffectual efforts
to overpower it. The following legend one of the
party told concerning it:—One of the Brownes of
Westport, the grandfather or great-grandfather of the
present Marquis of Sligo, was a wise man in general,
and noted for that wisdom that looks after the main
chance, adding house to house and acre to acre.
Happy the grandson or great-grandson of such a
man, even suppose that in the long run it should
befall the founder of the inherited greatness, as it
befell the great Browne of Westport. He, it seems,
insulted a friar—why or how the legend does not
tell—but the results were awful: the man, in the
midst of his magnificence, died miserable; and, what
is worse, his soul was sent to haunt yonder Billies
Rock in the form of an eagle,—it is well the friar
was so merciful as not turn him into a cormorant—
and *there*, perched on that lonely sea-pyramid,
undergoing his penal metempsychosis, was the solemn
osprey. The live-long day, he stood proud and melancholy, like Lord Altamont, only in feathered instead
of robed magnificence—when happily came on the
days—the glorious and liberal days of Catholic
emancipation; and perhaps one of the reasons of

Lord Sligo's voting so strenuously for that *great* and *healing* measure was to disenchant his progenitor. Be this as it may, the vote was given—the gratitude of the priests knew no bounds—and they showed it—for on the day on which the noble marquis said in his place in the house of lords, CONTENT, up flew the eagle from the Billies—up, I say, soaring until he pierced the clouds, and entered the empyrean. But was he never to come back? never again to grasp, with his yellow talons, the black point of his old perch? He was—he was—emancipation is *not* a final measure. Justice for Ireland is yet to be done. The noble marquis had gone a great way—but not far enough—and he came to a sulky stop. His odour has, therefore, got bad again in the nostrils of those who can command heaven and Lord Melbourne. The too late conservatism of Sligo is visited on the great-grandfather.* And old Altamont is come back to the Billies, there to stay until mass is said

* From what I have above said, and from remarks I have ventured on respecting the Marquis of Sligo's lodge at Delphi, I would not have it for a moment supposed that his family (or indeed himself) are low in my humble estimation—quite the reverse   I consider that there is not a county in Ireland that owes so much to a single family as Mayo does to the Brownes. They first introduced obedience to the laws into this district, where the gentry set the example of lawlessness, and carried their measures more by sword and pistol than by peaceful processes.   Mr. Bald, the engineer, who has executed the large and admirable map of Mayo, has furnished me with the following memorandum, to whose truth I fully accede—

" During the period of the Right Honourable Denis Browne's being generally foreman of the grand jury of Mayo, the map of

in Westport house, and the black slugs are driven
out of Ireland.

Speaking on the present occasion of the fishing
on this coast, what I heard from the coast-guard's
officer was corroborated. The fishing has been
latterly most unsuccessful. Besides the failure of
the fishery in shore, that on the sun-fish banks,
twenty leagues out to sea, has almost gone to nothing.
The priests of Achill have made some hazardous
ventures, in the way of prophecy, respecting the fish.
Last year, previous to his dues being collected, and
no doubt on that occasion to keep the people in good
humour, his reverence prophesied an abundant take
of fish. Alas! to the utter disappointment of the
people, and discountenance (if any thing could put

the county of Mayo was executed under his direction. The
road from Castlebar to Ballina by the Puntoon—the road from
Castlebar to Belmullet at the great harbours of Blacksod, and
Broadhaven in Erris—the roads from Westport to the Killeries;—the road from Newport to and through the island of
Achill, commencing at Mollyranbee, and terminating at near the
western extremity of that island—the road from Killala, along
the north coast, and on to Belmullet—the road from Bangor to
Corraan Achill—the Tulloghan road, with many other lines,
were surveyed and laid out by Mr. William Bald, the civil
engineer. Even the line of road passing through Barney
Lough Talt was, at the recommendation of Mr. Bald, changed
by Mr. Nimmo to a more eligible one, viz. from Swineford to
Ballina by Foxford. There were also many small fishing piers
erected on that coast by the Fishery Board, of which board
Mr. Browne was one of the most active members. Mr. Browne
gave powerful aid and assistance in procuring the extension of
the Grand Canal from Shannon Harbour to Ballinasloe. There
was an activity and an energy combined in all his actions; and
since the period of his decease, no roads, nor harbours, nor
general county improvements have been carried on."

him out of face) of the priest, the year was the worst
for fishing ever remembered.*

Having rested ourselves, we started up to face the
mountain, which is said to be 2500 feet high, therefore loftier than Croagh Patrick. The way we
ascended, though long and wearisome, was gradual;
and from this easiness of ascent of what I knew to
be lofty, I considered that we were to descend as
easily on the other side, and so get down to the
cliff, which I knew was very bold, overhanging the
ocean. So thus we toiled along, my companions

---

* The following statement was related to me, which, I believe in the main, to be true, shows to what lengths the priests
venture with these poor people. It was notorious that the fish
did not approach the coast as formerly : a reverend gentleman
accordingly went through the villages, assuring the people, that
God had, in anger for their allowing Nangle and his jumpers
to fix themselves in the island, built up a great wall in the sea,
to hinder the fish from coming in from the deep sea ; but, if
the people would subscribe, and pay him properly, and have no
more to do with the settlement, he would say a mass upon the
sea-shore, that would throw down the wall, and let the fish in,
as before. Accordingly, those people subscribed pretty generally along that part of the island most distant from the settlement ; and the priest, to fulfil his part, set up an altar on the
shóre, to say his mass ; but when he attempted to light his
candles—which is necessary to be done for the due celebration
of the office—the wind blew them out, and the service could
not be done. The wind was obstinate against the mass, and
jealous, perhaps, of the priest's attempting to *raise it* against its
wish, and so, for a long season, it continued obstinately obstre-
perous. This seemed to have cooled the people's confidence,
and rather sceptical whispers went abroad concerning the priest
and his sea wall. It was further stated to me, that when the
reverend gentleman tried the same method on the northern
side of the island, in those villages nearer the settlement, it
would not do there. No subscription could be got up, and no
attempt made to throw down the wall.

talking of other things besides the character of the
mountain, when all of a sudden we entered the
cloud that was now sweeping thick and cold all
around; and I should have gone on, taking advantage of what I conceived was a level summit before
me, were I not held back; and, lo! we were at the
edge of a tremendous precipice, down which to look
was enough to turn giddy *any* head, and against the
edge of which the 'cloud struck, and then rolled up
curling, and swept along eastward; for on this day
the wind came gently from the ocean.

Waiting a while patiently until the cloud passed
over, we were shortly gratified by the mist becoming
more transparent, and we could see, but not clearly,
forward towards the ocean; but downwards the vision
was complete, and we could observe 2500 feet below us,
the great ocean, heaving against the cliffs of the
shore that basked in light, and their dark and
lichen-tinted colours grandly contrasted with the
azure billows that heaved in so beautifully blue,
and then changed, with admirable and instant muta-
bility, to snow-white foam, as they were shattered
along the rocks.   Here we were, then, upon a
precipice about 2,000 feet high, that went down
almost plumb; and then *there* was an inclined plane
covered with the debris of the upper stratifications; and
then, about 200 yards further on or so, there were cliffs
about 300 feet high, against which the waves washed.
The top of this extraordinary mountain was certainly
very sublime, and perhaps the mist made it seem

grander, as it now came on thick and dripping, and then rose and partially passed away.

Our chief employment (as I suppose it has ever been of all who have stood on the verge of a great precipice) was to cast down stones and watch the time of falling, and the noise and impetus of the mass as it bounded, and smoked, and shattered itself in pieces below. But it was pleasanter to go a little lower, still keeping along the precipice, which retained its perpendicularity, but was not high enough to catch the stratum of clouds. Here we sat—the cloud just festooning, as it were, a raised-up curtain over our heads, and all below was serene; and from the lowest edge of the precipice' at this point there extended underneath us a pretty little vale, in which was a tarn, so smooth, so shining, and so clear, that it might have been taken for a mermaid's looking-glass; and yet, though of fresh water, it was so near the edge of the ocean (but perhaps some hundred feet above it) that you might imagine you could empty its contents with a syphon.

While sitting here and looking out north-eastward, where was spread out before us the great extent of Black-Sod bay—then northward the low, sand-hilled shores of the Mullet—the rock-defended islands of Innisgloria and Inniskea, with their light-houses and watch-towers—I observed that in such a place, and in an island that got its name from eagles, it would be disgraceful to the "genius loci" if he would not show us an eagle or two. The observation was

scarcely made, when upward, from a ledge of rock
beneath our feet, sprung a noble bird, and we could
see him open his beak and shiver his feathers, just as
a wild beast would stretch himself when rising from
his lair; and then he soared directly over our heads,
took a wheel round, as much as to say, I don't understand what these fellows want here, and, keeping
close to the stratum of clouds that was still incumbent on the topmost cliff, he kept afloat exactly under
it, as if coasting along a ceiling, and then struck
away northwards, taking his direction towards the
highlands of Inniskea. One of the company mentioned his having visited Inniskea; and that, as usual,
the people are beset with gross superstition. They
have a wooden idol there, left by a holy priest, who
said that as long as it was preserved with reverence,
no loss of life by shipwreck would happen to any of
the islanders, who always worshipped the idol before
venturing to sea. He said that (as he was informed)
this idol was once stolen by smugglers, who supposed
that they carried their palladium while they kept
this wooden saint on board; but from the day they
stole it until it was returned, which, with all repenting
speed, they hastened to do, they were persecuted by
a revenue cruizer, and vexed by storms, and driven
up and down on the ocean; for how could they have
luck when they had no grace, and stole from the
Inniskeans their teraphim, their little god.

Inniskea is not only celebrated for its idols, but for
a crane that has lived alone without mate or offspring,

old as the twinkling stars; and there it is, and there
it will be until the day of judgment. But what is
more important, it is noted for its spirits. Oh
whiskey, thou art a darling, delicious, dangerous
crathur; and you are made here in perfection. The
gay and pleasant author of the " Wild Sports of the
West" tells us that he emptied a Dutchman!!!
freighted with this nectar in one night, and only
inherited a headache for his pains in the morning.
May he never do it older, say I. Beyond Inniskea
I was shown the direction of Innisgloria, a more
northern isle. Here, as the story goes, bodies buried
will not corrupt. The living people can, therefore,
see their dead progenitors, with their teeth and skin
whole and sound, and their nails and hair perfect
and still growing; so their descendants, to the tenth
generation, can come, and with pious care, pare the
one and clip the other. There was no one in company who had been on the island to verify this *fact,*
which is so well established in the minds of the
people, that there is a strong desire to be buried
there, and many bodies are kept overground until
they are not sweet, waiting for fair weather to waft
them to Innisgloria. I have no information as to
whether they recover from putridity when laid in
GLORIA.*

* " Nunc superest tredecim gentis miranda referre,
    Quæ comprensus erat metris Flahertius illis.

    Insula Inniskea scriptis ut fama priorum,
    Credula commendat, regio qua prominet Irras,

Having looked sufficiently long northwards, we determined again to mount the highest parts of the mountain, and skirt along the precipice until we gained the loftiest eminence; and by this time the cloud had in a great measure gone off; and though every now and then a winged wool-pack passed, and in passing struck the sublime edge of the precipice, yet you could see downwards and onwards—downwards to behold the ranges of the mighty rocks that show here, by indications that cannot be mistaken, that the disruption of what has now left this wondrous *façade* bare, was as instantaneous as it was powerful. The look-out to ocean was sublime. Oh! what would I not give to stand here, if possible, and witness a tempest from the west; but even as I did see it, it was elevating to the mind,—filling you with grand conceptions of God's creation, and raising your imagination to consider what the mind may yet take in, when escaped from this mortal coil; and the untrammelled intellect can see, understand, and more intensely adore the God of the ocean and the mountain—the God of power, and oh! thanks be to

Oceani in fluctus grus est ab origine rerúm,
Unica, sideribus minimè consumpta coævis.

Cernere Innisgloria est Pelago, quod prospicit Irras'
Insula avos, atavos solo post fata sepultos,
Effigies servare suas vegetisque vigere,
Unguibus atque comis, hominum caro nulla putrescit."—

*From a Latin Poem, descriptive of Ireland,
by Sir William O'Kelly, of Aughrim.*

Jesus, the pardoning God of love. Upwards of 2000 feet must have given a great field for vision; yet you strained your eyes as imagination urged its impossibilities. Though you well knew that nearer than America no land was, you looked and looked, and yet nothing was to be seen but the lights and shadows, cast by the slow moving clouds along the surface—not a sail to break the uniformity of this sublimely solitary watery waste.

I say that there are evident indications here of Slieve Croghan being sliced down, and left, as it were, a palpable remnant of some great convulsion. Here are, in my view, incontestable proofs of this event; for just behind the precipice where it is highest, and about 20 feet from the brow, an interior chasm is seen, forming an enormous and rugged fissure for hundreds of yards ·along—in some places hundreds of feet deep; and this shows that when the mighty blow was given, and while half the mountain was falling down, this crack took place. It was but a chance that this great slice did not go down along with the rest. Though now confirmed in this belief, I have been long assured that a great change has taken place in the western coast of Ireland; that a great disruption and sinking of the land has occurred; and *that* subsequent to the existence of man, and the erection of some of his primeval monuments. If there be a well supported statement of remote tradition, it is *that* of there having been a great tract of land in the western ocean, that sunk at once by some natural

2 c

convulsion.* I consider also that this great submersion took place when that part of the continent
called Ireland was inhabited; and I ground my belief,
not only on the universal tradition prevailing along
the whole western coast, but also from the fact, that
in one place a Cyclopean wall and building on the
coast of Erris, not far from Killala, has been torn
asunder by the very same disruption. And that on an
island, now separated from the main land by an
enormous chasm not only the stratifications of the
rock correspond, but also the ranges of stones forming
the Cyclopean wall.† I therefore consider that the

* We learn from Plato and other Greek writers, that, at a
very remote era, a large island in the Atlantic Ocean was swallowed up by the sea, and with its numerous animals and people.
This may have taken place when the Euxine and the sea of
Asoph broke their banks, and when the opening was made at
the straits of Gibraltar.

† Mr. M‘Pharlane, in his Statistical Survey of Mayo, gives
the following account of this singular and important curiosity at
Downpatrick, ten miles along the coast, westward from Killala.
Please goodness, if allowed health so long, I will visit this spot
next summer.

" After travelling from Killala, about nine miles due west,
you gradually ascend upon a neck of land, which stretches on
to the ocean, narrowing to a point, until you arrive at a precipice, three hundred measured feet from the bottom to the top,
upon which the sea is always rough, and dashes itself in enormous billows. About the same distance of three hundred feet
out to sea, stands a rough perpendicular rock of the same height
as the main land and precipice. It is of a triangular form, and
terminates conically from a broad base to top, the surface of
which is about sixty yards round. On the top appear, to the
naked eye, the ruins of some building. There is, in the mainland precipice, an angular indention—and an angular prominence corresponding to it, in the opposite rock—not only the
prominence and indention of the fracture, but the colour and
quality of the rock seem to correspond. Within a one hundred

people who built Stonehenge, Abury, and Carnac—
who raised our stone circles, pillars, cromleachs, and
giants' graves—who formed New Grange, and erected
our Cyclopean walls and cahirs—were in existence at
the time of this great physical phenomenon—to this,
I say, bear witness all the old story-tellers of the
west. In Connemara, where Plato's name never
reached, they will tell you how the beautiful western
land sunk beneath the waves; and standing of a summer's eve on the shores of Ardbear or Renvyle, an
old man will say to his son, "Look out there where
you now see nothing but the waves dancing in the
sunbeams, there is 'our lovely land,' and it will one
of these days make its appearance."

In no place is the belief so strong as in the county
of Clare: there they consider a whole barony to have
gone down, and it fell away from the cliffs of Moher
and the precipices along Malbay; Mutton Island being
but a remnant of the great loss; and when Mr.
Burton went, in the year 1765, in search of the
Ogham monument, called Cuneen Miul's Tomb, on
the side of Callan mountain, which rises about seven
miles inland from Malbay, the people would not be
persuaded that it was to copy a parcel of scratches
upon a flag that he was come so far—but it was to

and thirty yards of the extremity of the neck of land, a strong
grouted wall, seven feet broad, and nine high, runs across the
point, from sea to sea, about sixty yards. The gateway is very
narrow and strong. Every thing seems to indicate the rock and
building to have originally belonged to the main land, and the
cross ramparts to have been the fortifications of the Castle."

find the key of the enchanted island that lay buried
in Cuneen's tomb he came; which key, if found,
would bring up the "lovely land"* in all its beauty,
with a fine city in the middle of it, the inhabitants
of which would be so generous as to divide their
wealth with all good Irishmen—their long-lost countrymen.

The general opinion is, that though the great part of
the land is gone down into the depths of the ocean,
there are parts of it, consisting of beautifully wooded,
and verdant isles that are still over water, but are
kept from the ken of man by enchantment. This
is O'Brazil. This the happy land to which St.
Brendan† and his companions sailed in the skin-
covered skiffs, and remained for seven years in its
sunny fields, flowing with milk and honey. This
is the land that rises all so suddenly to the view
of the men of Antrim or Innishowen. They see it
now rising in all the luxuriance of hill and vale, and
then evanishing, the baseless fabric of a fairy vision.
This is the land that the Welsh have their poetical
tradition of; the Flathinnis, or noble island, that lies
surrounded with tempest in the western ocean—this
the island which, in *fact*, Ortelius laid down in his
map of Europe, 300 years ago, as the island of
O'Brazil.

---

* The banks, forty miles off shore, where the sun-fish are
caught, of course, are parts of the sunken land. So may be
the banks of Newfoundland.

† See Appendix.

I am satisfied, then, that a great disruption has taken place. I have observed it, I say, at Horn-head, in Donegal—at Achill—at Moher—at Malbay, and Kilkee. The conviction on my mind is, that Ireland, as it now stands, is but the eastern headland of the continent of Atlantis. It is altogether unlike Britain in its formation. The great coal measures of England and Scotland, and all their superior sandstone and oolite strata, exist not in Ireland. What is called mountain limestone in England is the surface stratum of the lowest parts of our island. In England, in the caves, sand gravel and marl pits, in the tertiary and diluvial beds, are found the remains of mammoths, rhinoceros, and sundry animals of prey or pasture now belonging to the tropics. In Ireland no such thing—not one organic remain is found in our tertiary or diluvial strata; and in our alluvial beds but the one single species—but indeed that makes up for all—the peculiar animal characteristic of a great, distinct, and separated continent— the gigantic deer.

I have often wondered, when contemplating the horns and skeleton of this magnificent animal, how it could exist in an island so small as Ireland—how stalk, with its horns spreading out twelve feet and more, through its thick, tangled, and circumscribed woods. No: this creature was certainly intended for a larger range—for the wide-spreading prairies and lofty steppes of a great continent; and it appears to me that the specimens dug up now in our moors,

incumbent as they generally are on marl, show, that
while the remainder of this continent sank below
the ocean, its eastern headland, now called Ireland,
rose above its former level; and that in this great
transition, the Atlantic deer that happened to be in
its eastern parts were destroyed.

CHAPTER XVIII.

VILLAGES OF KEEM AND KEEL.

Legends connected with the sunken land—Innis Bofin enchanted and disenchanted—Legend of Adam and Eve—Fairies—What happened Phelim the devout—He puts a finish on a fairy—Story of a heavenly windmill—The fall of its mill-stone—The Most Rev. Father M'Hale's infallibility brought to a NON PLUS—Power of Elements on Slieve Croghan—Descent to Keem village—Its position—Good for mutton—Author a Castle-builder—A digression on Irish landlords—Extravagance of the Achillians as to houses—Quantity scarcely atones for quality—Coast-guard station—House and economy of one—Not fit for the Most Rev. M'Hale's "HOLY GARDEN"—To be temperate against one's will—Amethyst mine—Iron as good a cure for cattle as lead for men in Achill—Village of Keel—Position—Appearance—Capabilities—Reception—Some incivil—Some good humoured—Return to settlement.

WHILE sitting resting ourselves on the great interior chasm behind the precipice of Slieve Croghan, I gave to my companions the theory and *suppositions* it is founded on, which I now offer to the reader. They all seemed amused and interested in the discussion; and the schoolmaster, whom I have before alluded to as acting confidentially for the priests in Innis Bofin, said—" Sir, what you say is, I am sure, true. At any rate, I have often heard of the enchanted island called O'Brazil in Bofin. Indeed, according to the natives, that isle was once a part of the enchanted land; and I'll tell you, if you please, how it was disenchanted, for once it was *invisible* like all the other, in the far western sea, and was only spied at times, and then passed away again like a fog bank.

"Well, sir, as a man and his son, upon a long day in summer, was out in his coragh, a-fishing mackarel, far away from the island of Omay, of which he was a native, and had brought a coal of turf with him, neatly settled in the bottom of a lump of blue clay, in order to broil the mackarel when they were hungry—and now they had got into a misty part of the sea, which was very *quare* all out ; and they heard birds singing, and sheep bleating, and cattle lowing, as if they were close under the land, and still these men knew that they were some leagues from shore. So, with this, he happened to hook one of the finest mackarel ever his eyes beheld; and he says to his son Darby, ' Boy, jewel, we'll just have this fine fellow for our dinner ;' and, with that, he takes the coal* of turf off the clay between a clipstick, and begins to blow to light it up, when, as it happened, some of the fire fell overboard, and, would you believe it ? all at once, a beautiful island burst on his view, just within five fathoms of his boat, and he had nothing to do but push on shore, and look about him. Now, this Paddy of Omay, it seems, was a cute fellow : he saw what the coal of fire had done. So, do you see, he wraps his coal up close in a handful of sea-weed, and on he marches to make discoveries; and had not gone far, when he saw a beautiful

---

* The general opinion is, that no enchantment stands against fire taken from the hearth; this is an old determination, as appears from the statement of Giraldus Cambrensis, which the reader will find in the appendix.

lady, all dressed out in a gown and petticoat of green, driving a white cow before her. I'm sure he was mighty pleasant with himself at the sight. 'Come,' says Pat, 'this is the owner of the place, and it well becomes such a *clane*, pretty lass, to own such a purty little bit of land, and I'll just be going after her— while, do you, Darby dear, keep the cow in sight, and, if possible, catch a hould of her. I'd like to handle the cattle, and see whether they're good for milk.' So, he makes up to the lady, and Darby to the cow; and not very far off was a pretty little inland lake, just such a one as we were looking at from the bank there just below us—but here, mind you, that the father had the coal with him; but Darby had not. So, when the boy, as he was directed, caught the cow by the tail, she gave him a kick that sent him sprawling; and when he got up, the cow was gone, and nothing in his hand but a long stem of sea-weed, very like, indeed, to a cow's tail. But the father followed the lady, and she, the crathur, neither kicked nor spoke uncivil, but seemed mighty much afraid of the coal of fire. So, in this way, he advanced, and she retreated, until she found her back to the lake, into which, having no other escape, she plunged, and the isle has been disenchanted ever since, and is called the Innis Bo-fin—the Island of the White Cow. From this tradition, the people all along the coast expect, that some time or other, greater and finer islands will be disenchanted; and they say that, when fishing, some twenty leagues off shore, for the sun-fish, often a fog will rise out of the water on the banks which lie around, and, while in the middle of the fog, they hear the sweet singing of birds— they smell the fragrance of sweet flowers—lambs are heard bleating, and calling for their dams—and all around, floating on the waves, are seen the leaves of apple-trees and oaks; and then the fog rises, and nothing is seen but the foam curling on the billow, and the tossing of the porpoise."

Let me, sir, before I have done, tell you one legend more which these Innis Bofiners narrate:

There are two lofty rocks that stand out by them- selves a league or more. They are remarkable for their slender and exact form, not unlike two gigantic human creatures. They are called the Boughal and the Colleen—the Boy and the Girl. The tradition is, that they fell down from heaven—the Boughal stands upright, the Colleen leans as upon one side: this is accounted for by the statement that the male was innocent until the female was tempted and fell. It is the dark idea that these rocks represent Adam and Eve, and that as two eagles make their nest on these rocks, roost together, soar away together, come home together, and in the season make here their nest, so these must be the souls of Adam and Eve.

I took occasion here to observe to Mr. C——r, " I suppose that Bofin being so lately disenchanted is still in some measure the resort of fairies and such 'good people.'

"O certainly, sir—perhaps no where are the people

so assured of their existence, or where they are so
often (if you believe them) seen and felt too. The
hills are full of them—in dark nights, when they
cannot go out by the light of the moon, for they love
to dance upon the hill-side—they are heard romping
and carousing *within* the hills—they carry away children, and make them do service and wait on them in
their night excursions—they enter the dairies of those
who have plenty of milk and butter, and there they
eat and drink cleanly but not voraciously, and it is
considered that they can be killed, *when caught, only*
by the stab of a black-hafted knife. I have heard,"
says Mr. C——, "one of the Bofiners say, that there
was one of these 'good people' much more dangerous
and mischievous than the rest—he was full of frolic
and mischief at the same time: once, as a Bofiner
was going along the side of a hill, a shower of herrings came down, bleeding fresh from the sky, and
lay, with their beautiful green backs, all around, and
a voice came down from a little flying cloud—'Come,
Phelim, broil and eat'—but no!—Phelim would not
touch one of them, for he very well knew, that if he
once eat of their meat or drank of their drink he
would be enchanted, and for ever after, until the day
of judgment, live amongst them.

"But this audacious fairy went too far, at length,
with his jokes, for he chose to play his pranks
on a confraternity man, who wore the scapular,
and carried a black-handled knife in his pocket; so
as this man was going by the rath side, up came the

fairy with a long flagger in his hand, very like a sword,
and mighty playful, but little knowing who he had
to deal with, he hits the man a blow across the chops
with his flagger, when the other, very cross, drew
out his black-hafted knife and gave the little fellow a
dig in the ribs, so the fairy gave a groan, and the
man ran away home—the blood of the ghost was
found on the blade of the knife in the morning, and
moreover its body too was found, but dissolved into a
heap of slime, just like the jelly that you will often
see in a bog, which every one knows is what remains
of a dead frog."

I can only record one more matter of "Glamour,"
drawn from the rich stories of Mr. C——, of what he
heard while schoolmaster at Bofin.

In an island, or near it, is a huge millstone which
all the people assert dropt down from the sky where
the fairies had a windmill—how else, as they say,
could it come on the island, or for what use could it be
brought, seeing that there never was a mill there since
the world began. Mr. C——r's informant, speaking
of this millstone assured him he saw it descend from
the clouds, and that when it came down, they found
some of the meal on it which the fairies had been grind-
ing in the upper regions a few minutes before. The day
was breezy when it descended—in a shower of snow
it came down, floating gently in the air like a table-
cloth; who could doubt this fact after such attestations
and particularities respecting its origin. It is now in
a small island called Omay near Clifden; and, reader,

when you go to Connemara, as, no doubt, if an Irish tourist, you will, you can go to Omay and satisfy yourself about the millstone.

I cannot give up Bofin without alluding to the Most Reverend Father M'Hale's visit to this very civilized place, and which is, to use his Grace's own expression, the "Garden of Jesus Christ," because a Protestant has not yet contaminated it by his residence.

This island is sacred to St. Colman, who erected a college here for the Saxon students who had been at the college of Mayo, but were driven from thence by the jealousy of the Irish collegians. Now this Colman blessed a well here, and made it holy, and so it is that there are two wells near each other, and in process of time men forgot which was the real blessed one, and thus they were in unhappy doubt, until in the year 1836, the *great Bishop* came to confirm the children, give dispensations, and bless the coast and its fisheries; and in their difficulty about the well, they consulted THE INFALLIBLE. But, alas he did not condescend to decide, but said, with great discretion, that if they performed their DUTY with the requisite disposition, it was not much matter which of them they went their rounds about. He, himself, however, took off his hat, bowed his knee, and repeated something like a prayer before one of the wells.

All this while, occupied as I have been with O'Brazil and the fairies, and Innis Bofin, and Doctor M'Hale, I have forgot that I was standing two thousand five hundred feet above the level of the sea, on the precipice of Slieve Croghan, and it is time to leave it; so giving a long, last look at the grandest cliff I ever have beheld, or ever shall see, we all went down its eastern side, and were not twenty feet on our descent until there appeared no more evidence that this sublime precipice was within so few feet of us than if we were on any other mountain of the same height.

I did not fail to observe the decomposing power of the elements at this great elevation; the whole formation, like that of most of the summits I am acquainted with in Ireland, is composed of compact quartz rock of the most homogeneous character. A few yards back from the precipice the whole *boggy* surface is covered with a pure white sand composed of the rock disintegrated and powdered by the winds and rains that here operate so constantly. Our descent was rapid for two reasons, first, that the mountain, though very lofty, was not difficult; there were no obstructions from chasms or bog, an exceedingly compact and hard conglomerate formed the rocks on this side, composed of square, not rounded, masses of quartz bedded in the closest possible silicious cement. The mountain on this side forms a sort of large gorge, looking towards the south, and protected from the east and west winds by ridges that form the northern part of Clew Bay, on one side, and the southern part of Achill on the other. Here, for about one thousand feet from the level of the sea are very green sheep

pastures which reach down to the little village of
Keem; and here, as I am told, is fattened some of the
sweetest mutton in the county of Mayo. By the way,
the village of Keem is not only remarkable for the
fine hill pastures that are around it, but also for its
magnificent position and for its singular character.

Slieve Croghan embraces the vale in which it lies
within its sublime gorge, to the north and west; open
to the south-east, and protected from the roaring
Atlantic by Moilog head. There is just under the
village a yellow stranded bay, as smooth and firm as
sand can be, up which the blue billows heave and dis-
perse in white foam most musically; possessing, therefore, this soft sunny aspect, and this great shelter all
is green and fertile around. Then, such a prospect;
the many interior isles of Clew Bay eastward, all green
and gentle in their forms and aspect; westward, the
larger and exterior ones, the outworks of Europe,
as I may call them, against the Atlantic, the lofty and
cliff embattled Clare, Cahir, Davelin, and Innisturk;
and then the Lord of the southern horizon—the
Reek—the Holy-head of the west. I think I have
never seen such a position for a great man's castle;
if I were Sir Richard O'Donnell, and had, along with
his eighty thousand acres, half as many pounds, I
would build my castle here, make it my summer residence, spend my time, and my thoughts, and my
patience, and what common sense Providence has
gifted me with, in endeavouring to improve my island
and my people; endeavour to educate them; endea-

vour to give them a taste for comfort and for decency;
elevate them up to a standing of self respect; teach them
or get them taught, to know that true religion was a
reasonable service; that when embraced it always
makes the slave a freeman; that there is no occasion
for another to stand between the sinner and his God;
that it is always right to think that the spirit of
priestcraft is dangerous when popular force and
passion are made to work in the way of getting
rid of the priests' enemies, and promoting, un-
disturbed, his own unquestionable views. Thus the
landlord, making use of his proper influence, gradually, temperately, firmly, evidently disinterestedly,
nay more, evidently ready to make great pecuniary
and personal sacrifices, what a field he would have
here; what a great theatre for the exercise of Christian philanthropy; yes, but where is such a landlord
to be had; I might go to and fro through the British
empire and hardly find such. I might find men
with prudence without zeal, and men with zeal without prudence, and might find one ready and one willing,
but suffering under the sins of his forefathers and not
able; and another politically or religiously unquali-
fied; and he *dare* not do the good he would for fear
of his sect or his party. Such being the case, I think
it must be allowed that good landlords, as well as good
tenants, have been very scarce in Ireland, and sure I
am its evils have in a great measure flowed down from
the rich upon the poor; and that if there was an Irish
Dante to arise, his bitter and gloomy satire would

allocate in his Modern Inferno, a large district for the bad landlords of the last century; yes, room, much room, ample room and verge enough for the crowds coming down from where aristocrats were basking in their club-house selfishness and forgetfulness of duty.

Keem, I said, was a singular village; it is only inhabited in summer—who would suppose that the Achillians had such a superfluity of houses, that they had both their winter and summer residences. The Greenlanders and Esquimaux are so changeful, from their excessive vicissitudes of heat and cold— but here I was surprised to find empty every house but two, (and these were the residences of the coast-guard, all with their doors fastened and untenanted; and certainly such miserable wigwams, I had never before seen—all built, as I have already described, without gable-ends. It seems the owners of the village of Keem, and the renters of the adjoining district, have other houses in a distant part of the island, where they spend the winter and spring; thence they come when their oats and potatoes are planted and spend the summer months, herding their cattle on these heights, and leading a pastoral life. Thus in Switzerland they have their chalets on the hills, and in old times in Ireland the creaghts (as they were called) had their boolies on the mountains; but I don't think I ever saw a summer-herding VILLAGE before.

I said that two of the coast-guard lived here, and what a lonely life they must lead in winter, in this

2 D

extreme western end of Achill, when the villagers go home leaving them entirely by themselves. But speaking of one of the party, the only one I met, if ever I saw a man well adapted, from patient, pious Christian resignation, to live within the circle of his own family, while the howling tempest was hurtling all without—it is Mr. Hamilton—I say Mr., for he had the manners and bearing of a gentleman, in the best sense of the word—a fine, tall, handsome seaman as ever I saw—he invited us into his cottage, spread before us his cleanly dressed, plentiful, but frugal fare, and made our most desirable entertainment still more acceptable by the heartiness of his welcome. And then his poor lowly residence was rendered as comfortable as neatness and order could make it; and his tidy wife, and beautiful healthy, mannerly children; and his collection of books to beguile away the long winter's evening, all having a religious tendency, all leading the sinner's trust to Christ; and there was one convenient handy spot where the Bible was always to stand, not for show, not for pretence, not as I have seen it in the houses of some, with dust on the cover, so that you might write with your finger thereon, the owner's character, and that was sluggard? No, the Bible was *here* a USED book, and the eldest boy was brought up, not ostentatiously, not unseasonably, but at our own request, to show that he had been duly instructed in its holy truths; and, indeed, he satisfied us that, as far as parents could go, he had been reared in the fear of the Lord.

Here there was a man, perhaps in as lonely a place as any in the British isles, and he had all the means of contentedness about him, because he was in the face of his God, with the humility of a Christian believer doing his duty to his country and to his family. Dr. M'Hale, in a late rabid letter, which he has written to Lord John Russell, has complained that Protestants should be quartered as coast-guards on this island: it offends his Catholic exclusiveness, his view of what "a garden of Jesus Christ" should be, but all I wish is, that said Lord John Russell could see this coast-guard of Keem and his little homestead, and I think he would hesitate before he would pluck this flower of civilized life from amidst the weeds of barbarism that are growing all so lustily in this Roman garden.

Here let me acknowledge a little weakness; I was grievously disappointed, even while thus treated as he best could by this hospitable coast-guard. I had for hours been walking over the lofty mountains. I was in a state of great lassitude, heat, and perspiration, so thirsty that I panted for a drink; I dared not touch water, my stomach never could bear milk. Oh! that I had a little wine or spirits—ay, spirits— ye stern souls of the Temperance Society, I honestly confess that, as I had no chance of wine, I modestly and slyly hinted that I would be glad of a little drop of a dram. But no, Mr. H. was a strict Temperance Society man; and, ah me, I had just to get cool quietly and as I might before I could assuage my burning thirst with spring water.

"But rest assured, sir," said Mr. H. "you will get home better, and find less bad consequences from your walk, doing *as you must*, without any spirits."

"Perhaps so," said I. At all events I did do, and that safely, without the *crathur*.

Near Keem Mr. H. showed us where the large crystals of amethysts are found—it is on the slope of the hill, and by the side of the road that leads from Keem eastward, and about three hundred feet above the level of the sea, that they are, or rather have been, found. It is in the gravel and rubbish, the *debris* of the higher ranges of the mountain, and always with their points downwards, and broken at the apex of the crystal that they are found. From the ground being much run over, and from there being no plan or science exhibited in the search, the specimens are now very rare, but I am sure that if any intelligent person were to come here and employ men to work in a proper way, there would be obtained an abundant supply of this very beautiful mineral.

We were now on our return home, and our road lay eastward, keeping nearly along the southern coast of the island. One of our company showed me just on the road-side what the people used as a cure for their sick cattle—it was a mineral substance that appeared on the surface of the hill, and being nearly black, was evidently either bog iron ore or manganese. I had no opportunity of testing it—my informant said it was considered a sovereign remedy for all sickness in cattle, and was given infused in water:

it is about as simple and perhaps as efficacious as the old woman's bullet. These Achillians certainly make short work of the materia medica.

We had now to pass through one or two villages on our way homewards (a toilsome and rather uninteresting walk along the lowlands, if I may so call them, of the island,) and as these villages are much under the influence of the priest, I certainly was anxious to observe how our party, known as it was to belong to the "SETTLEMENT" would be treated as we went through. The village was larger than any I had yet seen, but the same want of any sort of regularity or decency—no street—the cabins all dropped, as it were, here and there; no such thing as a cabbage garden. One or two corraghs or wicker boats covered with pitched canvas, were lying with their bottoms up on the strand—the place had a strong smell of putrid fish and sea-weed, and altogether it was a savage place, nasty in the extreme. I was still very thirsty and so was my friend—partly to assuage thirst and partly to see whether a cup of cold water *would* be given, I requested one of the men to go (which he rather unwillingly consented to do) up to one of the houses and ask for a drink of water; the man was sternly refused; we went a little further, and boys began to hoot, and women readily joined in the outcry, and "*jumpers, jumpers,*" were then exclaimed, and some other expressions in Irish, denoting scorn and hatred, but no stones were thrown; and I observed that the men joined not in the outcry, but kept a strict silence; they neither saluted nor insulted us.

On walking across a pretty long sandy strand, and crossing a small stream that flowed from a lake, half a mile or so in the interior, we struck inland towards the north. The village we left is, I believe, called Keel. Here one of my companions said that it was the intention of Sir R. O'Donnell to build a house, form a demesne, and make the island his summer residence. I confess, I would, as I said before, prefer building at Keem ; but here he would have a fine opportunity of improvement ; I never saw a tract of country more capable. A great extent of moorland, that only wants the expenditure of capital, and that a small one, to make it productive. Abundance of sea-weed and sea-sand ; a pretty lake, whose shores could be converted into rich meadows. I am sure that there are five thousand acres about Keel that could be made worth a pound an Irish acre.

Striking inland, towards the north, the "settle-ment" lying on the northern shore, we met, for it was now growing duskish, a number of men returning from their day's labour. Mr. Baylee, let us meet whom we might, always accosted them civilly in Irish. Some touched their hats, and made a good-natured reply ; others passed on, and made no answer. One man, when accosted with the usual address, "God save you," with a horrible scowl of his eye, and an expression of malice I have seldom seen equalled, replied, "may the devil damn you, and all belonging to you." This excited the wrath of the labouring man from the settlement, who had attended us, and he exclaimed in Irish, "may death crush *you*, you unmannerly brute ; why do you answer gentlemen in this way?" For this wrathful outbreak of the man, he was immediately, in the presence of the fellow who called it forth, reproved by the schoolmaster, Connor, who quoted the injunction of St. Paul, "not to return railing for railing, but, contrariwise, blessing." Another fine healthy active young man met us, with his loy or gowl-gob on his shoulder ; Mr. Baylee, as usual, saluted him, and he replied right civilly. He even stopped to speak to us, and inquired where we had been, and who the strangers were, pointing to us. Thus encouraged, Mr. Baylee ventured to say some words of a religious tendency, to which the other answered, that he was ready to wish us all well; that he was any thing but one that would abuse or injure a man for his religion, but he would wish to have his own religion let alone.

"Well, but suppose your own religion (says Mr. Baylee) is not the true one."

"Oh ! sir, God bless you ; let me alone. How could the likes of me argue with a minister like you. I leave all that to the priest. Here I am, as you see, a *loy-man*, (pointing to the loy, over his shoulder,) *but no lawyer*." With this *pun*, quite satisfied, the young fellow sprang across the bog-drain that divided the road from the potato-garden, and he was off across the ridges in an instant.

The night had fallen on us before we reached the settlement, and right glad was I, as I believe was every one of the party, when we got where each of us was to sup and sleep ; and, reader, I don't care how active or young you may be, but if ever you visit Achill, and take the same excursion that I did, you will, I rest assured, be as willing as I was to enjoy the creature-comforts of a good repast and a soft bed.

CHAPTER XIX.

DEPARTURE FROM THE SETTLEMENT.

Prepare to return from the settlement—Infant School—National School of
Dugarth—A gymnasium—Walk from the settlement to Achill Ferry—
Proposal for a LIBERAL settlement—Is the patriotism of Liberals but talk ?
—What Achill owes to Mr. Nangle—He blessed the island with the presence of two Archbishops—Speech of Titular—Situation of the priests of
Achill—Voluntary system operating on character and conduct—Consequences of dependent poverty—Anecdotes—The priest of Dunevir, and
the pig and purgatory—Anthony O'B—— and his station—A religious controversy over a cup—A precaution before death—How many masses a
heifer is worth—A holy well can kill as well as cure—Achill theology
and sacred history bearing upon the natural history of goats—Adam
and Eve, and the Doul Duff—Mr. B——'s apology for controversy—A
challenge to conciliation—And no more at present.

WE were to return next morning, and make our way
to Castlebar. The two missionaries, Nangle and
Baylee, had both, previous to my arrival, (which was
quite unexpected,) made arrangements to proceed to
Dublin on the day subsequent to the departure of
the Archbishop of Tuam. This plan Mr. Nangle felt
obliged to adhere to; but Mr. Baylee kindly consented
to defer his journey for one day, in order to show me
the lions of Achill. This he had done, as I have
above recorded, and, on the following day, we all
determined to set out after breakfast. I enjoyed, on
that morning, the privilege of divine service. I went
into the infant school, the hobby of the *Achill St.
Luke*, Dr. Adams. I saw what no one, ten years ago,
would have dared even to suppose feasible in such a
place, a number of pretty creatures, about thirty chil-

dren, (I, indeed, forget exactly how many,) clean, neat, healthy, and happy—all under that lovely discipline that makes primary instruction a matter of playfulness, and allows the young being, just budding into rationality, to be joyful while it is learning. I envy not the feelings of that man, let him call himself what he may, that would say that those who had succeeded in establishing such a school as this, were evil doers, and who would wish that Dr. M'Hale and his priests should eradicate all, and send the fox to peep out of its desolated windows of this institution.

Before my departure, I had occasion to go through the village of Dugarth, on my way down to the seashore, in order again to inspect the place among the cliffs where the stratum of primitive limestone lies incumbent on the gneiss, and crops out on the edge of the sea.

I have already spoken of this village—it is not worth any farther notice—it is but a congeries of dens of barbarism, and must give place shortly to habitations more fitted for educated men. But one of these dens or wigwams caught my notice, because, on it was a board, on which were painted the words, NATIONAL SCHOOL. This I was determined to enter, and accordingly I stooped to do so.

Well, of all the school-houses ever I entered, the National school-house of Dugarth was the most miserable. At the time I saw it, there were no scholars. It was about nine o'clock in the morning; none were in the house—if house it could be called, consisting of but one room—three little children seemed but just risen where they had been sleeping for the night, in a sort of crib, at the left hand side of the door. Opposite the door of this apartment, which was about fourteen feet in length, were stones ranged along the wall, on which were placed two loose boards, which were for seats for the scholars. At the right side of the door, were a parcel of dirty stinking ozier creels, intended to carry fish or turf. These were the whole furniture of this National Gymnasium, and so it might well be called ; for, I believe, that the scholars were as nearly naked as the apartment. I asked where was the master : the eldest child replied in Irish, and, therefore, what it said was to me unintelligible, and I had to depart without further information, and this was the National School of Dugarth. One would think that Mr. Nangle had decoyed the Education Board to allow this gymnasium to assume its imposing name of "National," and stand there as a foil to set off his own admirably appointed schools, not a furlong distant. I should certainly like to see the inspector's last report of this academy ; or, could it be possible that it was no National School at all, and that the priest had the board fixed up to satisfy the natives, who, poor things ! were thus satisfied with the *name* of a school. "*Lucus a non lucendo*," "*Schola a non scholando*."*

* I suppose it may be considered by many who will take up this volume that I am very deficient in not speaking more on the subject of education, and more especially . here where I have come across the school of Dugarth. But I am free to aver that I have no desire to discuss the subject. I do not feel that, on this subject, I have sufficient information, or had opportunity of adequate observation.

About eleven o'clock we left the settlement for the
Sound which divides Achill from the mainland: the
distance is about ten miles. As I had got walking
enough the day before, my friend and I procured a
pony, on which we agreed to ride and tie (as the
phrase is) for that distance. Mr. Baylee, a Scripture-reader, and two or three more who were going
to the Sound, accompanied us. There is a road the
whole way, which, with others in the island, were
constructed some years ago, more I believe to give
employment to the people in time of scarcity than
any thing else. These roads are now let to go to
ruin. The mountain torrents in many places tear them
up; and it would appear that the natives set little
value on them, as they carry what they want on the
backs of horses, and often, for want of four-footed
animals, on their own. Mr. Baylee and the others
walked; indeed this worthy and admirable man is
singularly adapted for the missionary work, for his
body and mind seem indefatigable. He appears to
me as if he could talk and walk for ever; he is all
energy. I certainly was sorry that I had not the
power of staying longer at Achill settlement; in many
ways it was interesting to me, and I was certainly
desirous of informing myself and being able to give
information to others of a more accurate character. I
would have also wished to have sojourned in the island,
and had communications with the natives previous to
my going to "the settlement," in order that I might
have known, as far as they would tell, their opinions

respecting the strangers that had come amongst them.
But this *at least I* could not effect, and I must leave
it to others to do so *if they can.* And here I must
observe that I wonder much that some person or
persons, who object to the mode pursued by Mr.
Nangle in forming and carrying on this colony, do
not try a settlement of a different nature in Achill, or
in the similarly neglected, wild, and barbarous districts of Connemara or Erris. Why not establish a
settlement, where, by introducing better modes of
rural economy, setting examples of cleanly, regular,
and sober habits, showing the natives by well tried
experiments, the advantages attending the winter
feeding of cattle, the cultivation of green crops;
also by giving premiums for house industry and
cleanliness amongst the females, and establishing
schools for the teaching of needle-work. I say, even
suppose literary and religious instruction were quite
left out of the question, why do not some of your
patriots, your liberal *well wishers* for the good of
Ireland, bestir themselves? why in this way confine
themselves to *benevolence,* while all the BENEFICENCE
is left to Mr. Nangle and his supporters. Of course
as we went along, I had much conversation with Mr.
Baylee and his *cortége.* The Scripture-reader, who
came with us, seemed a very intelligent man, and I
would say, considering his position, singularly moderate. He described to me with much effect, the
different parts, if I may so speak, the two archbishops, Doctors Trench and M'Hale, played while

discharging their episcopal functions on the island.
I have before said, that to Mr. Nangle it is altogether
owing that the two prelates should honour thus this
hitherto neglected spot with their gracious presence.
It would seem that the Roman prince descended, as it
were, like one of the eagles of Slieve Croghan, with
a pounce.* He came as a Boanerges, a son of thunder,
and behind him a fiery tail of priests in awful coil,
and every thing that could dazzle and subjugate the
savage mind was resorted to. The arch-prelate, in
his paraphernalia, with mitre on his head, crozier in
hand, clothed in amice, chesuble, and stole, invested
with his papal pall, the peculiar token of his dignity
as primate of Connaught. There he stood, as we
may suppose Balaam stood on Pisgah, (when summoned by Balak,) looking down on "the settlement,"
and ready to wither it with his curses, if God would
so permit; and he did what Balaam dared not do, he
took up his parable against it and prophesied, and

---

* If we are to believe the pleasant author of the " Wild
Sports of the West," the eagles of Achill have a national school
therein, more efficient than that of Dugarth, where they teach
the young idea how to pounce. " This morning (says he) the
eagles descended from their rocky habitation, accompanied by
two eaglets evidently to teach their young to stoop and lift
their prey.   The old birds tore up the turfs from the mountain
side, rose up high in the air, and then dropt them—the eaglets
in their turn stooped and took them up again—this was frequently repeated, and the course of instruction having lasted
half an hour, the eagles mounted to their eyrie, leaving their
progeny safe in their nest, and sailed off on the rising breeze to
provide for their evening meal." This author further observes,
that these eagles have a great *penchant* for black fowl, therefore
the Achillians never keep a black hen—as far as I could see they
kept little domestic fowl of any kind.

ventured to foretel that all would go to ruin, and leave
nothing behind but a cursed memory of the mischief
it attempted to do to Achill. I may as well give the
words of this prelate while he *foretold*, with all the
assurance of a prophet, and *cursed* with all the ritual
exuberance of a Romish pontiff : " Some of the bro-
therhood (meaning some belonging to the settlement)
have already fled from the utter derision of the people,
others are preparing to follow their example, finding
or feigning a convenient apology in the unwholesome-
ness of the atmosphere. The Achill mission is
already another tale of the numerous failures of fraud
and fanaticism, and its buildings, now unfinished,
are like the tower of Babel, (his own tower at Tuam
as I have shown, is more like that,) a monument of
the folly and presumption of its architect. Whoever
thus, in future, should contribute to such a project,
will not only be the dupe of delusion but the willing
agent of imposture."

Well, two years and a half after this, the settlement, instead of being deserted, instead of its buildings being left unfinished, or tenanted by the daws
and Royston crows, throve so much that its increasing population of adult children, absolutely required
that the Protestant archbishop should, when holding
confirmations through the rest of his diocese, come
into Achill, which he accordingly had done immediately previous to my arrival, and there he confirmed
twenty-eight persons, nineteen of whom were the
children of parents that had been Roman Catholics.

The appearance of the Protestant archbishop was quite a contrast to that of the Roman.

Dr. Trench, the brother and the uncle of an earl, appeared at Achill without either show or pretence. He came on a jaunting-car, he could not be distinguished from the two other clergymen who attended him, except by his age, and venerable, but humble demeanour. The people seemed astonished at his not, as his rival, "assuming the god and shaking the spheres of Achill;" therefore, some almost doubting the reality of the thing, asked, can this gentle man be an ARCH*bishop?* but the doubt was soon removed—all saw when they looked to the scriptural definition of bishop, that his calling was to bless and curse not, and so that worthy man, after performing his episcopal functions with the simple dignity and decorum that belong to the Christian bishop, went away pleasing and pleased, and it was hard to tell whether the people were more satisfied with him, or he with the people.

The titular archbishop, in the October of this year, 1838, again visited the island; again he cursed and threatened. On this occasion, in his address to the people, he stated that before the coming of this cursed people (meaning Mr. Nangle, &c.) this island was the garden of our Saviour: "and I hope," (says he, "that I shall have my prayer from our Saviour and the blessed Virgin, that this island shall be again what it formerly was."

The conversation I had with the Scripture reader

and Mr. Baylee, as we were proceeding to the sound, exposed to me what "a garden of our Saviour" Achill was. I have already shown what was their civil and moral state before the coming of this "cursed people." I will now show what was their religious state; and certainly, if but a small part of what I heard were true, there was not in the wide range of Christendom a more neglected, and more ignorant people. Without desiring at all to infer that the priests of Achill were worse men than others, yet, from the poverty of the people, and the undesirableness of the place as a residence, it may be supposed that very inferior persons were allowed to remain in such a charge. Accordingly, under the worst of all religious systems, the voluntary, the priests, if they pleased to live in Achill, must live to please, and please too, a savage people with whom they must associate, and, if possible, govern, not by opposing their vices and superstitions, but by making use of both, as means of procuring a very precarious income; and I do hold, and that not only respecting Achill, but the whole of the kingdom, that a great deal of the superstition, and immoral practices connected with that superstition, that prevail at this day, are owing to the necessity the priests and friars are under to keep well with the people in order to get their alms and dues. I will adduce one or two anecdotes that I heard from the Scripture readers, and schoolmaster of the settlement, to show how the priests stood with the people. There was resident in

2 E

the village of Duniver, a Father O'M——, the predecessor of the present Father Connolly, and in the
same village dwelt a poor, struggling fellow, who had to
support his aged parents, that, unable to work, sat
by the hob in his cabin, and in their turns dropt into
the grave. Now, his mother died first, and to use
my informant's phrase, "there were five shillings
coming to the priest out of her death." The poor
son neglected to pay this due, for the best reason,
because he had it not to pay, and by-and-by the
father died, and five shillings more were " coming to
the priest out of *his* death;" this was too much money
for the priest to lie out of, so he demanded, insist-
ingly, his due.

"Give me time, father," says the poor man,
" until I sell the pig, it's a fine slip, and wait till
Shrovetide, father jewel, and my blessing go wid
yees, and I'll do my best to fatten it for your reverence's sake and my own."

"Ah! thin, Darby, you deceyver, do you think I'm
an omaudawn all out, to be out of my money so long,
and I wanting, as I do, a dacent suit of clothes to go to
meet the bishop. I'll do no such thing, you beggarly
spalpeen. But I'll tell you what I'll do, I've the best
of good feeding for the pig myself; and Darby, I'll
take her from you, and allow you as much, after paying myself, as any one else would give you—maybe
more."

So the man gave him the pig, and it in due time
fattened, died, and was hung up in his reverence's

kitchen, and supplied him with bacon when he needed flesh food, for many a day; and after a decent time elapsed, and Darby did not find that the priest was forthcoming with the balance due on the pig, he went to him and humbly put him in mind of the agreement.

"Oh! yes," says the priest, "I do remember that I did promise to give you the value for your pig over and above what was due to me, and so I will, Darby; when you yourself die, avick, you shall have the value, and more than the value, in masses for your sowl, so be content, my child, it's well you have the likes of me to keep father, mother, and yourself, and all for a little slip of a pig, out of purgathory."

Another anecdote may suffice on this head:— Anthony O'B—— was one of the snuggest men in Achill, he had more cattle on the hill side than any other in the village, and here it was that the priest, as of course he should, determined to keep a station. So when the confession was heard, and the penance imposed, and absolutions given, the dinner came, and Anthony, to be sure, was not the man to disgrace his name by stinting his reverence. So there was plenty of bacon and some cabbage, (which is scarce in Achill,) a side of Keem mutton, and to wash all down, pails full of whiskey. Now, the priest had a mighty sound head, and though he drank with any man and would fill bumpers with you, if your eyes were shut, yet he never forgot the main-chance—so when they had drank a great deal, and the hearts began to open, though the tongues faltered, a controversy (such as it was) arose about religion, and his reverence insisted that no mortal man would or could go to heaven without masses being said for his soul, and that one mass said before death was worth four masses said afterwards: "Because, do you see me," says he, "according to the proverb which you all know, 'a stitch in time saves nine.'" "Well," says Anthony, "it is certainly wise to settle for my sowl before I die, seeing as how it is the safest way, and seeing as how those I'd leave after might think more of themselves than of me. I have a pretty little thrifty baste, as any running on the side of Sleive-more; and now, your reverence, how many masses will you say for that said brindled heifer?"

"Anthony, as I love you, you shall have forty."

"No, father dear, you sha'nt have her, unless you say fifty." So upon this they nearly fell out; but as the saying is, they split the difference, and shook hands on it, and by-and-by the priest, as he could not go home, was put to sleep with Tony, and it seems they did not agree in the night, for there was a great noise and uproar, and all the people had to get up, and both were found wallowing on the floor, and it was hard enough to put them back into bed again, or keep them there. The next morning, Anthony was sorry for his bargain, and wanted to keep his brindled heifer, but it could not be, all the neighbours gathered round and said he should be as good as his word with the priest. Accordingly the heifer was given, and of course the masses were said.

At all events Anthony O'B——e from that day afterwards never throve—his stock died off one after the other, and to use his own phrase, he never since had one cow to look in the face of another.

The consequence of all this insufficiency and vulgarity of mind, as well as manners, in the priests, was, that the people were given up to the most absurd superstitions, and had the most ridiculous and abject notions respecting what they called their Christian faith. *Well worship* was, as through all the west, a most important point of religion. I was shown one of their holy springs, and while it was dirty and sordid in the extreme, it showed evident marks of the resort of pilgrims by the muddy tramplings of the votaries all around. I think a well of water, bubbling up from a limestone rock, with the little shells and minute particles of sand ever dancing, and sparkling, as it were, "instinct with life," beneath its waters, translucent as the surrounding air, and these waters, as thus they spring from their pure source, running off playfully and pratlingly over their pebbly bed—I say this is a lovely and refreshing sight, and it is no wonder that in dry and hot climes some beneficent deity should be as it were identified with these much desired fountains, and it is quite in keeping to see all around the fresh and varied vegetations of nature fostered and yet kept from weedy and choking abundance by the hands of pious taste. But there was nothing of beauty, taste, or assiduity connected with this ugly, green-mantled, and weed-obstructed

water, which was only more disfigured and vulgarized
by the filthy rags that were fastened on stones about
it, for there was not even a bush on which to hang
them—the ugliness and offensiveness of the place
was not diminished, in my conception, by being
informed that a man came here to do penance some
time (not very long ago,) and was found next morning smothered (not drowned, for there was not water
enough for that) with his face downwards in the well;
the man, it is supposed, came drunk to do his devotions—there is no other way of accounting for his
perishing. The people, though they in general look
with fear and repugnance on the place where a man
is found to have died suddenly, yet frequent this well,
and drink the water wherein a dead man had lain
steeping the whole night.

I have said that the people have the most mean
and degrading opinions respecting Christianity and
its divine Author and followers. How could it be
otherwise, when no Bible, even in the possession
of the priest, was, perhaps, ever in Achill until Mr.
Nangle arrived. One of the people who assumed to
know somewhat, on being asked why St. Peter was
called the rock, said it was because Christ made him
his altar and always said mass upon his back. Another—and I hope here the reader will pardon the ludi-
crous nature of the illustration I am about to introduce; and whether pardoned or not, as I am about to
show how far the island of Achill was heretofore "the
garden of Jesus Christ," I *will* detail what I have heard.

I say one Achillian asked another—"Paddy, ma bouchal, can you explain to me the reason why all goats I have ever seen have their tails turned up, when the sheep, as every one may observe, have theirs hanging downwards *dacently* and purtily?" "Why then I'll tell you, Larry. Once on a time, when our Saviour was persecuted by the wicked Jews, and they hunted him from place to place to have his life, he met a goat, and would have hid himself under her, but the nasty and wicked *baste* turned up its tail and exposed him to his pursuers; so with that he ran off, and seeing a sheep at hand, he went on all fours, and hid himself under her, and she, the kind crathur, dropped down her tail and fixed herself low and careful so as to hide him from all eyes—and from that day forth, the goat's tail turns up, and the sheep's tail falls downwards." Another, and I have done: Here is the Achillian description of the fall and recovery of man—"Adam and Eve were in paradise, as happy as the day was long; they had plenty to eat and nothing to do, and were as innocent as a child is after a christening; and so it was that the devil was passing by one day and peeps in over the stone wall that was all around the garden, mighty high entirely, and he saw Adam and his wife so comfortable and quiet, not having a hand's turn of work to do; so the devil was mighty angry at this, and says he, "I'm much mistaken if I don't spoil your sport;" so he tried to get in to do his mischief, but the good angels were too cute for him—if he went to bounce over the

wall there he met an angel with a drawn sword—if
he attempted to slip under the gate, there he met St.
Peter, ready to strike him back with his key—"So,"
says the devil, " I'll be up to them," and he changed
himself into a doul duff;* and so, though black and
ugly, (for he could not change himself into any thing
purty,) he crept under a dock-leaf, and there remained
until night, when he slyly wriggled himself into the
garden." Well, my story's too long to tell how the
enemy over-persuaded Adam and Eve to eat of the
apple; but they did it, that's sure, and all the world
went wrong. "So, after a very long time, the good God
had pity upon a poor unhappy world; and he says to
the angel Gabriel—' Go down upon earth, and as the
world has been lost by a sinning woman, you must
find out a perfect one who will set all to rights.' So
Gabriel got his directions what to do, and down he
flew, and, of course, he flew so as to land near the
right place. As he was going along, he met a great
number of people going to prayers, for it was Sunday;
so passing them, a little further on he sees a neat,
clane, sweet-faced, little colleen as ever went to confession, sitting by a well side, and she was a putting on
her shoes and stockings, having washed her feet very
dacently. So, says angel Gabriel to her—' Hail Mary!

---

* A doul duff is a black colœopterous insect, somewhat in the
shape of an earwig, but perfectly black, about an inch long,
which turns up its tail as if to strike whenever approached—it
is really a hideous creature, and the Irish have an intense antipa-
thy to it, and, as a representation of Satan, always kill it when
they can.

what are yees about and where are you going?' So she ups and told him, mighty civil, that she was preparing to go to MASS, and that *properly* as became her father's daughter." I need not proceed with the remainder of the *history*, enough is told to give an example of how the truths of sacred story are vulgarized and perverted; how the *mass* is made the important affair at the expense of all truth and chronology; and how, instead of the poor people being elevated up, and humanized by a lofty, pure, and rational faith, the religious system is brutalized and brought down to their grovelling comprehension; and so whatever true Christianity may do to elevate and humanize mankind, it is proved here, as well as all over the world, that its Roman representative only depresses and lies as a great nightmare terrifying and oppressing the world.

I believe I have exhausted all my recollections concerning Achill, and it is time for me to quit the subject. But, before I conclude, I would just repeat a conversation I had with Mr. Baylee, respecting the mode of controversy adopted by him and Mr. Nangle, and indeed by all persons connected with the settlement, with their adversaries, the priests and their confraternity men: and I took leave to ask, might not a gentler and less offensive attack be made on the false doctrines and superstitious practices of Rome, and be attended with better effects; or might it not be still better to preach the Gospel without controversy, and show by a holy and circumspect life and conversation that *here* was a more excellent way? To this his reply was, that to be sure the language he and his friends used would not be expedient before a cultivated audience, such as might be collected where education and good manners had given a finer polish to the mind; but that it was absolutely necessary to speak *coarsely* to *coarse* minds; that a people who really exhibited very little delicacy in their language or conduct, must be approached, if you wish they should understand you, by downright statements, couched in language adapted to their own daily conversation. That in this way Luther, living in coarse times, used the broad coarse language befitting his time and companions; and that as what he wrote and spoke, though now considered vulgar and gross, were not either one or the other in his own day and country, so now what may be objected to in Dublin or in England, as unfit for ears polite that love paraphrase, still is suitable language for the western meridian in which they are located; and though it might befit those who, on their becoming senators of the British empire, had declared that transubstantiation was a damnable and idolatrous tenet, to whisper elsewhere in more gentle mood, that it was only an amiable and venial error. Yet it did not become *him* or *his* friend to compromise their doctrine, lower their colours, or bow either the knee to Baal or the head to Rimmon. Their colony, he said, was established in *direct* hostility to popery; that it lost all claim to a religious and proselyting establishment if they treated that *gently*, which was like the nettle, a thing

that when only touched *lightly*, stung the hand
severely, but when grasped lustily, might be plucked
and eradicated without injury. Moreover, he said,
it might be well for those who sat at home at ease,
who saw Romanism, as it were, tired out and painted
like Jezebel, looking so alluringly fine at her window,
to speak softly of the gaudy mischief; but those who
saw it roaming in all its reckless and poisonous vigour,
in the places where it may do as it likes; it was for
them and them only to know how best to oppose it,
and wrestle against it with success. He finally observed, and here I beg leave to say, and without
expressing an opinion of my own on the subject, that
I am only recording the substance, and not the *ipsissima
verba*, of our conversation, that enough had been done
already in the gentle and conciliatory way, and *that*
without any success; and, he must say, that before
your conciliators should venture to condemn decidedly
the mode of proceed ng at Achill, they should either
point out any place on earth where *their* mode of
operation had succeeded, or have patience and fortitude to try such a method in Ireland, and report
progress.

APPENDIX.

No. 1.—Page 99.

In a MS. in Marsh's Library, I find the following
account, which settles the matter respecting the disputed
passage. In the ancient registry of the possessions of the
see of Clonmacnoise, which was transcribed in the thir-
teenth century by direction of Bishop Muercheartach from
the original entries which were written in the life of
Cearan, "fearing lest it might be obscured and lost." The
original MS. of this registry was, as Archbishop Usher
(in his report to King James's Commissioners of the state
of the diocese of Meath) states, in existence in his time,
but had been lately conveyed away by the practice of a
lewd fellow who hath thereupon fled the country; tran-
scripts, however, were in the hands of the Archbishop and
of his friend, Sir James Ware, who got it translated into
English by Dugald M'Firbiss, and the autograph of that
translator is preserved in the British Museum, amongst
Ware's MSS. In this registry, after stating that
O'Rourke had given for his right of sepulture at Cluain,
seven cells or churches in his territory, with as much land
attached to each of them as could be ploughed in 48 days,
it proceeds thus: there was a controversy between
M'Granail and Fergal O'Ruairk, because M'Granail had
got no place for a tomb in Cluain and did stop the
building of a church there for O'Ruairk. Afterwards
M'Granail got a tomb in the place of sepulture allotted
for O'Ruairk. Wherefore that M'Granail, which was
Brian M'Granail, bestowed for his part 48 ploughs in the
aforesaid Killaghthain, so that the bishop of Cluain had in
Killaghthain, ninety-six plough-days in all, whence it came
that a Comorbe or Corbe was sent from Cluain to Killaghthain, who used to receive the bishops of Cluain's rents,
viz. two beeves and three hogs at St. Martin's eve, and

two beeves and one hog from every one of the six churches mentioned before in O'Ruairk's country; then follows the above cited passage stating how O'Ruairk built the steep Castle or Tower.

In the annals of the four masters it is stated that in the year 1124, "Operimentum Campanilis, (Cloictighe) Cluan-macnoise factum per O'Maloneum vicarium Ciarani.

As a proof that these towers were places of retreat, it may be stated that in the annals of the four masters and others, the burning of persons who had retired to those towers was often effected; that of Slane is thus recorded: Campanale (Cloicthighe) Slanense Combustam ab Aliegenis cuma bundantia reliquiarum et religiosorum hominum simul cum Caonocharo Prælectore et Baculo Patroni et Campana optima Campanarum.

To obviate the danger arising from being burnt while in the towers, by foes from without, some of the towers show in the doorways provision for a double door.

No. 2.—Page 169.

Cathol Crove Derg, according to tradition, was the natural son of Roderick O'Connor by a low-born maiden of the name of Moran. Roderick's wife, hearing of the unfaithfulness of her husband, and of the pregnancy of his concubine—she herself being childless—felt in extreme the pangs of jealousy; and in her malicious mood sent for a Scotch witch to consult her how best to put a stop to the birth of the hated child; and the witch, obedient, (as Lucina was found on a like occasion,) directed that nine hazel rods should be twisted in a knot of her own contriving, and so hung up against the gable end of the royal residence; and she asserted that unless this magic knot were untwisted Garouge Nevorane (or in plainer terms, the concubine Moran) could never be delivered. Of course poor Moran's time came; and for nine long days she underwent the severest of all pangs, and still there was no strength to bring forth—*tantummodo manus dextra infantis protrusa et exinde rubra fuit.*

An old woman in attendance upon poor Moran all this while, suspecting that what was so unnatural must arise from malicious witchcraft, and shrewdly suspecting the queen, went forth and accosted her highness as she was walking, proud and melancholy, in the lawn opposite her palace. She besought some nourishment for a poor female who had just been brought to bed, and was sick and weak. " What is the woman's name?" says the Queen. " Garouge Moran, please your majesty, who is delivered of a fine boy." On hearing this, the disappointed queen, considering that she was deceived by the Scotch enchantress, ran to the gable end, cut the knotted hazel rods in bits with her skein, and of course Moran was in a thrice safely delivered. Her son was the famous Cathol of the red hand, who was never received or acknowledged by his father; but during his reign worked as others for his daily bread. He was reaping oats, as the tradition goes, when the news arrived of his father's death; he at once threw down his hook, went to his father's palace, claimed, according to the law of tanistry, the vacant throne, and being elected to it, showed himself worthy to be King of Connaught. The O'Conor Don is said to be descended from Cathol Crove Derg.

The monk of Boyle thus records the demise of Cathol: 1223, Jan. Cal. Cathol Croderg O'Connor, King of Connaught, and King of the Irish in Ireland, died in the Abbey of Knockmoy. The best Irishman that came from the time of Brian Boroihme for gentility and honour; the upholder, mighty and puissant, of the country, keeper of peace, rich and excellent; for in his time tithe was paid and established in Ireland first legally. Threshold meek of belief and Christianity, corrector of transgressors and thieves; the banisher of the wicked and robbers; the defender of the right cause; clement and courageous; to whom God gave great honour in this world, and everlasting life in heaven, dying in a monk's habit, overcoming the world and the devil.

No. 3.—Page 188.

" The general characteristics (says he) of the class of society I speak of, are dissipation, idleness, and vanity; every man with a few acres of land, and a moderate revenue, is dignified, as a matter of course, with the title of esquire; and, be his family ever so numerous, or the incumbrances on his little patrimony ever so great, he must support a pack of hounds, entertain with claret, or if not able, with whiskey, keep a chaise and livery servants, and, in short, ape his superiors in every respect. Meanwhile, his debts are increasing, his creditors growing clamorous, and every industrious occupation which might relieve his distresses neglected, as utterly beneath the dignity of a gentleman. The numerous instances of this which occur, cannot fail to have a very serious and powerful influence in the obstructions of national industry and employment. The bad debts of men of business are more numerous in Ireland than can well be imagined; such must considerably injure and obstruct the industrious; those sums which should be saved for the younger children of the family, and laid out in the establishment of some industrious occupation that would enable them to afford employment to thousands of their countrymen, are either squandered in idle extravagance, or, if collected from the fortune which the hopeful heir-apparent may obtain in matrimony, are employed by those on whom they are bestowed in pursuing the laudable example they have been accustomed to from infancy; but the influence of such example is still more extensive; its ruinous contagion extends to the most inferior ranks. The labouring hind quits his spade to pursue his landlord's pack of beagles on foot, and at night intoxicates himself with whiskey, while the master enjoys a similar pleasure with liquors more refined and palatable. To the one source are we to trace those nuisances to every rank of society, denominated *bucks* and *buckeens*. Such, in general, are either the eldest sons of gentlemen of small property we have described, or the younger children of those possessed of larger, who have received their scanty pittance, of which the augmentations by industrious means is never once attempted, and the final dissipation one would imagine deemed impossible. To stand behind a counter, superintend a farm, or calculate in a counting-house, would be beneath the dignity of such exalted beings, and disgrace the memory of their *gentlemen* ancestors; but would not such pursuits be finally beneficial to their country, and more grateful to their own feelings, than a mode of life which dissipates the funds which should be employed in industry, and corrupts the manners of the people, ruins the health, and annihilates the fortunes of the individuals in general, and, at last, finally, leads them to subsist as mendicants on the charity of some more opulent relation?

It is disgusting to see such beings gambling at a hazard-table, bustling at a horse-race, quarrelling over their claret, or hallooing after a fox, perhaps in an equipage they have neither inclination nor ability to pay for. Let us turn from the picture; the only satisfaction attendant on its examination is, that the species are daily diminishing."—(*See Doctor Crump's Essay on Providing Employment for the People.*)

No. 4.—PAGE 222.

On a day as holy Patrick, with his blessed company, approached a certain river called Dabhall; and because it was late, and the sún setting, it was determined to spend the night on the banks, and pitch their tents upon a beautiful meadow adjoining. Presently the prelate proceeds to the stream, therein to wash his hands and his face; and while in the act of scrubbing his gums and his teeth—and while, perhaps, too hardly rubbing what was over loose from age—one of his teeth by a chance spit, or as it may be better said, by divine ordinance, was cast into the water. As soon as his disciples heard this, they, with intense industry, sought for the tooth in the stream, but with all their diligence could not find it. But when night came on, amidst the darkness, the tooth, lying at the bottom of the water, cast up a splendour like one of heaven's bright stars, so much so that all abiding in the vicinity of the river were drawn to behold and get possession of it. And so the tooth being taken up was brought to the holy father, and it was by him and all present dedicated to the honour and glory of God; and the saint, in the place where it was found, built a church, placed the tooth under the altar, which place immediately became eminent for many miracles, and is called to this day Clueyn Fiacal—that is, the Church of the Tooth.—*Colgan Trias Thaum Sexta Vita St. Pat. page 85.*

No. 5.—PAGE 318.

" Then St. Patrick, according to the example of our Lord, went forth in the forty days of fast before Easter, into the desert of Cruachan Aigle, and there he sat upon a stone, with four stones on the four sides of him; then a mighty multitude of black birds, or rather of demons, kept flying over his head, and grievously they impedimented his praying. But Patrick sounded his bell, and sent them trooping off into the sea, and immediately a host of angels, in the form of snow-white birds, came flying round the mountain, and chorused soft music for his solace. While in the mountain he put up three petitions; the first was, that every inhabitant of Ireland who did penance at his last hour should not have the gates of hell close him in; the second was, that no aliens or barbarians should inhabit the island from that time forth until the day of judgment; the third was, that four years before the day of judgment the sea should cover the island. When he was about to descend from the mountain he blessed the island, sounded his bell, and all the inhabitants of the whole land heard plainly the sound thereof."

I have within these few days heard from my friend Dr. Wilde, that Patrick's Bell—THE BELL!!!—is still in existence, and in possession of a poor man near Ballinrobe, in whose family it has been handed down from father to son from time immemorial. This man, on particular station days, brings it up to the Reek, where it is offered to each pilgrim to kiss, and each kiss is *paid for;* it is also brought about the country and passed round the bodies of those afflicted with disease, and of pregnant women—altogether the owner has a profitable estate in the Bell.

Colgan has a note upon the second petition of Patrick, in which, while he acknowledges that aliens and heretics had got possession of the land, yet, to save the credit of the saint, says, that he meant that pagans should not receive possession of Ireland. After all, in the friar's view, a heretic is not so bad as a pagan.

There is much scepticism abroad about St. Patrick. Some suppose there was no such person, as Ledwich; others suppose, as Sir William Betham, that there were many Patricks. I am disposed to think, that, as the persons who brought Christianity to Ireland came from the Roman provinces of Britain and Gaul, they were called PATRICIANS, a name of honour not unusually assumed in the latter days of the Roman empire, and still more generally attributed by those amongst whom they travelled, as the

English are at this day usually called milord; thus there might have been Palladius the Patrician, and Cœlestius, the Patrician. Higgins, a learned, but fanciful, absurd and sceptical writer, makes short work of Patrick.

In the *Celtic Druids*, Chap. V. Sect. xliv., I have said, " Thus there is an end of St. Patrick. I shall not repeat the reasons which I have given for that opinion, which are quite sufficient for its justification. A learned and ingenious gentleman has written a life of St. Patrick; and Nimrod says, " Firstly, and most obviously, the express tradition that St. Patrick's fosse and purgatory were the fosse and *necyia* of Ulysses. Ogygia (moreover) was the isle of Calypso, in which Ulysses sojourned; and Plutarch informs us that it was situated five days' sail to the west of Britannia, and that there were three other islands near it. From the south-east of Britain, where the Romans used to land, it would have been a five days' journey to Ireland for ancient navigators. The first name of Ulysses, before he came to be styled Ho-dys-eus, was *Nanus*; and the first name of St. Patrick was *Nanus*. In Temora, the bardic capital of Ireland, *Nani* tumulum lapis obtegit, and it is one of Ireland's thirteen mirabilia. Ulysses, during his detention in Aiaia, was king of a host of swine; and Patrick, during a six years' captivity in the hands of King Milcho or Malcho, was employed to keep swine. Ulysses flourished in Babel, and St. Patrick was born at Nem-Turris, or the Celestial Tower; the type of Babel, in Irish mythology, is *Tory* Island, or the Isle of the *Tower*. At the time of its expugnation Sru emigrated from the east. Rege *Tutane* gestum est praelium campi Turris et expugnata est Troja Trojanorum; but Tutanes is the Teutames, King of Assyria, whose armies Memnon commanded. Ulysses was the Roiranus (or King) whom a dolphin saved, and whom all the dolphins accompanied from Miletus; his son Telemachus, whom a dolphin saved, was the bard Arion; but Arion was King of Miletus in the days of Priam, King of Troy; and as Miletus was a considerable haven of Asia Minor in Homer's time, it is the most probable place of Ulysses's departure. But a great consent of tradition brings the colonists of Ireland from Miletus. Miletus, father of Ire, came to Ireland in obedience to a prophecy." The above is a very small part of the similitudes between Ulysses and St. Patrick; but it is enough to confirm what I have said in the *Celtic Druids*, and to blow the whole story of the saint into thin air. I believe that the whole was a Romish fable.

Nimrod afterward goes on at great length to show how the story of St. Patrick is accommodated to the ancient Homeric Mythos, and Patricius and the Pateræ to the saint; and he particularly notices a famous ship-temple, described by General Vallancey in the Archaeologia. Now I think it is quite impossible to date this great stone ship after the rise of Christianity. This at once raises the strongest probability, indeed almost *proves* that the stories of Ulysses, King Brute, &c. &c. detailed in the old monkish historians, are not their invention in the dark ages, as they are now considered by all our historians, and as such treated with contempt, but are parts of an universally extended Mythos, brought to the British isles in much earlier times, and as such in a high degree worthy of careful examination. The proof of any part of this Mythos having existed in Ireland or Britain before the time of Christ, opens the door for the consideration of all the remainder, and is a point of the greatest importance. —*Higgins's Anacalypsis, Vol. I. page* 367.

No. 6.—Page 371.

On a certain day, as St. Patrick was going about preaching the Gospel and healing all manner of disease, he met by the wayside a tomb of astonishing size, (being thirty feet long). His companions observing this, expressed their opinion that no man could have ever arrived at such a size as to require such a grave. Whereupon the saint replied that God, by the resurrection of this giant, could persuade them, provided they were not altogether slow of faith. For just at that time there existed much doubt respecting the truth of the general resurrection. St. Patrick therefore prayed fervently that his statements might be borne out by facts, and that thereby the scruples of doubt might be eradicated from their minds. And lo a wonder—wonder heretofore in past ages unheard of— For the man of heavenly might approaches the sepulchre; he pours out his powerful prayer; signs with the staff of Jesus the tomb. And up rose the giant from the grave; and there he stood before them all, in stature and countenance most horrible; and looking intently on St. Patrick, and weeping most dolorously he cried, " Immense gratitude I owe you, my lord and master, beloved of God and elect; because that at least for one hour you have snatched me from out the gates of hell, where I have been suffering unspeakable torments." And he besought the saint that he would allow him to follow him; but the saint refused, giving for his reason, that men could not bear to look without intolerable terror on his countenance. When being asked who he was, he said his name was Glarcus, son of Chais; that heretofore he was swineherd to King Laogair, and that about 100 years ago he was attacked and killed by one Fin M'Coul in the reign of King Cairbre. St. Patrick then advised him to believe in the Triune God and be baptized, if he would not return to his place of torment, to which the giant joyfully agreed; and then he returned to his grave, and he was delivered, according to the word of the saint, from his place of suffering.—*Colgan Trias Thaum Sexta Vita Sat.*, *page* 83.

No. 7.—Page 388.

In Colgan's Acta Sanctorum, page 721, the account is given " De egressione familiæ St. Brendani," and therein it is narrated how St. Brendan got information from a certain St. Barinthus, of a paridisaical island in the western ocean, to which he had once sailed under the instruction of a hermit living an ascetic life in one of the islands off the western coast of Ireland. How, said Berinthus, thus instructed, sailed through seas covered with fogs, so that they could not see from stem to stern of the vessel; and how, at length they touched on land, all whose fields were flowery, and whose forests bore sweet fruit; and how, when he went into the interior he met a person in shining garments who desired him to return; and leave the discovery to one more favoured of heaven. St. Brendan hearing this from his friend St. Barinthus, and assuming that he was the chosen for the adventure, departed with fourteen of his confraternity to the island of Arran, where flourished the wise and the good St. Endius; from whom receiving much wise and holy advice (for there is no doubt but that the saint of Arran

knew more of the remote west than any other person)
St. Brendan departed for his own country in Kerry—
there to see his parents before he ventured on his voyage.
Having there with much prayer consorted with them for
a brief space; in a little bay at the foot of that mountain,
which, to this day, is called St. Brendan's Hill, he and
his companions constructed a vessel such as is still used
along that coast, framed of wattles, over which were ox
skins stretched and made waterproof with pitch and tallow,
and taking in provision for fifty days they set sail, and
proceeding against the summer solstice, ("navigantes contra
solstitium æstivale,") they had a prosperous wind, so that
for fifteen days they never shortened or changed sail; but
on the fifteenth day the wind ceased, and they took to their
oars, at which having laboured long and much, the man
of God, St. Brendan, at length said to his fellow voyagers,
"Cease your toils; we will commit ourselves to the Lord,
in whom we trust; we will hoist our sail, and, without
using oar or helm, abide the leadings of Providence." So
on they sailed, not knowing whither; sometimes they had
wind, sometimes not; they refreshed themselves but once
during the day, and that was before the hour of evening
prayer; and at length reached the lovely land of promise, where they remained seven years.

So far I have contracted Colgan's account, who promised
to give a fuller history of the adventure of St. Brendan and
his followers when he came to the 11th of May, the day
sacred to St. Brendan. But Colgan never published
more than the acts down to the end of March; and I
have not yet come across, though I know it is in existence,
any account of St. Brendan's actions during his seven
years' sojourn in this transatlantic country. But let
us try and connect this discovery of St. Brendan, which I
am quite certain was not pure monkish invention, and
which when stripped of the superstitious *verbiage* in
which it is involved, contains in the main much veri-
similitude. Now we find it stated in the introduction to
the account of the Icelandic Discoveries of America, published lately at Copenhagen, page xxxvii. that the Shaw-
neese Indians, who some time ago emigrated from Florida,
and are now settled in the Ohio, have a tradition that Florida was once inhabited by white people, who were in the
possession of iron implements, &c. &c. &c.; and judging
from ancient account of the habits, language, and tenets of

this white race, they must have been an Irish, Christian people, who, previous to the year 1000, were settled in that region. The powerful chieftain, Arc Marson, of Prykanies in Iceland, was in the year 983 drawn thither by storms, and was there baptized. The first author of this account was his cotemporary Rafn, sirnamed the Limerick Trader, he having his residence in Limerick. This Rafn, or as he is in other accounts called, Ari, sailed to what he called Whiteman's Land, and dwelling there for some time, returned, and named it *Great Ireland.* The original Icelandic of the passage is quoted in the second volume of the Anthologia Hibernica. In the preface to the Copenhagen work the following circumstance is narrated:—
" In the year 983, Gudlief Gudlauson sailing from Dublin to Iceland, was driven by north-east winds to the land above alluded to, and found a Norwegian dwelling there, by whose means he was rescued when about to be put to death by the natives; he in a short time safely returned to Dublin and reported that the people he was amongst spoke what resembled the Irish language."

No. 8.—PAGE 388.

The compiler of the MS. history of Ireland, preserved in the library of the Royal Irish Academy, written about the year 1636. He, as quoted by Hardiman in his Irish Minstrelsy, vol. 1, p. 138, speaks of the sunken land thus:—
" The Tuatha Danaans, coming in upon the Firbolgs, expelled them into the out islands which lay scattered on the north coast, and they themselves were served the same measure by the Clanna Miledhes; but what became of the remainder of them I cannot learn, unless they do inhabit an island which lyeth far out at sea on the west of Connaught, and is sometimes perceived by the inhabitants of Uaile and Iris. It is also said to be sometimes seen from St. Helen's Head, being the farthest west point of land beyond the haven of Calbegs, now Teeling Head, bounding the bay of Killibegs in Donegal; likewise several seamen have discovered it at sea as they have sailed on the western coast of Ireland; one of whom, named Captain Rich, who lives about Dublin, had of late years a view of the land, and was so near that he discovered a harbour, as he supposed, by the two headlands

on each side thereof, but could never make the land, although when he had lost sight thereof in a mist which fell upon him, he held the same course several hours afterwards. This I am bold to assert by the way, because I have heard a relation thereof from many credible persons, and particularly from the said Captain Rich; although in many old maps (especially maps of Europe and maps of the world) you will find it by the name of O'Brasil, under the longitude of 13°, and the latitude of 50° 20'; so that it may be those famous enchanters now inhabit them, and by their magic skill conceal their island from foreigners. Yet this is *my own* conceit, and would have it taken for no other."

So strong was the belief at this time in the existence of O'Brasil, that a fictitious account of a voyage thither found circulation in 1675. The story purports to be told in a letter from one William Hamilton of Londonderry, to his cousin in London, and is entitled " *O'Brasil, or the Enchanted Island, being a perfect relation of the late discovery and wonderful disenchantment of an island on the west of Ireland.*" The tale itself is sufficiently absurd, but the writer states some collateral facts worth noticing; as that on first coming to Ireland he heard many stories which were common in every man's mouth concerning the island of *O'Brasil* which multitudes reported to be often seen from the coasts of *Ulster*. Again he expresses his wonder at having found it laid down in many maps both ancient and modern; and still greater surprise at what moved his correspondent's cousin " who was a wise man and a great scholar to put himself to the charges and trouble (in the late king's time) to take out a *patent* for it when it should be gained;" on which there is this note — " There is nothing more certain than that a patent was taken out for it in the late king's days." He further adds, " since the happy restoration of his majesty that now reigns, many reports have been that it has been disenchanted or taken, yea at the time of the sitting of the last parliament in Dublin, (in the year 1663,) one coming out of *Ulster* assured the House of Commons (whereof he was a member) that the enchantment was broken, and it gained; but it proved not so ; and about two years after, a certain Quaker pretended that he had a revelation from heaven, that he was the man ordained to take it with a new ship built by his inspiration, &c. ; and in order thereto he built a vessel, but what became of him or his enterprise I never heard," &c.—(*See Hardiman's Irish Minstrelsy, V. I. pp.* 369, 371.)

It may here be remarked that the island, as known to the Irish, is properly called *Hy Bresail,* corresponding with the Bresilium of Hadrienus Junius, being accented on the first syllable, not as in the present name of Brazil proper; and that in this respect it agrees with the old name, as known to Chaucer, in whose verse the accent is thrown back; so also Marston, in his satires, used the word with a long penultima, some time after the name had been imposed on the country which now bears it—" God bless his honour's running *Brasell bowl.*"—*Marston, Sat.* 11, from which it appears that this wood was also turned to the manufacture of utensils. Such, also, seems to be the pronunciation indicated by the spelling of the word in the other evidences. The affix Hy used in the Irish name, as in Hy Mania, Hy Niellam, &c. &c. is nearly equivalent to *Clan,* as in our Clan-Breasal, meaning the tenantry of or country occupied by the descendants of Brasail, which is still a common Irish name.

For these observations I am indebted to my friend Mr. Ferguson, who lately read a clever, pleasant paper on the subject, before the Royal Irish Academy.

No. 9.—PAGE 329.

In order to show with what fidelity tradition is preserved amongst the Irish, I think it well to quote the following passage from an author who wrote 500 years ago, and whose work is so scarce that it is quite impossible that the Connaught schoolmaster should have ever seen it. Yet his tradition is almost identical with the statement of Gerald Barry:—

Giraldus Cambrensis Topographia Hibernia, book 2, chap. 12.

"Inter alias vero Insulas est una nuper nata, quam phantastica vocant, cui talis eventus originam dedit:—Die quodam sereno emersit in mari, cumulus terræ non modicus, ubi nunquam, antea terra visa fuerat videntibus et admirantibus insulanis. Quidam enim ex iis dicebat balenam vel aliam beluam marinam monstrosam esse ;

alii vero considerantes quod sine omni motu persisterat;
dicebant nequaquam, sed terra erat; ut vero hanc
contiguitatis conditionem certitudo discrimerent, electi
juvenes de insula quadam propinquore illuc navicula
remisque adire statuerant. Accidentes vero tam propè
ut applicare jam se arbitrati fuerint tanquam in mare
descendens ab oculis eorum insula prorsus evanuit.
In crastino, vero, similiter, apparens eosdem juvenes
simili delusione decepit. Tertio tandem die senioris
cujusdam consilio accidentes sagittam igniti ferri in
insulam promiserunt et sic applicantes terram stabilem
et habitabilem invenerunt. Multis itaque patet argumentis
phantasmati cuilibet ignem semper inimicissimum."

TRANSLATION.

Amongst other islands there is one lately come to light,
which they call the Phantom Island, which was discovered
in the following manner: On a certain calm day a mass
of no small size emerged from the sea, where never before
land was seen by the now wondering natives. Some
indeed said it must be a whale or some other monstrous
creature of the deep; but others considering how steady
the mass appeared, asserted that it must be land; and in
order to arrive at a certainty, certain young men were
chosen to row thither in a boat, and they accordingly
pulling towards it, and now almost touching the land,
found that, as in an instant, the island vanished from their
sight. To-morrow, however, as it appeared again, the
same young men tried, and that in vain, to reach it; but
on the third day, pursuant to the advice of an old man,
they on approaching shot an arrow tipped with red hot
iron towards the shore, and then landing they found a
land steady and habitable. By many arguments it appears
that fire is altogether inimical to any thing that is
phantastic.

THE END.

Dublin: Printed by JOHN S. FOLDS, 5, Bachelor's-walk.

BOOKS FOR TOURISTS IN IRELAND.

PICTURE OF DUBLIN, or Guide to the Irish Metropolis; containing an account of every object and institution worthy of notice—with a brief description of the surrounding country, and its geology. With a large Plan, and thirteen Views, 7s. 6d. cloth, or 8s. bound.

" A book to be read in England or Scotland, as well as Ireland; we are bound to give our warmest praise to the work, which is alike creditable to the city and the spirit of the publishers."—*Morning Register*.

" A geological paper on the vicinity of Dublin adds much to the value of this estimable little volume."—*Athenæum*.

GUIDE TO THE COUNTY OF WICKLOW. Small 8vo. map and plates. 5s. cloth.

GUIDE TO KILLARNEY AND GLENGARIFF. New Edition, small 8vo, map and plates. 5s. cloth.

GUIDE TO THE GIANT'S CAUSEWAY, and the Coast of Antrim. Small 8vo. map and plates. 5s. cloth.

" No tourist ought to set foot in Ireland without these little works, they are worth a dozen living guides such as the inns supply. Our personal knowledge of the routes described enables us to speak confidently of their correctness."—*Sun*.

A CRUISE round the South-East Coast of Ireland, in a four-oared gig. Small 8vo. 1s.

Dublin: WILLIAM CURRY, JUN. and Co. 9, Upper Sackville-street. Sold by all the respectable Booksellers in the United Kingdom.

MAPS, PLANS, &c.

MAP OF IRELAND—constructed for Fraser's Guide, and corrected to 1839. 3s. 6d. in a case.

PLAN OF DUBLIN. 2s. 6d. in a case.

MAP OF THE ENVIRONS OF DUBLIN. 2s. 6d. in a case.

MAP OF THE COUNTY OF WICKLOW. 2s. 6d. in a case.

ROAD MAPS OF IRELAND—noticing every town, village, hamlet, and gentleman's seat on the different roads.

The following are now ready, neatly coloured, and mounted for the pocket, one shilling each :—

DUBLIN TO BELFAST,	DUBLIN TO CORK,
DUBLIN TO WEXFORD,	DUBLIN TO LIMERICK.

KIRKWOOD'S MAPS AND PLANS, beautifully printed on enamel cards. One shilling each.

DUBLIN,	IRELAND,
BELFAST,	WICKLOW.

MAP OF THE SHANNON, from its source to the sea. Price sixpence on a sheet, or one and sixpence mounted.

Dublin : WILLIAM CURRY, JUN. and Company, 9, Upper Sackville-street. Sold by all respectable Booksellers.

WORKS ON IRELAND.

KILKEE—Two months at Kilkee, a watering place in the County of Clare, near the mouth of the Shannon; with an account of a voyage down that river, from Limerick to Kilrush. By Mary J. Knott. Small 8vo. plates. 6s.

BALLYBUNIAN—An account of the caves of Bally-bunian, County of Kerry. By William Ainsworth, Esq. with engravings on copper and wood. 8vo. 4s.

THE SHANNON—Observations on the Inland Navigation of Ireland, and the want of employment for its population, with a description of the River Shannon. By C. W. Williams, Esq. Second Edition. 8vo. with a large map. 3s. 6d.

A HISTORY OF IRELAND—from the raising of the Siege of Derry, in 1689, to the surrender of Limerick in 1691. By the Rev. John Graham, A.M. 12mo. 6s.

TRUE STORIES, from the HISTORY OF IRE-LAND. By John James M·Gregor. 3 vols. 18mo. 10s. 6d. half bound.

FLORA HIBERNICA—Comprising the flowering plants Ferns, Characeæ, Musci, Hepaticæ, Lichenes, and Algæ, of Ireland, arranged according to the Natural Order; with a Synopsis of the genera, according to the Linnæan System. By James Townsend Mackay, M.R.I.A. 8vo. 16s. cloth.

GUIDE TO THE ROYAL DUBLIN SOCIETY'S BOTANIC GARDEN, GLASNEVIN. By Ninian Niven. Small 8vo. with plates and plan. 4s. 6d.

TALES OF IRELAND. By William Carleton, Author of Traits and Stories of the Irish Peasantry, small 8vo. with etchings by Brooke. 7s. 6d. cloth.

Dublin : WILLIAM CURRY, JUN. and Co. 9, Upper Sackville-street—Sold by all Booksellers.

CHEAP AND COMPLETE EDITION,

In small 8vo. 7s. 6d. bound in cloth,

INCIDENTS OF TRAVEL

IN

GREECE, TURKEY, RUSSIA,

AND POLAND,

BY JOHN G. STEPHENS, ESQ.

" These travels are written by a clever, good-humoured, and lively American, who has a marvellous faculty for getting along, and putting a great deal into little room ; and one, moreover, who interests and entertains his reader exceedingly. At Cracow the traveller closes his lively and entertaining narrative, which we cordially recommend both for information and entertainment."—*Tait's Magazine.*

" One of the most companionable and entertaining volumes we have had in our hands for many a day."—*Glasgow Constitution.*

" We have seldom met with a livelier writer, or a pleasanter travelling companion."—*Scottish Guardian.*

" We have derived no little pleasure from the perusal of this volume, and can commend it to the public as a lively and agreeable book."—*Edinburgh Advertiser.*

SCENES FROM THE

LIFE OF EDWARD LASCELLES,

Late Midshipman on board his Majesty's Ship Hesperus.

In two volumes, small 8vo. with Etchings by Cruikshank.
12s. cloth lettered.

Dublin : WILLIAM CURRY, Jun. and Co., 9, Upper Sackville-street. Sold by all Booksellers.

Lightning Source UK Ltd.
Milton Keynes UK
UKHW021043141122
412173UK00007B/1481